Evangelising for the Third Millennium

The Maynooth Conference on the New Catechism
May 1996

Edited by Maurice Hogan SSC and Thomas J. Norris

VERITAS

First published 1997 by
Veritas Publications
7-8 Lower Abbey Street
Dublin 1

Copyright © The individual contributors 1997

ISBN 1 85390 342 6

British Library Cataloguing
in Publication Data.
A catalogue record for
this book is available
from the British Library.

Cover design by Banahan McManus Ltd, Dublin
Printed in the Republic of Ireland by Betaprint Ltd, Dublin

CONTENTS

INTRODUCTION

In one of its most inspirational documents the Second Ecumenical Vatican Council wrote lines that seem to capture both the spirit and the aim of that great stirring of minds and hearts: 'This Synod wishes to set forth the true doctrine on divine Revelation and its transmission. For it wants the whole world to hear the summons to salvation, so that through hearing, it may believe, through belief it may hope, through hope it may come to love'.[1] The Council had this clear pastoral and cultural focus, since the bishops of Vatican II held the conviction that if the men and women of our times could hear afresh the authentic voice of Christ, they would believe in a new way, grow deeper in hope and learn to love more concretely. A Gospel simplicity impelled the Council to announce 'the gift of God' (Jn 4:10) which shines on the face of Jesus Christ and radiates into the hearts of true believers (see 2 Cor 4:6). It was the same Gospel candour which inspired the Church to opt for a universal Catechism on the occasion of the Extraordinary Synod of 1985, the year which marked the twentieth anniversary of the conclusion of the Council.

A national conference
A national conference on the Catechism of the Catholic Church, itself 'the catechism of the Second Vatican Council' (Pope Paul VI), could have no more appropriate purpose than that of attempting to present the vision and the content of this unique

'gift of God' (Pope John Paul II) to the People of God of our times. This was in fact the aim of the National Conference which took place at Maynooth from Monday, 13 May 1996, until the following Ascension Thursday. Requested by the Irish bishops, the organisers, all members of the Faculty of Theology at Maynooth, concentrated for the previous year on one clear goal, namely, the presentation of the spirit, vision and content of the new Catechism.

To propose the faith again

The faith given once for all to the saints (Jude 3) needs to be proposed to each new generation. Each generation is in fact a new continent to be won for Christ, as many have stressed in our times. The particular character of our day only serves to intensify the urgency of this task. At the close of the second millennium and the opening of the third, there is a pressing need in Ireland for such care. Ireland needs a new evangelisation, albeit *à l'irlandais*.

This conviction perhaps explains the request of the Irish bishops that the symposium adopt a clear *catechetical and pastoral* focus. Accordingly, the event had the simple aim of serving the significant religious educators such as bishops, priests, parents, teachers, catechists and all those involved in the worlds of education and pastoral care. The conference would highlight the Catechism as a reservoir for catechesis and as a providential instrument for the new evangelisation which the circumstances of the age have thrust upon us.

Proof of the vitality of the faith

Now a universal catechism is a daring, even an adventurous, undertaking. It was particularly so in the light of the ferment generated by the event of the Council whose work and insight required time to assimilate. It was this consideration that, more than anything else, delayed for twenty years the decision to compile such a proclamation of the faith of Catholics. It is adventurous in many respects. 'Since the faith is the same yet the source of ever new light',[2] its contemporary elaboration requires the illuminating grace of the Holy Spirit. It is he who leads into all truth (see Jn 16:13) and accompanies the Church along the roads of history until God's eschatological design for humankind and human history eventually rhyme.

In that way 'the Church constantly moves forward toward the fullness of divine truth until the words of God reach their complete fulfilment in her'.[3] A catechism has to take the risk of capturing this dynamic unfolding of the one faith. Nothing in fact that is antiquated and weary, nothing that is mere convention, nothing that is flat will convey the Gospel today, since the Gospel is young with the very youth of God. In the memorable words of Pope John XXIII at the opening of the Council, 'One thing is the deposit of faith, which consists in the truths contained in sacred doctrine, another thing is the manner of presentation, always however with the same meaning and signification'.[4] This Catechism sets itself the twofold task of stating 'the unfathomable riches of Christ' (Ep 3:8) and of finding the 'form' or 'dress' most appropriate to this statement.

The second adventure has to do with the strong ecumenical item on the agenda of the Council. The Catechism of the Council of Trent, more popularly known as the Roman Catechism, had the task of transmitting the teaching of that Council. This teaching, however, sealed the divisions of Western Christianity which had been occasioned by the Reformation. Inevitably the Tridentine Catechism became a key instrument in the Counter-Reformation.

The Second Vatican Council recovered the ancient perspectives of the early Fathers who saw the Gospel as the Word of Life (Ph 2:16) for all of humankind. It underlined the four great dialogues which are mentioned in Pope Paul VI's *Ecclesiam suam* and run through the sixteen documents of the Council.

This new Catechism of the Second Vatican Council, however, coming as it does after a pastoral council with this vigorous strong ecumenical mission, has the task of healing those divisions, and of promoting the unity for which Christ came, suffered and rose again (see Jn 17: 21f). That work of reunification, however, is a high and arduous goal: it made its own special demands of the compilers of the Catechism.

In the third instance, while the New Catechism holds out to catechists and catechetical writers a unique opportunity, this very opportunity is bristling with difficulties. Some of these have to do with the appropriate communication of the Catechism to the local Churches. The soil for such inculturation needs preparation and time and a special quality of listening if the Catechism's text is to be heard and to be capable of inspiring future local catechisms. It requires in a special way the gradual assimilation of the authentic thought-patterns of the Council on which it is constructed.

The categories of the Council

Here we are face-to-face with the genuinely original categories of the conciliar synthesis. This Catechism challenges the whole People of God to assimilate these categories and to live by them. For example, the Council repeatedly stresses the divine-human sociality of the faith, the fact that the Church is a 'people made one from the unity of the Father, the Son and the Holy Spirit'.[5] It identifies in 'the new commandment to love as Christ loved us(cf. Jn 13:34)' 'the law' of the People of God.[6] The Gospel word 'unity' lies at the very heart of the faith *as the Holy Spirit wants the Church to live at this point of her pilgrimage.*

Christian spirituality, however, has been largely individualistic; now it must discover 'the brother for whom Christ died' (1 Cor 8:11) as an essential step on the way to the God of Jesus Christ. In the words of Henri de Lubac, 'Fundamentally the Gospel is obsessed with the idea of the unity of human society'.[7] This is quite impossible, however, without a radical change of horizon. Otherwise the Catechism will not be able to escape the dilution and flattening that come from being filtered through obsolescent modes of thought and outdated patterns of action. The Church in Ireland needs to *be prepared for its reception*. 'New wine in new wineskins'(Mk 2:22).

An overview of the contributions

The volume which you hold in your hands contains the papers of the Maynooth Conference. These do not exhaust, or even aspire to exhaust, the substantial content of the Catechism. With its 2665 paragraphs, its almost 700 pages and its thousands of citations, that would have been an impossible task and, in the circumstances, an unwise one. Instead, the chapters address in an orderly fashion the four organically connected sections of the Catechism. The result is that the fourfold structure of the Catechism itself determines the structure of this volume and the sequence of its chapters. There is also a logical sequence in the subjects treated and this permits the reader to read any single chapter or any set of chapters gathered around one of the four component areas.

'A rich treasury of doctrine'

In his formal opening of the symposium Cardinal Cahal Daly pointed to the character of the Catechism as above all else 'a rich treasury of doctrine'. He stressed the principle that the truth of faith requires dogma, and 'dogma inspires wonder, contemplation, adoration, total self-giving'. The Catechism 'is rich biblically; it is rich patristically; it is rich liturgically and spiritually'. Above all, 'the Catechism is a great instrument for the formation of the Christian mind'.

'The unity of the faith'

As editor-in-chief of the Catechism Archbishop Schönborn of

Vienna had more to do with the shape and content of the Catechism than anyone else. His presence at the conference was a singular providence as his address ably demonstrated. He highlighted the Catechism's purpose as that of 'the unity of the faith' and its irreplaceable function in presenting the faith 'as one organic whole'. The one faith in the many cultures and in the many centuries must be guaranteed if the life and the truth given to humankind in the life, death and resurrection of Jesus Christ are to continue in any meaningful sense. It is this one faith which makes the innumerable believers spread out in space and time into a people, the one People of God living by and from the truth of 'one Lord, one faith, one baptism'(Ep 4:5).

'The holy face of Jesus'

Professor John Saward of Philadelphia identified the doctrinal key of the Catechism as its Christ-centredness: 'in Him she believes, by his sacraments she is sanctified, his commandments she obeys, his prayer she addresses in the Spirit to the Father'. By means of a genial employment of the four icons prefacing the four sections of the Catechism he demonstrated how the whole work manifests 'the holy face of Jesus'. Professor Saward's address truly turned ears into eyes.

'The Trinity and the Cross'

Fr Breandán Leahy unpacked the theology of revelation and faith on which the whole edifice of faith and sacrament, of morality and prayer is founded. He stressed the variety of the strands composing this theology, and pointed up the Catechism's identification of the trinitarian and paschal mysteries as the core mysteries of the faith. The Blessed Trinity is revealed in order to be lived, but it is the mystery of the Crucified Son which alone reveals *how* it is to be lived. His judicious use of concrete experiences of living the words of the Gospel illustrates well the key moments of the contribution, conferring on it a unique quality, a touch of attractive liveliness.

'The mysteries of Christ's life... the sacraments'

Moving from the area of the profession of faith to that of its celebration in the sacramental economy, Fr Sean Collins, OFM, located the great merit of the presentation of the sacraments in 'its solid contextualisation of sacramental life. This is done in three ways – in the trinitarian economy of salvation, in the mission of Jesus Christ, and in the life of faith and conversion of the Christian community'. In a fascinating way he makes us dwell upon the authentic anchoring of the sacraments in the momentous, as well as the ordinary, experiences of human life, and in the concept of blessing that 'embraces the whole of God's work... from the beginning until the end of time' (CCC 1079). Since this work focuses on the event and person of Christ, 'the mysteries of Christ's life are the foundations of what he would henceforth dispense in the sacraments' (CCC 1115 and 1117).

The language of rights

Moving into the third part dealing with morality, Professor Janet Smith began by asking the question, 'Why did the authors of the Catechism create so much work for themselves – and so much reading for us – by devoting the longest portion of the Catechism or nearly 300 pages in the English edition to the subject of morality?' She provides the answer in the light of a response to 'modern concerns' and the Catechism's faithfulness to 'the inherited moral vision of the Church'. For her own part, she singled out for consideration the Catechism's deployment of the language of rights, highlighting their worth and limitations in moral discourse, and the emphasis placed upon the theme of conscience.

Conscience: 'the aboriginal vicar of Christ'

Dr Teresa Iglesias picks up again the theme of conscience, highlighting its dramatic role in enabling 'faith to put down roots in personal life... faith shining forth in personal conduct'.[8] Like

Dr Smith, she welcomes the fact that the Catechism chose to present a 'new treatise' on the subject. As 'the aboriginal vicar of Christ',[9] conscience provides the personal guidance necessary to turn the one and only life each human being has into a holy journey. The exposition is crowned by highly practical suggestions for those with the task of educating conscience, be they priests, catechists or parents.

The Commandments and the vocation to life in the Spirit

While the Roman Catechism deals exclusively with the Ten Commandments in its section on the moral life of Christians, the New Catechism has a significantly different viewpoint. The Commandments appear only after a lengthy situating in man's vocation to life in the Spirit. Professor James McEvoy deftly unpacks key 'aspects of the theology of the Decalogue with a view to deepening the appreciation of its significance when viewed from the Catholic perspective'. In pursuit of this goal he takes the reader on a tour of the several stages in the treatment of the Commandments in the course of history from revelation until today. The result is a splendid survey not only of the theology of the Commandments but also of much of contemporary moral theology.

'The specific and unique nature of Christian prayer'

The concluding part of the Catechism deals with prayer. Its exposition has already struck responsive chords far and wide. Fr Bede McGregor, OP, delves into the material with a perceptive eye. In particular, he attempts 'to underline the specific and unique nature of Christian prayer in the context of other forms of prayer and meditation found in other religious traditions and contemporary new religious movements'. The 'priestly prayer' of Jesus shows 'that what we are as a Church whose innermost life is unity in love' is the final key to the specific nature of Christian prayer. It is also the secret of both *effective* and *missionary* prayer. This and many other elements of this talk are enough to inspire the reader to go to the text.

Translating the Catechism into the Irish context

The Catechism demands an appropriate translation into the Irish scenario. Bishop Donal Murray of Limerick took up the issue in a thought-provoking manner. While the Catechism is clear and serene in its exposition of Catholic doctrine, our culture is now deeply affected by the imperatives of productivity, sensuality and success. These set up a wavelength that renders the message of faith difficult to hear and even more difficult to follow. 'We can see growing around us a culture in which it seems possible to speak about who we are while making no reference to our Creator or to our ultimate destiny, no reference to the origin and purpose of human life.' The whole Catechism may be read as a sustained response to these questions of personal and national identity.

'Faith becoming living, conscious and active'

In the final analysis the responsibility for the pastoral and catechetical deployment of the Catechism resides with the bishops. As the sign of Christ the teacher in the local Church each bishop has the vital task of making 'people's faith become living, conscious and active through the light of instruction'.[10] Archbishop Michael Neary of Tuam stressed how a bishop 'needs to unite clergy and catechists into a team' and to do so 'in a manner adapted to the needs of the times, that is to say, in a manner corresponding to the difficulties and problems by which people are most vexatiously burdened and troubled'.[11] Here perhaps is to be found the real challenge of the Catechism: to 'illumine with the light of faith the new situations and problems which had not yet emerged in the past'.[12] This calls for an informed dialogue among Irish Catholics, a discerning listening by the bishops and pastors of the Church in Ireland, and the courage to speak the full truth of the faith in love (Ep 4:15).

The indestructible support of faith

The conference concluded on Holy Thursday evening with solemn celebration of the Holy Eucharist by Archbishop Desmond Connell as principal celebrant. In his homily the Archbishop pointed to the fact that 'the Church's memory is the gift of the indwelling Spirit'. This memory, however, is an access in the present to the great events of revelation and salvation in Christ. The same Holy Spirit enables the people of God to realise that 'the visible presence of our Redeemer passed over into sacraments; and so that faith might be more noble and firmer, sight gave way to doctrine, the authority of which was to be accepted by believing hearts enlightened with rays from above'[13]. A great Irish theologian, the Venerable Columba Marmion, has shown that the realities of Jesus remain forever 'as the epiphanies of Christ's person, surpassing somehow the flux of time as the words and actions of a man who is God'. It is this faith now formulated afresh in the Catechism which 'is the indestructible support of the faith of her children'.

A set of workshops

A major component of the conference was a set of workshops which took place each afternoon, conducted by experienced leaders in the many fields of catechetics around the country. The workshops covered areas such as the Catechism and the preaching of the Lectionary, the modern catechetical programmes, the senior cycle of religious education, liturgical and personal prayer in the schools, and the Catechism as an instrument of parish and adult catechesis. This part of the symposium facilitated a lively interface between the Catechism and those involved in a broad range of pastoral and catechetical activities within the Irish landscape.

A symposium does not simply happen. It requires multi-dimensional preparation. The Maynooth Symposium wishes to record its deep gratitude to the College's late lamented President,

Monsignor Matthew O'Donnell, for his practical help and sincere encouragement. The event is also indebted to many groups of people, such as the cloistered monks and sisters of Ireland who accompanied the occasion in prayer, and to many individuals too numerous to mention by name who gave generously of their time, talent and resources during and since the event. May the God who loves generous givers be their ultimate reward. In the meantime may they have the joy of seeing the seed they helped plant in May 1996 germinate, grow and bear fruit in the minds and souls of Irish men and women.

Maurice Hogan SSC
Thomas J. Norris

1

THE CATECHISM OF THE CATHOLIC CHURCH AS AN INSTRUMENT OF EVANGELISATION

Opening Address by Cardinal Cahal B. Daly

On behalf of the Irish Episcopal Conference and on my own behalf, as well as in the name of Maynooth College, I welcome you all to this college and to this conference. I warmly thank the committee who have worked so hard in planning and organising the conference, and I congratulate them in assembling such a distinguished panel of speakers on various aspects of the theme, 'The Catechism of the Catholic Church as an Instrument of Evangelisation'. They have taken special care to ensure that the conference would not merely be an academic exercise, but would be oriented towards the homiletic, catechetical, pastoral and spiritual use of the Catechism at personal and parish and diocesan level. This conference is sure to make a valuable contribution towards the utilisation of the Catechism as an instrument of formation in faith, of spiritual enrichment and of evangelisation, in a time of profound social and cultural change; a time literally of the transvaluation of all values, challenging all of us who are Church to do everything in our power to ensure that that transvaluation is permeated by the leaven of the Gospel of Jesus Christ.

Distinguished speakers

I particularly welcome Archbishop Christoph Schönborn, Archbishop of Vienna. He is the principal redactor of the Catechism, one who, more than any other single person, is responsible for the shape and content of the Catechism.

Archbishop Schönborn was born in the former Czechoslovakia in 1945. He entered the Dominican Order and made his profession in 1964. In 1970, he was ordained priest. He was Professor of Theology in the University of Fribourg in Switzerland, and in that capacity, he served for ten years as a member of the International Theological Commission. The Holy Father appointed him secretary of the commission charged with the editing of the Catechism, and he became its principal editor, piloting it through successive drafts with incredible energy and erudition, under the direction of Cardinal Ratzinger. The Catechism was, of course, the subject of very wide consultation across the universal Church, and Cardinal Ratzinger gave masterly reports on its progress at several successive Synods of Bishops. Father Schönborn was appointed Auxiliary Bishop of Vienna in 1991, and was named Coadjutor Archbishop and shortly afterwards Archbishop of Vienna in 1995. He is the author of several books, chiefly in the area of Christology. We are privileged in Maynooth and at this conference to have such a distinguished speaker address us on the volume to which he has devoted so much time and labour and learning. I assure him of a very warm welcome to Ireland and to Maynooth. A predecessor of his, Cardinal König, is a good friend of Ireland and, indeed, an honourary Cavan man, not unknown in Croke Park. May we hope that Archbishop Schönborn will also come back to Ireland, for perhaps a longer stay in the future. Shortly he will address us on 'the vision of the Catechism', and tomorrow he will deliver a lecture to the members of the conference and to a wider public on 'the Catechism and the challenges of faith today'.

I do not need to call attention to the other conference speakers; as you can see from your programme, they are a distinguished group, coming from Ireland and overseas, particularly from the United States of America. I sincerely regret that I cannot be present for the whole of the conference, since tomorrow I go to Lourdes, to join the Armagh Diocesan Pilgrimage there.

A thesaurus of doctrine

The Catechism is indeed a 'thesaurus', a rich treasury of doctrine. It can rightly be called one of the great fruits of the Second Vatican Council. It is described by Pope John Paul II, in the Apostolic Constitution which accompanies it, as 'a sure and authentic reference text for teaching Catholic doctrine'. The Pope goes on to say that it is 'offered to all the faithful who wish to deepen their knowledge of the unfathomable riches of salvation'.

The Catechism is richly biblical; Cardinal Ratzinger remarked at one of the Synods of Bishops that there are more scriptural references in the Catechism than there are in the whole corpus of documents of the Second Vatican Council. The Catechism is rich also in its references to the early Christian writers, whom we know as the Fathers of the Church. It is significant that the great modern renewal of theology, which preceded and prepared the Council, particularly in the French and German-speaking countries, drew upon two sources; firstly, a renewal of Catholic scholarly study of the Bible, and secondly, and subordinately, a renewal of the study of the early doctors of the Church, the Fathers, who were themselves steeped in the scriptures. The range and relevance of quotations from the Fathers of the Church in this Catechism are most impressive. These quotations are not given in any display of erudition; they nourish faith; they nourish the faith of the men and women of the late twentieth century and the eve of the twenty-first, just as much as they nourished the faith of Christians of the first five centuries. This is indeed a volume of which all Catholics can be proud. The words of the renewal of baptismal promises are applicable to the Catechism:

'This is our faith; this is the faith of the Church; and we are proud to profess it in Christ Jesus, our Lord.'

Dogma

It is sometimes suggested nowadays that Church doctrine should not be precisely and clearly defined, but should have blurred edges. To many minds, dogma seems man-made, triumphalist, intolerant, some would even say fundamentalist. 'Dogmatic' is almost always used pejoratively. Dogma is seen as the destroyer of mystery.

The opposite is the case. Dogma is the preserver and safeguard of mystery. The history of dogma shows that the great dogmatic definitions resulted from theological disputes in which one party or the other sought to give clear and rational explanations of truths of faith, thus reducing faith to the level of human philosophy and eliminating the essential character of revealed mystery. So it was with the great christological dogmas, the dogma of the Trinity, the dogma of the Divine Motherhood of Mary. Indeed, all the Marian dogmas are rooted in the christological dogmas of the Incarnation, the Redemption and Grace. Various theories purporting to explain these doctrines rationally became recognised by the Church as 'heresies', a word which one could almost exactly translate as 'selective theories', and the Church defined the truth precisely, but defined so precisely as mystery, as truth beyond reason, though not contradicting reason. This is the truth which inspires wonder, contemplation, adoration, total self-giving. Dogma is the very opposite of human explanation of mystery; dogmas are statements of a mystery beyond human explanation. Romano Guardini wrote: '[Dogmas] make one realise how fathomless the mystery is…. A dogma does not explain but safeguards the whole. It is like a wall built about a sacred spring to keep the contents from running out.' The metaphor of the wall around the spring comes from St Augustine.

It is in this sense that Cardinal Newman could declare that the first principle in his journey into Catholic truth was 'the principle of dogma'. In the *Apologia* he wrote: 'My battle was with liberalism; by liberalism I mean the anti-dogmatic principle and its developments. I have changed in many things, in this I have not. From the age of fifteen, dogma has been the foundation principle of my religion; I know no other.'

His second principle was that of 'the truth of a certain definite religious teaching, based on the foundation of dogma', namely: 'There [is] a visible Church, with sacraments and rites which are the channels of invisible grace.'

The Catechism is faithful to these great principles of Cardinal Newman. It is rich in its doctrine of the Sacraments. The words of the Catechism, like the words of faith itself, 'are spirit, and they are life' (cf. Jn 6:63). The Catechism is, I have said, rich biblically; it is rich patristically; it is also rich liturgically and spiritually. Abbot Anscar Vonier of Buckfast Abbey, though he died in 1938, can be called a precursor of the Second Vatican Council. One of his books has the title *The Christian Mind*; it was published in 1920. The Christian mind, he says, is one formed 'through practical assimilation of the wondrous truths of the Incarnation.' I see the Catechism as a great instrument for the formation of the Christian mind. That mind is characterised by conviction of Christ's power and victory. Vonier writes: '(Many people) are devout in Christ, but not powerful in Christ. Yet, if the Son of God is anything, He is the first and greatest World Power'.

Christian Doctrine of its very nature leads to prayer; and the Catechism concludes with a magnificent chapter on prayer, comprising a reflection on each of the petitions of the Lord's Prayer. The Catechism answers to Karl Rahner's demand for a 'theology on its knees'. The Catechism has an inspiring doctrine of the sacraments, of worship and of prayer. It has a splendid presentation of Christian morality, seen, not as a set of negative prohibitions, but as a positive challenge, an invitation to the struggle to become more truly human, by becoming more like to Christ, the most fully human of the sons of Adam, because truly the Son of God.

The greatest of these

All Christ's commandments are summed up in love. It can indeed be said that the whole of the Catechism of the Catholic Church is oriented towards love. The prologue to the Catechism quotes its great predecessor, the Roman Catechism, which said:

> The whole concern of doctrine and its teaching must be directed to the love that never ends. Whether something is proposed for belief, for hope or for action, the love of Our Lord must always be made accessible, so that anyone can see that all the works of perfect Christian virtue spring from love and have no other objective than to arrive at love.

In this, the Catechism re-echoes words from the baptismal liturgy of the early Church. The fifth-century Theodore of Mopsuestia said to catechumens preparing for baptism: 'In reciting the Creed, you are entering, through your bishop, into a solemn covenant and pact with God to persevere in charity before God.'

Indeed, the Catechism could well define its whole purpose in the words of St Paul in his First Letter to Timothy: 'The only purpose of this instruction is that there should be love, coming out of a pure heart, a clear conscience and a sincere faith' (1:4).

May that be the fruit and blessing of this conference.

2

MAJOR THEMES AND
UNDERLYING PRINCIPLES

Archbishop Christoph Schönborn

'*Iuvenes Bostoniensis, Leningradiensis et Sancti Jacobi in Chile induti sunt 'Blue Jeans' et audiunt et saltant eandem musicam.*' I very well remember the day I heard these words. The Latin may fall short of Ciceronian standards, but the impact was far-reaching. We would probably not be gathered here today if Cardinal Bernard Law had not launched the idea of a Catechism emanating from the Second Vatican Council.

Speaking on the very first day to the bishops gathered for the Extraordinary Session of the Synod in 1985, he was the first to bring up this idea. I was present as a theologian and I remember the impact of this simple, clear argument: 'We have to teach faith', he said, 'in a world that becomes more and more a global village'. In a world where young people all over the world wear the same blue jeans, should it not be possible to express faith in a common language? It is not only possible, it is even necessary, and this mainly for two reasons: first because the world has definitively become one, sharing the same problems, the same anxieties and hopes; and second because faith in itself is one.

Unity is an essential feature of Christian faith. This vision of one faith in one world has not only fired Cardinal Law's inspiration. It became the driving force of the Synod's discussions about the idea of a Catechism.

At the end of the Synod, the Holy Father made the idea his own. When, a year later, in November 1986, he addressed for the first time the commission charged by him with the preparation of this Catechism, he emphasised this aspect of unity which became the most important underlying principle of the whole work: 'The Catechism you are called upon to draft follows in the wake of the Church's tradition, not for the purpose of replacing diocesan or national catechisms, but to serve as a point of reference for them. It is not intended therefore as an instrument of dull uniformity, but as an important help to guarantee the unity of faith which is an essential dimension of that unity of the Church which flows from the 'unity of the Father, Son and Holy Spirit'.

The last words are a quote from St Cyprian's 'De unitate ecclesiae', quoted in *Lumen gentium* 4, to be found in paragraph 810 of the Catechism.

The unity of faith this Catechism is supposed to strengthen is not 'dull uniformity', it is the unity that flows from the perfect and infinite unity of the living and loving God, Father, Son and Holy Spirit. Looking for the basic principles underlying the Catechism, this principle of unity seems to be the most important of all. Paragraph 11 states: 'This catechism aims at presenting an organic synthesis of the foundations and essential content of Catholic doctrine as regards both faith and morals.'

What is said here is (or should hold) good for every catechism. A catechism is a synthesis of the essentials of faith.

The very idea of a catechism depends on the assumption that such a synthesis is possible. My impression is that much criticism of this Catechism concerns – implicitly or explicitly – this assumption. In 1983 Cardinal Ratzinger, in his famous conferences given in Notre Dame de Paris and at Lyon, focused attention on this crucial point when he analysed the reasons for the universal dropping of catechisms and the breakdown of classical catechesis in the late 1960s. He saw the profoundest reason in the fact that 'one no longer has the courage to present the faith as an organic whole in itself, but only as selected reflections of partial anthropological experiences, founded in a certain distrust of the totality. It is to be explained by a crisis of the faith, or more exactly, of the common faith of the Church of all times.'

The puzzling impression conveyed by many books for religious education in my country is that of 'bits and pieces', of flashlights here and there, like in a TV-clip, but not the building up of a synthesis, an organic view of faith.

How does the CCC respond to this challenge? Let me underline three aspects of this unity:

1. the principle of hierarchy of truth;
2. the unity of the Church's tradition in space and time;
3. the realism in approaching the content of faith.

1. HIERARCHY OF TRUTH

The first and most severe criticism against the 'Projet Révisé', the 'Revised Project' sent out to all the bishops in December 1989, was neglect of the *'hierarchia veritatum'*. Most of you well remember this point. Not that it was always clear what the different critics really understood by this concept of the Second Vatican Council. Cardinal Ratzinger said several times in this context that 'hierarchy of truth' does not mean 'a principle of subtraction', as if faith could be reduced to some 'essentials' whereas the 'rest' is left free or even dismissed as not so significant. 'Hierarchy of truth' means, he said, a principle of organic structure. It should not be confused with the degrees of certainty; it simply means that the different truths of faith are 'organised' around a centre. Therefore it is right to require that a Catechism shall correspond to this principle, and in this sense the many criticisms brought forward in the consultation of all the bishops helped the Commission to heed this principle.

How does the CCC respect this principle of hierarchy of truth? Mainly via three criteria for the organisation of the whole work:

a) The Mystery of the Blessed Trinity as the centre of the hierarchy of truth;

b) the Christocentric approach, and finally;

c) the fourfold plan of the Catechism, intrinsically expressing a principle of organic structure.

The mystery of the Trinity

'The mystery of the Most Holy Trinity is the central mystery of Christian faith and life. It is the mystery of God in himself. Therefore it is the source of all the other mysteries of faith; it is the light that illuminates them. It is the most fundamental and essential teaching within the "hierarchy of the truth of faith"' (GCD 43). 'The whole history of salvation is identical with the history of the way and the means by which the one true God, Father, Son and Holy Spirit, reveals himself to man "and reconciles and unites himself with those who turn away from sin"' (GCD 47) (CCC 234). Following this indication of the GCD the Catechism is articulated in a profoundly Trinitarian way. From the very first paragraph the Trinitarian dimension is central. It is the overall perspective of the Catechism because it is the centre of the Christian faith:

'God is infinitely perfect and blessed in himself. In a plan of pure goodness he freely created man to share in his blessed life. Therefore he is close to him at all times and all places. He calls him and helps him to seek, know and love him with all his strength.

Through his Son, whom he sent in the fullness of time as the Redeemer and Saviour, the Father gathers all mankind, scattered and divided by sin, into the unity of his family, the Church. In Christ and through him, the Father invites all men to become his adopted children in the Holy Spirit and so heirs of his blessed life' (CCC 1).

All that needs to be said about Christian faith and life is directed to this centre: the communion in the blessed life of the Most Holy Trinity.

'The final end of the whole divine economy is the entry of

God's creatures into the perfect unity of the Blessed Trinity. But even now we are called to be a dwelling of the Most Holy Trinity' (CCC 260).

We could go through the whole Catechism and see how this Trinitarian view runs like a thread through the book. May I just briefly indicate some points at which this thread is more plainly visible.

- The missionary dimension is present from start to finish: the divine missions of the Son and the Holy Spirit continue through the mission of the Church; they are the divine source from which all missionary and catechetical activity stems (cf. CCC 1-3; 257; 690; 849-856; 859, etc.)

- The work of Creation is the common work of the Blessed Trinity (cf. CCC 290-292); the same is true of the entire work of redemption and sanctification (cf. CCC 599-618). This is particularly underlined in CCC 648-650 on the resurrection of our Lord. It is explicitly stated for the Church: according to *Lumen gentium* she is 'the people made one by the unity of the Father, the Son and the Holy Spirit' (LG 4; CCC 810).

- The liturgy is seen, first of all, as the work of the Holy Trinity (cf. CCC 1077-1112), especially the Blessed Eucharist (cf. CCC 1358-1381). This holds true also for prayer addressed to the Father, to Jesus Christ, and to the Holy Spirit. And again it is true for the Christian life, which is seen in CCC 1693-95 explicitly as a life in communion with God – Trinity.

Karl Rahner, from the early 1950s, repeatedly complained that Catholic theology and piety had forgotten the Trinitarian dimension. The Catechism could help to refocus Catholic teaching and preaching around the 'hierarchy of truth'.

The Christocentric approach

The second focus in the hierarchy of truth is the mystery of Jesus Christ, true God and true man: 'There is no other name in the whole world given to men by which we are to be saved (Ac 4:12) than the name of Jesus,' as the epigram to the Catechism says.

The Christocentric accent in the Catechism is not opposed to the Trinitarian view: it is through the Incarnation of the Eternal Son, His life, death and resurrection that the Father is revealed and the Spirit is given. Therefore catechesis, to be Trinitarian, has to be Christocentric. Paragraphs 426 to 429, introducing the christological section, therefore insist that 'Christ is at the heart of Catechesis'. Quoting Pope John Paul II's *Catechesi tradendae*, the Catechism states:

> At the heart of catechesis we find, in essence, a Person, the Person of Jesus of Nazareth, 'the only Son from the Father... full of grace and truth,' who suffered and died for us and who now, after rising from the dead, is with us forever. To catechise is 'to reveal, in the Person of Christ, the whole of God's eternal design reaching fulfilment in that Person. It is to seek to understand the meaning of Christ's actions and words and of the signs worked by him.' Catechesis aims at putting 'people not only in touch but in communion, in intimacy, with Jesus Christ: only He can lead us to the love of the Father in the Spirit and make us share in the life of the Holy Trinity'. (426)

The principle of the hierarchy of truth is again clearly stated in the next paragraph:

> In catechesis, 'Christ, the Incarnate Word and Son of God, is taught – everything else is taught with reference to him – and it is Christ alone who teaches – anyone else teaches only to the extent that he is Christ's spokesman, enabling Christ to teach through his lips. Every catechist should be able to apply to himself the mysterious words of Jesus: "My teaching is not mine, but his who sent me".' (427)

Christ is the overwhelming light that illuminates the whole exposition of faith, but also the ways of the *sequela Christi* in a 'life in Christ'. Catechesis of Christian morals, inspired by the grace of the Holy Spirit, is mainly a schooling in the new life in Christ. Therefore the prologue to the moral part ends with the following words:

> The first and last point of reference however for such catechesis will always be Jesus Christ, who is... the way, and the truth and the life. By looking to Jesus in faith, faithful Christians can hope that he will fulfil his promises in them and that, by loving him with the same love with which he has loved them, they may perform works corresponding to their dignity. (1698)

The fourfold plan of the Catechism

The Trinitarian and the Christocentric focus of the Catechism are supposed to help in the application of the principle of 'hierarchy of truth'. But there is a third aspect: the plan of the Catechism is in itself a message, a clear catechetical option expressed by Cardinal Ratzinger in a beautifully clear way in his 1983 speech in Paris and Lyon. Allow me to quote him:

> The structure of catechesis appears through the principal events in the life of the Church, which correspond to the essential dimensions of Christian existence. Thus is born from the earliest time a catechetical structure, the kernel of which goes back to the origins of the Church. Luther used that structure for his catechism just as naturally as did the authors of the Catechism of Trent. That was possible because it was not a question of an artificial system, but simply of the synthesis of mnemonic material indispensable to the faith, which reflects at the same time elements vitally indispensable to the Church: The Apostles' Creed (also known as the symbol of the Apostles), the Sacraments, the Ten Commandments and

the Lord's prayer. These four classical and master components of catechesis have served for centuries as the depository and résumé of Catholic teaching. They have also opened access to the Bible as to the life of the Church. We have just said that they correspond to the dimensions of Christian existence. That is what the Roman Catechism affirms in saying that we find there what the Christian should believe (the Creed – Symbolon), hope (Our Father) and do (Ten Commandments) and in what vital space he is to accomplish these things (Sacraments and Church).

Then, in 1988 the critical edition of the *Catechismus Romanus* (CR) was published by the Vatican Press, edited by Professor Pedro Rodriguez and his collaborators. These scholars have carefully studied the reasons for the plan and options adopted by the authors of the CR. They came to some noteworthy results which confirm Cardinal Ratzinger's view, but add some new insights.

A short look at the proportions of the CR is interesting: 22% for the Creed, 37% (nearly twice as much) for the Sacraments, 21% and 20% for the Commandments and the Lord's Prayer. There is a manifest imbalance in favour of the Sacraments, probably in part because of the sacramental controversy of the Reformation. Let us see now the proportions of the Catechism: 39% for the Creed, 23% for the Sacraments, 27% for the Commandments and 11% for prayer. Historical and circumstantial reasons have played their role in these proportions. Nevertheless they convey a theological and catechetical message. We can apply to the Catechism what P. Rodriguez said about the plan of the CR: 'The option is evident: The CR, before presenting to the Christian what he has to do, wants to express to him who and how he is; we find this quote of St Leo the Great: "Christian, remember your dignity". Only when he recognises the supernatural power that flows from his "being in Christ through the Holy Spirit", the faithful disciple of Christ can make the effort, with confident heart, without servile fear, to practise and to increase the Christian life according to the Decalogue.... Without the preceding doctrine of the Sacraments which implies also the teaching about the mystery of the Church and of justification – the precepts of the Decalogue seem to exceed our human capacity. But, basing ourselves on faith and sacraments, we look at them with confidence and vigour. This is a specific property of that catholic spirituality which attains a summit in the CR' (preface, pp. XXVI-XXVII).

This strong emphasis on the primacy of grace in both catechisms is underlined by the little statistic I have just given: In both documents the first two parts form by themselves nearly two-thirds of the volume. Taking this fact into account, we can apply to the Catechism what the editors said about the CR: 'In fact, the doctrinal order of the CR has not four parts, but presents itself as a magnificent diptych taken from the tradition: on the one hand, the mysteries of faith in God, the One and Threefold, as professed (Creed) and celebrated (Sacraments); on the other hand, the Christian life according to faith – faith working through charity – expressed in a Christian manner of life (Decalogue) and in filial prayer (Pater) (preface, p. XXVIII).

The message of this diptych is clear. Whatever method is used in catechesis, the CR and the Catechism do not impose any specific method – the primacy in catechesis is to be given to God and to his works. Whatever man has to do will always be a response to God and to his works. In both catechisms the *magnalia Dei* are 'the heart of the matter'. So far there is a clear catechetical option, but this choice is not optional, it is self-evident: it simply corresponds to the reality – God is first; Grace is first. This is the true hierarchy of truth. Catechesis therefore must lead primarily to the worship of God, to the proclamation of his great works, to the praise of his grace: *Misericordias Domini in aeternum cantabo.*

2. THE UNITY OF THE CHURCH'S TRADITION IN SPACE AND TIME

After having considered the hierarchy of truth a second aspect of the principle of unity underlying the idea and the realisation of the Catechism is the unity of tradition, including the Holy Scripture. The draft and the now published text of the Catechism have been criticised for falling short of a proper, scientifically correct use of Scripture and of tradition. The question is of great importance. Scripture has not only to be at the heart of theology, as *Dei Verbum* (21) states, but also of catechesis. But how can Scripture be used?

On 23 April 1993 the Holy Father addressed the cardinals, the diplomats and the members of the Pontifical Biblical Commission in a speech on the occasion of the centenary of Leo XIII's encyclical *Providentissimus Deus*, the anniversary of Pius XII's *Divino afflante Spiritu*, and the publication of an important document on 'The Interpretation of the Bible in the Church' by the Biblical Commission. The Holy Father affirms the legitimacy and the necessity of scientific biblical scholarship.

Exegesis must be attentive to the human aspects of the biblical texts; it must be open to all the disciplines that can illuminate the historical elements conditioning the biblical text. Together with Leo XIII and Pius XII, John Paul II vehemently approves these approaches. At the same time he insists upon the divine element in Scripture. In analogy to the Mystery of the Incarnation, Holy Scripture is the Word of God in human words. Therefore 'the exegete himself has to perceive in the texts the divine Word' (9), and the Holy Father quotes St Augustine: '*Orent ut intellegant*'. Spiritual life is a condition of Catholic exegesis. Another condition is 'the fidelity to the Church' (10). John Paul II insists on the need to read the Bible within the Community of the faithful. 'To be faithful to the Church', he states, 'means to join resolutely the stream of great tradition' (11). Scripture does not exist without the Church. To read Scripture within the tradition, but without neglecting the sound and solid results of critical exegesis, has also been the leading principle for the use of Scripture in this Catechism. It corresponds to the indications given by *Dei Verbum*.

It is obvious that a great amount of modern biblical scholarship is behind the Catechism, even if this is not explicitly expressed. Of course, a Catechism is not a monograph of exegetical science. It is not the task of this kind of book to discuss theories about early or late dating of the New Testament, about sources and '*Sitz im Leben*'. Nevertheless it is easy to see that, for instance, in the paragraphs on Jesus and Israel, very solid contemporary Jewish and Christian scholarship forms the background of the text.

But on the whole it is true that the dogmatic, the doctrinal use of Scripture prevails. Is this necessarily opposed to a proper historical reading of the Bible? Is the doctrinal framework of the Apostles' Creed, as used in Part I, an impediment to an exegetical approach? The strife between dogmatic and historical interpretation of Scripture has to be overcome for the sake of historical reality itself. In his famous book *Von Reimarus bis Wrede. Eine Geschichte der Leben-Jesu-Forschung*, published in 1900, Albert Schweitzer came to the conclusion that the search for the historical truth, for the true historical Jesus, always loses its orientation when it detaches itself from 'the rock of the Church's doctrine'.

Historical exegesis without the doctrinal reference tends, as history shows, to get caught in the suction of prevailing ideologies. As Schweitzer showed for the nineteenth century – and the same is still true for today – historical truth itself disappears from sight whenever the dogmatic ground of the Church's faith is abandoned. The deepest reason for this frequently attested fact is that the historical reality of Christian faith is in itself a dogmatic reality: the 'historical' Jesus truly is the eternal Son of God made Man, born in Bethlehem and living a Jewish life in Galilee. The historical quest for Jesus ever and again comes up throughout all historical layers against dogmatic ground: against the mystery of Jesus, true God and true Man. This unity – without confusion, without separation – of the divine and the human nature in Christ is the key for the right use of Scripture: 'The Son of God... worked with human hands, he thought with a human intellect, he acted with a human will, and he loved with a human heart' (GS 22,2; cf. CCC 470).

You may ask why I insist on these questions of biblical exegesis! It is because the use of Scripture in the Catechism follows these principles. This use is exemplified in the chapter on the life of Christ. In past decades a strong current of Protestant theology tended to establish a dichotomy between the so-called 'historical Jesus' and the 'Christ of faith'. This tendency has influenced large parts of catechetical literature (at least in continental European countries). From the very beginning the Pontifical Commission for the Catechism opted for a different approach: catechesis has its solid ground in the life of the Church, and especially in the liturgy. Every year the Church celebrates the entire cycle of the events of Christ's life: his birth, his baptism, his preaching and healing, his transfiguration and his passion, and finally his Resurrection and Ascension. When we celebrate these events, we remember real historical events which, at the same time, are true mysteries: the divine-human acts of our Lord, true God and true Man.

This approach has been used in the Catechism. It is an attempt to overcome an unhealthy division between a 'biblical' and a 'dogmatic' way of reading Scripture. In the life of the Church all the acts and words of Jesus remain present, and through faith and liturgy we enter into communion with Christ's life. A key text of the Catechism states:

> Christ makes it possible for us to live in him and for him to live in us all that he himself lived. 'By his Incarnation the Son of God has united himself in a certain way with each man'(GS 22,2). He calls us to become one with him;

as members of his Body, we are made to share in what he has lived in His flesh for us and as our model (521).

Parts Two, Three and Four of the Catechism are to be seen in the same perspective: how we are enabled to share in the mysteries of Jesus' life, death and resurrection. So also for the approach to the sacraments: 'The mysteries of Christ's life are the foundations of what henceforth Christ dispenses in the Sacraments through the ministers of his Church, because "what was visible in our Redeemer has now passed into the sacraments"' (St Leo the Great, *Sermo* 74, 2) (CCC 1115).

So also for the understanding of Christian moral life: 'When we believe in Jesus Christ, have entered into his mysteries, and keep his commandments, the Saviour himself comes to love in us his Father and ours, his brothers and sisters and our own. His Person becomes, through the Spirit, the living and interior rule of our activity' (CCC 2074).

Thus, Scripture has to be read within the life of the Church, and this life is a sharing of the divine-human life of Christ. The great number of quotations from the Church Fathers, the liturgies of East and West, the Councils, and from a multitude of saints are meant to support this kind of understanding of the Word of God. The witness of the saints, of a St Francis, a St Thomas Aquinas, a St Catherine of Siena, or the 'Little Flower', are, so to speak, living commentaries on the Gospel. Who better than a saint reads and understands Scripture? The testimony of the saints is so vital for our understanding of faith because they have lived the realities in which they and we believe. This leads me to my last point which I called 'the realism in approaching the content of faith.

3. REALISM

'This Catechism stresses the presentation of doctrine. Its aim is to aid in deepening the knowledge of the faith. By doing so it is meant to increase the maturity of the faith, to root faith in life and to make it evident through personal witness' (CCC 23).

This is exactly the challenge of this book: to be at once a clearly doctrinal work and to be a help towards living more profoundly and bearing more powerful witness to faith. Are these two aims compatible? How can the objective truth of the Church's doctrines and the intensely personal character of the believer's possession of them be brought in line? Archbishop Eric d'Arcy writes in a paper on 'The New Catechism and Cardinal Newman':[1] 'For many years anglophone catechists and faith-educators have had to work out of a theory that plumped heavily for the personal, subjective aspect only. This has had disastrous consequences for a whole generation's confident recognition of the objective truth of the Church's doctrines.' Archbishop d'Arcy quotes E.D. Hirsch: 'Believing that a few direct experiences would suffice to develop the skills that children require, Dewey assumed that early education need not to be tied to specific content. He mistook a half-truth for a whole. He placed too much faith in children's ability to learn general skills from a few typical experiences, and too hastily rejected the 'piling up of information'. Only by piling up specific community-based information can children learn to participate in complex co-operative activities with other members of their community.'[2]

And he comments on Hirsch: 'The first three sentences of this sum up all too well the theory in the dominant catechetics of the last twenty years. The fourth recalls the Church's constant recognition that, if her children are to share in the richly complex co-operative activities of the faith-community, they have to pile up an informed familiarity with the truths of the faith, and its tribal rites and customs and expectations. The Extraordinary Synod of 1985, when it requested a universal catechism, was squarely in line with that constant recognition.'[3] We are, indeed, badly in need of an up-to-date account of the place of doctrine in a complete education in faith. This would require overcoming a still very strong emotional antipathy to doctrinal catechesis.

Education of faith is more than merely 'experience',

'existential concern', 'emotional touch'. Faith has first of all to do with realities, with facts, not with notions or concepts: *'Fides non terminatur ad enuntiabile sed ad rem'* ('faith terminates not in proposition, but in realities'), said St Thomas Aquinas. We believe in the reality of the Incarnation of God's Eternal Word; the virginal conception is a real event, as is the Lord's Resurrection from the dead. But facts can be asserted in propositions. Faith without propositions is faith without facts. Newman said: 'Christianity is faith, faith implies a doctrine, a doctrine implies propositions'[4]. The Catechism states likewise: 'We do not believe in formulas but in the realities they express and which faith allows us to grasp ... Still, we do approach these realities with the help of the formulations of faith. These permit us to express and to transmit the faith, to celebrate it in community, to assimilate it, and through it to live ever more fully' (170).

The propositions of faith form a body of doctrine called in Christian language the *depositum fidei*. 'Guard the deposit' (1 Tm 6:20), 'guard the noble deposit' (2 Tm 1:14), St Paul says to his disciple. 'Guarding the deposit of faith is the mission which the Lord entrusted to his Church, and which she fulfils in every age'. These are the first words of John Paul II's Apostolic Constitution for the publication of the Catechism.

'What is 'the deposit'? Newman asks. 'That which has been entrusted to you, not which thou hast discovered; what thou hast received, not what thou hast thought out; a matter, not of cleverness, but of teaching; not of private handling, but of public tradition'.[5]

The Catechism is to serve the guardianship and the transmission of the deposit of faith. The Church has the duty, but also the right to express the fullness, the riches and the beauty of the 'faith that was once for all entrusted to the Saints' (Jude 3; cf. 171).

Doctrine is not opposed to life. How can we love without

understanding? Faith education must also be an education of the *intellectus fidei*. The understanding of faith deepens the trust in this faith and so the confidence in the way of life faith teaches us. The young generation particularly needs urgently to be helped in this confidence. As Newman stated:

> I want a laity.... who know their faith, who enter into it, who know just where they stand, who know what they hold and what they do not, who know their creed so well that they can give an account of it, and who know enough of history to defend it. I want an intelligent, well-instructed laity.... And one immediate effect of your being able to do all this will be your gaining that proper confidence in self that is so necessary for you.'[6]

And again Archbishop d'Arcy: 'Hence we will now be able to empower students to discover for themselves that the doctrinal infrastructure of the faith is just as intellectually serious, just as well grounded and articulated, and just as thoroughly incarnate in contemporary life, as are the other things they study'.[7] And he concludes: 'In the Catechism, the Church calls us to entrust teachers and students once more with the deposit which is their rightful inheritance'.[8]

3

SALVATION IS OF CHRIST THE LORD!
The Christ-Centredness
of the Catechism
John Saward

Christ be with me, Christ within me,
Christ behind me, Christ before me.
Christ beside me, Christ to win me,
Christ to comfort and restore me.

St Patrick's breastplate is the Lord Jesus. In the great King of Heaven's armour he fights, the sword of his Spirit he wields. Like all the saints, Patrick has one centre, one direction for the thoughts of his mind and the affection of his heart: the Father's eternal Word made flesh, the Son of the Virgin, the shining Saviour, Jesus Christ our Lord, true God and true man. And so I say, sláinte Naomh Pádraig do bheannaigh Éire, and I place myself happily under his patronage as I speak about 'The Christ-Centredness of the Catechism'.

By 'the Christ-centredness of the Catechism' is meant of course, the Christ-centredness *of the Church* as expressed in the Catechism, and when we say 'the Church', we refer, not to an abstraction, but to the living personality of the Catholic Church, Christ's dear Bride and our beloved Mother. In the pages of this book, the Church reveals the Christ-centred disposition of her heart: in him she believes, by his Sacraments she is sanctified,

His commandments she obeys, his prayer she addresses in the Spirit to the Father. She confesses of herself: 'The Church has no other light than Christ's ... [T]he Church is like the moon, all its light reflected from the sun.' She says of her catechesis: 'At the heart of Catechesis we find, in essence, a Person, the Person of Jesus of Nazareth, the only Son from the Father.'[1]

In this paper, I invite you to join me in trying to 'think with the Church', to listen to her as she speaks to us of her Lord and Spouse. Let us listen – and *look*. My reflections on each of the Catechism's four parts will begin with a meditation on the illustration, the icon, that prefaces it. This iconographic method is faithful, I believe, to the spirit of the Catechism. The significance of these pictures is doctrinal, not merely decorative. The Catechism in all four of its parts gives us teaching on the dogmatic and devotional importance of religious art. In Part One, citing the Second Council of Nicea, it shows us how the fashioning of sacred images is made possible by the Incarnation of the Son of God.[2] Part Two describes the place of icons in Christian worship.[3] Part Three explains how the veneration of images does not contravene the Divine Commandment.[4] Finally, in Part Four, the Catechism encourages us to have a 'prayer corner' in our homes, with the Scriptures and icons, in order to pray in secret before the Father.[5]

It is no accident that the Catechism has pictures. Each of the four icons, with its commentary, is a visual summary of the verbal teaching that is to follow. Let us listen, then, and let us look as the Church shows us the holy face of Jesus.

1. FAITH IN CHRIST

The first image in the Catechism is a fresco from the catacomb of Priscilla in Rome, dating from the beginning of the third century. It is an icon of the Incarnation. It shows Balaam pointing to the Virgin Mary and her divine Child. The prophet voices the hope of the Old Covenant and the longing of all fallen humanity: 'A star shall come forth out of Jacob, and a sceptre shall rise out of Israel' (Nb 24:17).

This prophecy was fulfiled in the birth of Jesus, the incarnate Son of God, conceived by the power of the Holy

Spirit and born of the Virgin Mary. Mary brought him into the world and gave him to all mankind. For this reason she is the purest image of the Church.[6]

A Marian Christocentricity

From the beginning, the Catechism shows us Jesus with Mary. The central Christ is the incomparable Sun of Righteousness, but he does not shine alone. He lights up a whole constellation, of which the brightest star is his Blessed Mother, the lowly Virgin in whose flesh and by whose faith he was made man. The Christocentricity of the Catechism is a Marian Christocentricity. 'What the Catholic faith believes about Mary is based on what it believes about Christ, and what it teaches about Mary illumines in turn its faith in Christ.'[7]

Our Lady is the supremely Christ-centred person and the surest way to a true Christ-centredness in faith and worship, in moral life and prayer. Her whole mission is to 'bring him into the world and to give him to all mankind'. For this she was predestined and created, for this she was engraced from her conception. To go to Jesus through Mary, therefore, to look at the Child in his Mother's arms, is to be Christ-centred in the purest and most beautiful way.

Everything in Mary has a reference to Christ. In Cardinal Newman's words, all her glories are 'for the sake of her Son'.[8] As the Church Fathers teach, and as the Catechism confirms, her greatest and glorious title 'Mother of God' is a veritable compendium of the Church's faith in the Incarnation:

> [T]he One whom she conceived as man by the Holy Spirit, who truly became her Son according to the flesh, was none other than the Father's eternal Son, the Second Person of the Holy Trinity. Hence the Church confesses that Mary is truly 'Mother of God' (*Theotokos*).[9]

Whatever the Triune God bestows upon Mary, whatever she by his grace is and does, is for Christ and his Church. It is for him and for us, therefore, as the Catechism shows, that she is a virgin – before, during, and for ever after giving birth. It is because of who her Son is, the eternal consubstantial Son of the Father, that she conceives him by the Holy Spirit without seed[10] and gives birth to him without corruption.[11] It is for him that she dedicates her whole self, in body and in soul, to remain a virgin for ever.[12] The Catechism affirms both the historical and corporeal reality of Our Lady's virginity and its saving significance, 'the reasons why God in his saving plan wanted his Son to be born of a Virgin'.[13] The Son of God becomes man in order to make all things new, to 'inaugurate a new creation',[14] to usher in 'the new birth of children adopted in the Holy Spirit through faith',[15] and so he is conceived and born, as St Leo says, 'in a new order, by a new birth'.[16]

In this first icon, in its very first words, the Catechism shows us the Blessed Virgin in relation to both Christ and the Church. It wants us to see the Church in Mary and Mary in the Church. To speak, as I spoke earlier, of the Church as person and Mother is more than metaphor, because, as the Catechism teaches us, 'at once Virgin and Mother, Mary is the symbol and the most perfect realisation of the Church',[17] the Church's 'purest image'.[18] The Church exists in Our Lady before a single Apostle has been called. Already, in the Incarnation, the Virgin Mary has the bodily and believing union with the Son of God to which his whole Church is called.

> Mary goes before us all in the holiness that is the Church's mystery as 'the Bride without spot or wrinkle'. This is why the 'Marian' dimension of the Church precedes the 'Petrine'.[19]

The Christocentricity of the tradition
The Catechism draws upon the Christology of the Church's tradition in all its Catholic richness – the Scriptures, the writings of the Fathers and the Schoolmen, the Councils of the Patristic

age, the words and lives of the saints, the liturgy of both East and West. Mother Church speaks to us through the Fathers of all seven of the great Trinitarian and Christological Councils of the first Millennium from Nicea I to Nicea II. The Catechism expounds the christological definition of faith of the Council of Chalcedon with the help of both the Councils which preceded it and of those which came after it and clarified its meaning. For example, we are given the teaching of the Second Council of Constantinople (553) that the 'one person, one hypostasis' referred to by Chalcedon is none other than the Second Person of the Blessed Trinity, the pre-existent divine hypostasis of the Word. 'Thus everything in Christ's human nature is to be attributed to his divine person as its proper subject, not only his miracles but also his sufferings and even his death.'[20] He who is crucified in the flesh for us is truly 'One of the Trinity'.

Particularly important for the Catechism is the sixth Ecumenical Council, Constantinople III in 681, at which 'the Church confessed that Christ possesses two wills and two natural operations, divine and human', which means that 'the Word made flesh willed humanly in obedience to his Father all that he had decided divinely with the Father and the Holy Spirit for our salvation'.[21] This dogma of the two natural wills will prove to be a fruitful source for much of what follows in the Catechism, not least in Part Four when it speaks of the Prayer of Jesus: 'Thy will be done'.[22]

A Trinitarian Christocentricity

In his 'Breastplate', St Patrick presented the mystery of the Incarnation together with the mystery of the Trinity.

> I bind unto myself the name,
> The strong name of the Trinity:
> By invocation of the same,
> The Three in One and One in Three;

> Of whom all nature hath creation,
> Eternal Father, Spirit, Word;
> Praise to the Lord of my salvation
> Salvation is of Christ the Lord!

The Church in her Catechism follows St Patrick and indeed all her Fathers. The central Christ of the Catechism is 'One of the Trinity', the Son who reveals the Father, the Son who with the Father is revealed by the Spirit.[23] The Catechism's Christ-centredness is Trinitarian. I am reminded of Balthasar's admonition:

> It is, of course, Jesus Christ who is the centre of our faith, but only the Christ who is the Father's Son, endowed with the fullness of the Spirit, the Christ to whom the Bible bears witness. No Christology without the doctrine of the Trinity (and, of course, vice versa).[24]

The Catechism draws on one of the classic themes of the seventh-century Greek Father, St Maximus the Confessor,[25] when it says that the wonderful 'mode' of Christ's human life and actions reveal his divine Trinitarian person: how he acts as man shows us who he is – the Father's consubstantial Son.

> Everything that Christ is and does in this nature derives from 'One of the Trinity'. The Son of God therefore communicates to his humanity his own personal mode of existence in the Trinity. In his soul as in his body, Christ thus expresses humanly the divine ways of the Trinity.[26]

Christ's 'personal mode of existence' is filial, the existence of the Son. In his humanity, as in his divinity, he exists 'towards the Father'. He lives for him, is devoted to him, obeys him unto death, even death on the Cross. In everything he is and does as man, in his every human word and action, 'in his soul as in his body', the incarnate Son opens up to us the inner life of the Trinity, his eternal life with the Father and the Holy Spirit. As St Maximus says, 'theology', that is the mystery of the Trinity, is taught us by the incarnate Logos himself, for 'He reveals in Himself the Father and the Holy Spirit'.[27]

The Catechism's Christocentricity is fully Trinitarian. It contemplates Christ in his filial relationship to the Father in the Holy Spirit. The very name 'Christ' *(ho Christos)* has a Trinitarian meaning: the incarnate Son is anointed in his humanity by the Father with the unction of the Holy Spirit.[28] Throughout the Catechism, the two divine missions, the sending of the Son by the Father and the sending of the Spirit by the Father and the Son, are presented as inseparable and interconnected. This can be seen in the virginal conception of Christ. As the Catechism says:

> The mission of the Holy Spirit is always conjoined and ordered to that of the Son. The Holy Spirit, 'the Lord, the Giver of Life', is sent to sanctify the womb of the Virgin Mary and divinely fecundate it, causing her to conceive the eternal Son of the Father in a humanity drawn from her own.[29]

The Holy Spirit blows where he wills, but where he wills to blow is in the direction of Jesus. His mission is to unite men to the Word made flesh. From the pierced heart of the Redeemer, the living waters of the Holy Spirit pour forth, and back to that heart do they carry us; only thus do we reach the Father. 'To be in touch with Christ, we must first have been touched by the Holy Spirit'.[30] Taking up a theme dear to the theologians of the Christian East, the Catechism concludes that there is a kind of 'divine self-effacement' in the Holy Spirit: he 'unveils' Christ, but he does not speak of himself.[31]

Christ the Saviour is One of the Trinity, and the salvation he brings us is a share in the life of the Trinity. This divinising communion with the three-personed God begins in this life by grace and is fulfiled in the life to come in glory – in the beatific vision, the Communion of Saints, the resurrection of the body, and the life everlasting.

The ultimate end of the whole divine economy is the entry of

God's creatures into the perfect unity of the Blessed Trinity. But even now we are called to be a dwelling for the Most Holy Trinity.[32]

Like St Thomas Aquinas in the third part of the *Summa Theologiae*, the Catechism begins the treatise on the Incarnation with a consideration of its purpose: why was the Word made flesh? In answer, it quotes the Apostle Peter: 'The Word became flesh to make us "partakers of the divine nature".'[33] It goes on to explain the meaning of this 'divinisation', quoting St Athanasius for the Greeks and St Thomas for the Latins, thereby proving that this doctrine belongs equally to the Christian West as well as to the East.[34] The theme reappears in Part Three on 'Life in Christ': the Sanctifying Grace of Christ, we are told, is a 'deifying' grace,[35] because it is 'a participation in the life of God', introducing us 'into the intimacy of Trinitarian life'.[36] Through our incorporation into Christ in Baptism, we become by grace what he is by nature: we are made sons-in-the-Son.

Christ in his Mysteries

> I bind this day to me for ever,
> By power of faith, Christ's Incarnation,
> His Baptism in the Jordan River,
> His Death on the Cross for my salvation.
> His bursting from the spiced tomb,
> His riding up the heavenly way,
> His coming at the day of doom
> I bind unto myself today!

Like Patrick, the Catechism contemplates Christ in his 'mysteries'. Every stage and state of his human life from the Virgin's undefiled womb to Joseph's unused tomb are fathomless stores of truth and grace, ever present and active in the liturgy of the Church. This approach may appear to be new, but in reality it is ancient, a recovery of the full proportions of the Christology of the Fathers and the medieval Doctors. It proves the

Catechism's debt to Aquinas, who in the third part of the *Summa Theologiae* follows his discussion of the Hypostatic Union with an exposition of the mysteries of the life of Jesus. In the paintings of the fifteenth-century Dominican blessed, Fra Angelico, this theology is expressed iconographically: in his scenes of the life of Jesus, Dominicans – Dominic himself or Peter Martyr – appear, so to speak, waiting in the wings, contemplating and adoring Christ, drawing upon his light and mercy.

The theology of the mysteries of Jesus was not forgotten by Catholic scholars in the intervening centuries. In the Baroque age, Cardinal Bérulle and the French School, with their mysticism of the 'states' of Jesus, kept the traditional doctrine alive, as did the saints who had the mission of serving a particular mystery – the Hearts of Jesus and Mary, the Holy Infancy, the Passion, Jesus in the Eucharist. In the nineteenth century, Matthias Scheeben incorporated the theme into his masterpiece, *The Mysteries of Christianity*, and at the beginning of our own century a great son of Ireland, the Venerable Columba Marmion, opened up Christ in his mysteries for the sanctification of priests, religious, and laity alike. In the 1920s, 1930s, and 1940s, the German Benedictine Dom Odo Casel proposed a controversial theory, brilliant in its intuitions but somewhat muddled in its metaphysics, about how the mysteries of Christ live on in the liturgy. In his encyclical *Mediator Dei*, Pope Pius XII, avoiding what he called 'vague and nebulous' formulations, showed how the mysteries of Christ are present and active in the Church as models of virtue and sources of grace. Finally, in its Constitution on the Liturgy, the Second Vatican Council taught that when she recalls the mysteries of redemption, the Church 'opens up to the faithful the riches of her Lord's powers and merits, so that these are in some way made present for all time; the faithful lay hold of them and are filled with saving grace'.[37]

The Catechism's teaching on the mysteries of Jesus is rich and all-pervasive. In Part One, it lays the christological foundation.

Nothing in the life of Jesus is futile or trivial. Everything – 'from the swaddling clothes of his birth to the vinegar of his Passion and the shroud of his resurrection' – is 'a sign of his mystery'.[38] These are the human actions and experiences of a divine person, and so, though finite in themselves, they have an infinite dignity and value.[39] The humanity of Christ, is the 'sacrament, that is, the sign and instrument, of his divinity and of the salvation he brings: what was visible in his earthly life leads to the invisible mystery of his divine sonship and redemptive mission'.[40]

In all of his mysteries, even from his Mother's womb, the Son of God is pouring out boundless riches – a treasury of revelation, redemption, and recapitulation. He is the eternal Word, and so his 'whole earthly life – his words and deeds, his silences and sufferings, indeed his manner of being and speaking – is Revelation of the Father'.[41] 'Redemption comes to us above all through the blood of his Cross, but this mystery is at work throughout Christ's entire life'.[42] So, for example, 'already in his Incarnation, by becoming poor he enriches us with his poverty'.[43] The Catechism draws on St Irenaeus's theology of recapitulation. The Son of God became incarnate from the Virgin in order to make all things new, to sum everything up under himself as Head, thereby giving creation a new beginning. By making the whole human journey, from the womb to the tomb, his own, the Son of God objectively bestows upon it a fresh and matchless dignity.[44]

Everything in Christ is for sharing. 'All Christ's riches "are for every individual and are everybody's property".'[45] Christ is our Head. With him, as St Thomas said, we are 'like one mystical person'.[46] Somehow, through his Incarnation, the Son of God embraces and bears within himself every single human being. That is why his mysteries can become ours. This sharing is, first of all, moral. In all of the mysteries Our Lord gives us an example. 'He is "the perfect man", who invites us to become his disciples and follow him.'[47] But the sharing is much more than moral. There is grace, new life and power, in each of the mysteries. Participation makes possible imitation.

> Christ enables us to live in him all that he himself lived, and he lives it in us. 'By his Incarnation, he, the Son of God, has in a certain way united himself with each man.' We are called only to become one with him, for he enables us as the members of his Body to share in what he lived for us in his flesh as our model.[48]

The mysteries of the life of Jesus are thus direct causes of sanctification. His infancy can make us childlike. His overcoming of Satan's tempting is a victory for all men. The immersion of his body in the Jordan gives a new vocation to water. Dying, he destroyed our death; rising, he restored our life.

The flesh: the hinge of salvation

The Catechism teaches with great gusto that 'the flesh is the hinge of salvation'. It is a true human body (animated by a rational soul) that the Son of God takes from the Virgin Mary.[49] In that body he suffers and dies, and in that same body he rises on the third day and ascends to the right hand of the Father.[50] Moreover, in and through his body, now glorified, the Son of God touches and heals us in the Sacraments.[51] Against all the Gnosticisms, ancient and modern, against all the attempts 'from Valentinus to Bultmann' to demythologise and etherealise the Resurrection of Our Lord,[52] the Catechism reaffirms its historicity and bodiliness. It is 'a real event, with manifestations that were historically verified'.[53] The empty tomb, though in itself not a direct proof of the Resurrection because 'the absence of Christ's body from the tomb could be explained otherwise', is nonetheless 'an essential sign for all'. When the Beloved Disciple sees 'the linen cloths lying there', he 'saw and believed', that is, 'he realised from the empty tomb's condition that the absence of Jesus' body could not have been of human doing and that Jesus had not simply returned to earthly life as had been the case with Lazarus'.[54] Given all the confirming testimonies, 'Christ's Resurrection cannot be interpreted as something outside the physical order, and it is impossible not to acknowledge it as an historical fact.'[55]

> By means of touch and the sharing of a meal, the risen Jesus establishes direct contact with his disciples. He invites them in this way to recognise that he is not a ghost and above all to verify that the risen body in which he appears to them is the same body that has been tortured and crucified, for it still bears the traces of his Passion. Yet at the same time this authentic, real body possesses the new properties of a glorious body: not limited by space and time but able to be present how and when he wills....[56]

The Son of God assumes the whole nature of man in order to redeem the whole nature of man. His Resurrection, indeed he himself, is 'the principle and source of our future resurrection',[57] 'even now by the justification of our souls (cf. Rm 6: 4), and one day by the new life he will impart to our bodies (cf. Rm 8: 11)'.[58]

The heart of Christ

The centre of the central Christ is his Sacred Heart. The Catechism refers to the teaching of Pope Pius XII in his encyclicals *Haurietis aquas* and *Mystici Corporis*:

> Jesus knew and loved us each and all during his life, his agony, and his Passion and gave himself up for each one of us... He has loved all with a human heart. For this reason, the Sacred Heart of Jesus, pierced by our sins and for our salvation, 'is quite rightly considered the chief sign and symbol of that... love with which the divine Redeemer continually loves the eternal Father and all human beings' without exception.[59]

This is a magnificent doctrine. In Gethsemane, on Calvary, when he carried the monstrous burden of my and every man's sins, the Son of God had me and every man, all his members, in his human heart. He knew me and loved me and gave himself up for me. Such a vast sweep of knowledge and love could not be merely natural. It is a supernatural perfection of the human mind and heart of Jesus through their union with the divine person of the Word. One of the Pius XII texts to which the Catechism refers in a footnote, explains it beautifully:

> But the loving knowledge with which the divine Redeemer has pursued us from the first moment of his Incarnation is such as completely to surpass all the searchings of the human mind; for by means of the Beatific Vision, which he enjoyed from the time when he was received into the womb of the Mother of God, he has for ever and continuously had present to him all the members of his Mystical Body, and embraced them with his saving love....[60]

Archbishop Schönborn has spoken of 'the secret presence of the Sacred Heart' in the Catechism.[61] The section to which I have just referred is relatively brief, but there are many other places where the Catechism invites us to contemplate the heart of man, the Heart of the God-Man. For example, with regard to the Passion, we are told that, 'by embracing in his human heart the Father's love for men, Jesus "loved them to the end".'[62] Finally, in Part Four, Christian prayer is presented as the conforming of our hearts to the Heart of Christ, so that, through him and in him, we can pray, 'Father, thy will be done'.[63]

2. THE SACRAMENTS OF CHRIST

Part Two of the Catechism is prefaced by a second fresco from the Catacombs. It shows the woman with the flow of blood, who was healed when she touched the cloak of Jesus through the power that 'went forth from him' (cf. Mk 5: 25ff).

> The Sacraments of the Church now continue the works which Christ had performed during His earthly life. The Sacraments are, as it were, 'powers that go forth' from the Body of Christ to heal the wounds of sin and to give us the new life of Christ. The image thus symbolises the divine

and saving power of the Son of God who heals the whole man soul and body, through the sacramental life.[64]

The sacraments and the mysteries

The sacraments of Christ in his Church continue and prolong the mysteries of his life on earth. The Catechism gives us this teaching, quoting from Pope St Leo the Great:

> Jesus' words and actions during his hidden life and public ministry were already salvific, for they anticipated the power of his Paschal Mystery. They announced and prepared what he was going to give the Church when all was accomplished. The mysteries of Christ's life are the foundations of what he would henceforth dispense in the sacraments, through the ministers of his Church, for 'what was visible in our Saviour has passed over into his mysteries'.[65]

We can unfold this teaching with the help of St Thomas's doctrine, derived from the Greek Fathers, that the humanity of Christ is the living, united 'instrument' of the divinity. It was through the instrumentality of his human nature on earth that Christ acquired grace for us, and it is through the instrumentality of that same human nature, crucified and glorified, in Heaven that Christ communicates grace to us. As principal efficient cause, the Triune God uses the humanity of the Son as an instrument to produce in us the grace which he merited by his mysteries.

Powers coming forth from the body

In the sacraments, power comes forth from the Risen Body of Jesus to heal and divinise us. Sacramental causality would seem to be physical and not merely moral. This is the teaching of St Thomas Aquinas, who tells us that the entire glorified humanity of Christ, body and soul, acts upon men, body and soul.[66] On earth, the bodily actions of the Lord Jesus expressed his mental thoughts and feelings; when he fell to the ground in Gethsemane, he showed the crushing weight of the grief in his heart. In heaven, his risen body serves his spiritual soul with exquisite ease, channelling the grace which in his love he wants to give us. The living waters of the Holy Spirit flow from the Father and the Son through the side of the Son, out of the wound in his heart.

In the seven sacraments, our Lord continues to do in his flesh now glorified what he did already in his flesh when mortal: using bodily things and actions to achieve spiritual effects. As St Thomas says, the power to sanctify us flows from the divinity of Christ through his humanity into the sacraments of the Church.[67] Or, in the words of Cardinal Journet, the sacraments are 'the hands of Christ extended in space and time'.[68] They are the means by which the incarnate Saviour reaches out to touch mankind, to extend his saving action throughout space and time – to heal and renew, to sanctify and divinise, to make us sharers of his life with the Father in the Holy Spirit. Jesus still touches us with his body, and from that touch power streams forth. The glorified flesh of God the Son physically radiates power – the power to make us holy and whole. We receive that radiation in the sacraments. Power goes forth from him to heal our bleeding wounds.

Re-presentation

In all of the sacraments, Christ touches us through his body, but in the Holy Eucharist, his Body and Blood, together with his Soul and Divinity, are really, truly, and substantially present under the sacramental species.[69] St Cyril of Alexandria says that the Word incarnate does not want us to be united with him only in spirit, by faith and charity, he wants us also to be united with him in the flesh. 'Why does the Mystical Blessing enter into us? Is it not to make Christ dwell there bodily through communion and participation in his sacred flesh?'[70] 'Truly, I say to you, unless you eat the flesh of the Son of Man and drink his blood, you have no life in you' (Jn 6: 53).

When speaking of the Holy Eucharist, the Catechism gives special attention to the doctrine of 're-presentation'. According to the Council of Trent, in the Mass the bloody sacrifice Christ offered on the Cross is 're-presented, its memory perpetuated until the end of the world, and its saving power applied'.[71] The Catechism likewise says that Christ's 'Passover' is 'made present' in the Eucharist, and so 'the Sacrifice Christ offered once for all on the Cross remains ever present'.[72] The Mass is a Sacrifice because 'it re-presents (makes present) the Sacrifice of the Cross, because it is its memorial, and because it applies its fruit'.[73]

On the altars of the Church, the two thousand years separating us from Calvary are set aside. 'In the Eucharist the Church is, as it were, at the foot of the Cross with Mary, united with the offering and intercession of Christ.'[74] When the Apostle says that the Sacrifice of Christ was offered once and for all', he does not mean that it is over and done with, locked away and inaccessible in the lumber-room of history. On the contrary:

> [A]ll other historical events happen once, and then they pass away, swallowed up in the past. The Paschal mystery of Christ, by contrast, cannot remain only in the past, because by his death he destroyed death. And all that Christ is – all that he did and suffered for all men participates in the divine eternity, and so transcends all times while being made present in them all. The event of the Cross and Resurrection abides and draws everything towards life.[75]

Once again we see how the two missions of the Son and the Spirit work together: in each celebration of the liturgy 'there is an outpouring of the Holy Spirit that makes the unique mystery present'.[76] This is manifested in the epiclesis, 'the intercession in which the priest begs the Father to send the Holy Spirit, the Sanctifier, so that the offerings may become the Body and Blood of Christ, and that the faithful, by receiving them, may themselves become a living offering to God'.[77] The Holy Spirit puts us into contact with the flesh and blood reality of the crucified and risen Christ. He unites us with his Body and in his Body.

3. LIFE IN CHRIST

The Catechism's third icon of Christ is a sculpture, the central section of a fourth-century sarcophagus discovered beneath the 'Confession' in St Peter's, Rome. It shows us Christ giving his new law to the Apostles Peter and Paul.

> As Moses had received the Old Law from God on Mount Sinai, now the Apostles, represented by their two leaders, receive from Christ, the Son of God, the Lord of Heaven and Earth, the New Law, no longer written on tablets of stone, but engraved by the Holy Spirit on the hearts of believers. Christ gives the strength to live according to the 'new life'. He fulfils in us what he has commanded for our benefit.[78]

Christ-centredness is for living, not just discussing. If the Lord Christ is 'centrally for us, if we believe in him and love him, then we must keep his commandments as transmitted faithfully by the Church (cf. Jn 14: 23f). Jesus must be the practical centrepoint of our lives.

> The first and last point of reference to this catechesis will always be Jesus Christ Himself, who is 'the way, and the truth, and the life' (Jn 14: 6). It is by looking to him in faith that Christ's faithful can hope that he himself fulfils his promises in them, and that, by loving him with the same love with which he has loved them, they may perform works in keeping with their dignity.[79]

As Christians, as those who in Baptism have been incorporated into Christ, our activity has to conform to the Christ-centredness of our being.

> Coming to see in the faith their new dignity, Christians are called to lead henceforth a life 'worthy of the Gospel of Christ' (Ph 1: 27). They are made capable of doing so by

the grace of Christ and the gifts of his Spirit, which they receive through the Sacraments and through prayer.[80]

The moral life is life in Christ: by his grace we live in him, and he in us. 'When we believe in Jesus Christ, partake in his mysteries, and keep his commandments, the Saviour himself comes to love, in us, his Father and his brethren, our Father and our brethren'.[81] It is by the sanctifying grace of Christ and the gifts of the Holy Spirit that we truly live in Christ as adopted children of the Father. The Holy Spirit is 'the interior Master of Life, according to Christ, a gentle guest and friend who inspires, guides, corrects, and strengthens this life'.[82] Here, too, the mission of the Holy Spirit is ordered to that of the Son: through the Spirit Christ becomes 'the living and interior rule of our activity'.[83] The new law *is* the grace of the Holy Spirit given in faith and working through charity.[84]

In the spirit of St Augustine and St Thomas, the Catechism gives us a morality of happiness, of beatitude and the Beatitudes. The Beatitudes reveal the goal of human life: participation in the happiness of the Triune God himself.[85] The sons of Adam have been wounded by his sin, and so they need the saving help of God to reach their final happy home. 'Divine help comes to him in Christ through the law that guides him and the grace that sustains him'.[86] The Ten Commandments and the Sermon on the Mount are the paths to heavenly happiness, paths we tread by the grace, virtues, and gifts of the Holy Spirit poured out upon us by Christ.

The Beatitudes are truly Christ-centred, not just because Christ proposed them, but because he personifies them; he is their centre. To live according to the Beatitudes is to live the life of Christ.

> The Beatitudes depict the countenance of Jesus Christ and portray his charity. They express the vocation of the faithful associated with the glory of his Passion and Resurrection; they shed light on the actions and attitudes characteristic of the Christian life; they are the paradoxical promises that sustain hope in the midst of tribulations:

they proclaim the blessings and rewards already secured, however dimly, for Christ's disciples; they have begun in the lives of the Virgin Mary and all the saints.[87]

4. Christ – the Way of Christian Prayer

The fourth icon in the Catechism comes from the Byzantine tradition. It is an eleventh-century miniature from Mount Athos.

> Christ turns in prayer towards the Father. He prays alone, in a deserted place. His disciples look on from a respectful distance. St Peter, the head of the apostles, turns towards the others and points to him who is the Master and the Way of Christian Prayer: 'Lord, teach us to pray' (Lk 11:1)

At the centre of the icon is the praying Christ. He is the heart and centre of Christian prayer, its master and only way, just as he is the centre of Christian faith, worship and morality. But Christ, though he is in a lonely place, is not alone. The icon depicts him as 'One of the Trinity', the incarnate Word 'turned in prayer towards the Father', contemplating the Father's face. By His human prayer, the Son expresses his eternal dialogue of love with the Father, and he invites his disciples to a share in that dialogue of love by the gift of the Holy Spirit. The icon portrays in colour and shape what the text of the Catechism preaches by words: Christian prayer is Christocentric and Trinitarian.

> [I]n the New Covenant prayer is the living relationship of the children of God with their Father who is good beyond measure, with his Son Jesus Christ, and with the Holy Spirit... [T]he life of prayer is the habit of being in the presence of the thrice-holy God and in communion with him.[88]

Peter expresses his poverty. He wants to pray, but he does not know how. This humble recognition of our inadequacy, says the Catechism, is the essential starting-point of all Christian prayer.

'Prayer is the raising of one's mind and heart to God or the requesting of good things from God' (St John Damascene). But when we pray, do we speak from the height of our pride and will, or 'out of the depths' of a humble and contrite heart? He who humbles himself will be exalted; humility is the foundation of prayer. Only when we humbly acknowledge that [as St Paul says] 'we do not know how to pray as we ought', are we ready to receive freely the gift of prayer. 'Man is a beggar before God'.[89]

We have everything to learn about prayer. The Catechism teaches us that man, made in God's image, has a 'capacity for God',[90] is restless until he rests in God, that he is in search of God.[91] And yet prayer is not a merely human accomplishment. It is not man who makes the first move in prayer. It is God who, in the heart of man, takes the initiative in drawing him to prayer, and who in the history of man has revealed to him the nature and purpose of prayer.

The history of salvation, the drama of the covenant, is the history and drama of prayer. The Catechism shows God revealing and giving the gift of prayer to the Patriarchs and Prophets. Finally, in the fullness of time, he reveals prayer to us in his Son made true man: 'The drama of prayer is fully revealed to us in the Word who became flesh and dwells among us'.[92] All the prayer of the Old Testament – the intercession and contemplation of Moses, the praise and supplication of David, the vigilance of the prophets - looks towards and is fulfiled in the Lord Jesus Christ! true God and true man.

The Catechism warns us that we must approach the praying Jesus in an attitude of prayer. He is our Master, our Teacher, who shows us how to pray. He is our Priest and Mediator through whom we pray. He is our kingly Head in whom we pray. But he is also our God to whom we pray who hears and answers our prayers. As the Catechism says:

> To seek to understand his prayer through what his witnesses proclaim to us in the Gospel is to approach the holy Lord

Jesus as Moses approached the Burning Bush: first to contemplate him in prayer, then to hear how he teaches us to pray, in order to know how he hears our prayer.[93]

Jesus prays

The Catechism teaches us that the prayer of Jesus is the 'human prayer'[94] of a divine person. It springs from his human heart, his Sacred Heart: 'The Son of God who became Son of the Virgin yearned to pray in his human heart'.[95] The Catechism applies to the prayer of Jesus the Church's teaching that the one Lord Jesus has two wills, the divine and the human. It is precisely with His human will, with his human mind and heart, that the Son prays to the Father: 'Jesus' prayer before the events of salvation that the Father has asked him to fulfil is a humble and trusting commitment of his human will to the loving will of the Father'.[96] Our prayer – our praying through, with and in Christ – is meant to be a prayer of obedience to the Father, the conforming of our unruly hearts to the loving and obedient heart of Jesus: 'Contemplative prayer is the poor and humble surrender to the loving will of the Father in ever deeper union with His beloved Son'.[97] At the centre of all Christian prayer is the petition 'Thy will be done'.[98]

The prayer of Jesus is human prayer, but he who prays it is a divine person, God the Son, and so how he prays, the manner of his prayer, is divinely unique. There is something new about the way Jesus prays. He does what no Son of Israel has ever done before: He addresses God as 'Abba Father', thereby revealing himself as eternal Son in relation to the Father.[99] His prayer is filial, the human prayer of the Son, and so is our share in his prayer: we pray as sons-in-the-Son. The Catechism makes mention of Our Lord's words to Our Lady and St Joseph in the Temple: 'I must be in my Father's house' (Lk 2: 49). It then comments:

Here the newness of prayer in the fullness of time begins

to be revealed: His filial prayer, which the Father awaits
from his children, is finally going to be lived out by the
only Son in his humanity, with and for men.[100]

The wonder and mystery of Christian prayer is that the eternal Son
made man pours his Holy Spirit, the Spirit of his Son, into our hearts,
enabling us also to pray, 'Father', 'Our Father'. As the true and natural
Son, Jesus prays 'Father' as of right. As adopted children, we 'dare to
say' 'Our Father' as a grace granted us by Jesus in the Holy Spirit.

We can invoke God as 'Father' because the Son of God
made man has revealed Him to us. In this Son, through
Baptism, we are incorporated and adopted as sons of God.[101]

Prayer to Jesus

We must not misunderstand the phrase 'way of Christian prayer'
as applied to Christ. It does not mean that we can only pray
through him to the Father. No, Jesus is true God from true God,
consubstantial with the Father, and so we rightly address our
prayers to him.[102] Over fifty years ago, in his encyclical *Mystici
Corporis*, Pope Pius XII warned against the error of believing
that we ought not to address our prayers to Christ, but rather to
the Father through Christ. (This was the error of the Arians in
the fourth century, who taught that only the Father was true
God; St Basil wrote his treatise on the Holy Spirit against the
Arian doctrine and way of praying and insisted that we must
give equal glory to the Father and to the Son and to the Holy
Spirit.) Pope Pius asserted against the error in its twentieth-
century form: 'It is necessary for all Christians to know and
clearly understand that the man Christ Jesus is truly the Son of
God, and himself truly God'.[103] He pointed out that during the
Sacrifice of the Mass we pray to and worship the Lord Jesus as
well as the Father: in the Kyrie, the Gloria in Excelsis, the prayer
Domine Iesu Christe qui dixisti, the Agnus Dei, and the priest's
prayer before communion.

The Catechism quotes a wonderful text from St Augustine:

He prays for us as our priest, prays in us as our Head, and is prayed to by us as our God. Therefore, let us acknowledge our voice in him and his in us.[104]

Similarly, in the paragraphs on The Prayer of Jesus, the Catechism declares: 'Our High Priest who prays for us is also the One who prays in us and the God who hears our prayer'.[105]

The Catechism has a lovely paragraph on the invocation of the Holy Name of Jesus. In a way, it is the simplest and most powerful form of Christian prayer. Mention is made of the Jesus Prayer, Devotion to the Sacred Heart of Jesus, and the Way of the Cross.[106] Contemplation is also defined Christocentrically: it is the 'gaze of faith, fixed on Jesus'.[107] As the old man of Ars said to his holy parish priest about how he prayed before the Blessed Sacrament, 'I look at him, and he looks at me'.[108]

Come, Holy Spirit!
The Church prays not only to the Father and to the Son, but also to the Holy Spirit, 'who with the Father and the Son is worshiped and glorified'. The Holy Spirit's entire mission is to unite men with Christ and so with the Father.

> 'No one can say "Jesus is Lord" except by the Holy Spirit.' Every time we begin to pray to Jesus it is the Holy Spirit who draws us on the way of prayer by his prevenient grace. Since he teaches us to pray by recalling Christ, how could we not pray to the Spirit too?[109]

The Catechism mentions the classical forms of prayer to the Holy Spirit in East and West: 'Come, Holy Spirit, fill the hearts of thy faithful', from the Pentecost Sequence in the Roman Missal, and 'O heavenly King, O Comforter, the Spirit of Truth', in Byzantine Vespers for Pentecost.

The Mother of God shows the way

'Christ does not live alone in his Church', says Hans Urs von Balthasar, 'He is accompanied by all the saints who fill Heaven, and will never more be separated from them'.[110] The Catechism teaches us that we take the Christ-way of prayer in communion with the Holy Mother of God and all the angels and saints in Heaven, amidst a 'cloud of witnesses'.[111] We can and should ask the whole company of Heaven to intercede for us, for 'their intercession is their most exalted service to God's plan'.[112] Above all we turn to Our Blessed Lady with whom and to whom we pray.

> Jesus, the only Mediator, is the way of our prayer; Mary, his Mother and ours, is wholly transparent to him: she shows the Way (*hodigitia*), and is herself the Sign of the Way according to the traditional iconography of East and West.[113]

The Queen of Heaven brings everything down to earth. She is the Church's supreme model in faith, charity, and union with Christ, and so she is also the supreme model, the living personification, of the Church at prayer: 'Mary is the perfect Orans (pray-er), a figure of the Church'.[114]

The drama and the beauty of Christian Prayer

To take the Christian way of prayer, the Christ-way of prayer, is, according to the Catechism, to plunge into a battle. 'Prayer is a battle. Against whom? Against ourselves and the wiles of the Tempter who does all he can to turn us away from prayer, away from union with God.'[115] In its section on Original Sin, the Catechism has already taught us that 'the dramatic situation of "the whole world [which] is in the power of the Evil One" makes man's life a battle'.[116] The Christian knows that he is committed from his Baptism and empowered by his Confirmation to engage in a perpetual war against the world, the flesh and the devil. The Catechism tells us that 'the "spiritual battle" of the Christian's new life is inseparable from the battle of prayer'.[117] The

Catechism's teaching is reminiscent of the theodrama of Hans Urs von Balthasar, which presents Divine Revelation as the 'drama' of the interaction of divine and created freedom. Likewise, the Catechism speaks of the 'covenant drama' of prayer.[118]

There is both compassion and challenge in this remarkable section of the Catechism: compassion for our weakness, a challenge to our complacency. It speaks of all that undermines our efforts to follow Christ in prayer: 'erroneous notions of prayer', the 'mentality of this present world' which disparages prayer, the experience of 'failure in prayer'. There is only one solution. 'To overcome these obstacles, we must battle to gain humility, trust and perseverance'.[119]

Once again, it is the light of the incarnate Word that the Catechism shines upon our difficulties in prayer. When we experience dryness, we should 'cling to Jesus in his agony and in his tomb'.[120] When we are tempted to think that our petitionary prayers go unanswered, we should remember the final petition of Our Lord's prayer in Gethsemane: 'Thy will be done.' 'Since the heart of the Son seeks only what pleases the Father, how could the prayer of the children of adoption be centred on the gifts rather than the Giver?'[121]

The Catechism's teaching on prayer is a 'theodrama'; it asks us to commit ourselves, to get involved, by our prayer, in the Church's struggle against the spiritual powers of evil. But this fourth part of the Catechism is also beautiful; it provides a kind of theological aesthetic of prayer. In Part Three it defines beauty as the splendour of truth: 'Truth carries with it the joy and splendour of spiritual beauty'.[122] Beauty is the radiance of the true and the attractiveness of the good. The Catechism sheds light on prayer, but it also seeks to move us, to draw us into prayer. It makes prayer awesome yet attractive, because it presents not an abstract theory, but a living person, the Lord Jesus, the Word made flesh, the Master and Way of Christian prayer.

Conclusion

I began with Our Lady and St Patrick, and with them I shall conclude: the Queen of Ireland and the Apostle of Ireland. In this month of May, it is good to remember that the Blessed Virgin is the Church's supreme model in faith and charity and union with Christ, and therefore also in catechesis. She 'brought him into the world and gave him to mankind'. She still brings him into the world and gives him to mankind. The Mediatrix of Grace has, as Hopkins said, 'this one work' to do, 'let all God's glory through'.[123] In all her great apparitions in this century and last she calls her children back to deeper faith in her Son, more devout use of his sacraments, to conversion of life, and to unceasing prayer – the full programme of the Catechism. At Knock, in contemplative silence, she points to the Lamb and his Sacrifice and calls us to share his innocence and enter into his prayer. The compilers of our new Catechism have taken great pains to make Mary present throughout as our Mother and model, as the purest embodiment of everything Christian and Christ-centred. At the beginning, she is the realisation of Christian believing, and at the end she teaches us the secret of Christian praying. In joyful communion, then, with the Mother of God, in the words of our father Patrick, let us commend ourselves anew to Christ our God:

> Christ be with me, Christ within me,
> Christ behind me, Christ before me,
> Christ beside me, Christ to win me,
> Christ to comfort and restore me.

4

REVELATION AND FAITH

Breandán Leahy

Introduction

During my studies abroad, I was involved in a project called 'Theology in Dialogue'. Its aim was to bring together lecturers and students from various faculties (theology, philosophy, psychology, history, science etc.) a few times during the academic year in order to have an exchange of learning, insight and research. On one of these occasions, a well-known Italian philosopher came along. Very much influenced by the Marxist school, he was a man of great intellect and willingness to dialogue. He had read an enormous amount of Patristic literature – in the original Greek or Latin! I can still recall the poignancy of the occasion as we reflected on the reality of Christian faith. He recognised it as something which close companions and dialogue partners had, but which he did not. We had so much in common that discussion with him was fascinating. But the question of faith intrigued him. I recall him saying: 'We share a common vision in so many ways, but I know that there is a reality that you call faith which I do not share.'

It is no surprise that the Catechism starts with the theme of revelation and faith because it is the presupposition of the whole document! In general terms, the Catechism talks of faith as the human response to the God who reveals himself to us. Specifically, the theme which I have been given to address, namely, revelation and faith, is to be found in section one of Part One of the Catechism, which deals with our search for God,

God's coming among us, an Advent which culminates in Jesus Christ and is then transmitted to us, and, finally, the theme of faith itself.

Just as in the Second Vatican Council, where you can pin-point the Dogmatic Constitution on Divine Revelation, *Dei Verbum* (the Word of God), as the place where the issues of revelation, its transmission, and faith are elaborated, and you then have to look at other documents such as the Pastoral Constitution on the Church in the Modern World, the Decree on the Church's Missionary Activity, the Declaration on the relation of the Church to Non-Christian Religions, and the Declaration on Religious Liberty, so too we have to look to the whole Catechism for the theme of revelation and faith. Our faith is articulated in the Creed (39% of the Catechism), celebrated in the sacraments (23%), translated into life in the two great commandments, love of God and love of neighbour (27%), and nourished through union in prayer with the Triune God of love (11%).[1] So, in this short article, we'll hardly do justice to the theme!

An observation: two languages

At the outset I want to make a general observation with regard to the overall 'tone' of the Catechism on revelation and faith. I believe it echoes the tone found in *Dei Verbum*. And here reference can be made to an interesting commentary by Ghislain Lafont on the Constitution on Divine Revelation in the Second Vatican Council.[2] I mention it because I believe the point he makes is also true for the Catechism. Lafont comments that if you compare the Constitution on Divine Revelation with its preceding Conciliar statements (Trent and Vatican I) you'll notice two 'languages' running throughout *Dei Verbum*.

The first language is *trinitarian* (revelation is distributed between the three divine Persons, each one having their own role, in other words, revelation as disclosed in the context of the

'Economic Trinity'), *communional* (revelation as directed towards the eschatological communion, but also as about a humanity shaped in a trinitarian way), *historical* (revelation described as a process which starts from the beginnings of creation right up to its accomplishment in Jesus Christ, and prolonged, in a certain manner, in its transmission, giving shape to Christian history). The second language found in the Constitution on Divine Revelation is more in terms of *creation/participation* (the question of our dependency on God and the autonomy of creation), *nature* (the divine nature as participable), *truth* (underlining the inalienable characteristic of the contents of revelation [deductive method, certitude and obligation]) and *individual assent* to the God who reveals.

Lafont suggests that whereas Trent and Vatican I use more theist/metaphysical language, it is the trinitarian/historic language which 'sets the tone' (although, of course, not exclusively) for *Dei Verbum*. And this is significant. In noting that this second language is to be found throughout the documents of the Vatican II, Lafont points out that there is a whole 'new style' which emerges from the Council in terms of the way we think and live in the Church, a 'new style' therefore with regard to doctrine, worship, Church institutions, theology and inculturation.

It is worth remembering Lafont's observations as we reflect on the theme of revelation and faith in the Catechism. It has been pointed out that one of the major achievements of the Catechism is its consistent presentation of the trinitarian character of the Creed.[3] Revelation is presented in terms of a history of salvation with stages and features which culminates in Jesus Christ who opens up for us a new realm of communion modelled on the life of the Trinity. All of this has great implications for a 'new style' of thinking and living the Church which itself is important for evangelisation, catechesis and preaching today.

I took part in the 1986 meeting in Assisi of all the world

religious leaders in prayer for peace. This was an amazing event, with all the Christian denominations together, and an array of vestments, colours and symbols from representatives of all the major world religions. In many ways, the meeting will remain as a masterpiece in John Paul II's pontificate. Those who participated knew they were in the presence of something different, a very new way of the Church, reflecting the Council's teaching on revelation and faith.

Revelation and faith as a manifold movement

In a consideration of revelation and faith as presented in the Catechism, it is good for us to reflect on any faith experiences we have had ourselves. When you have an experience of a new beginning in faith, where some breakthrough has been experienced or where a turn of direction has come in your life, then you know that faith is something that works itself, as it were! It's a gift. Your life changes course, your marriage relationship improves, a difficult relationship with some neighbours begins to be resolved, you discover an endurance in the midst of some seemingly irreconcilable situation or you begin to be able to bear your illness... all of this shows that your new step in faith is really an answer to God's first step towards you.

When we look at the Bible we find that this is the great discovery we are being told about in the Word of God. Certainly the Sacred Writings present us with a way to follow in life; a way to live out our lives; but it witnesses to this way because first and foremost it witnesses to God's way towards us. The Catechism reflects this faith experience rooted in God's self-communication, presenting revelation and faith as a manifold movement. We shall follow the Catechism's presentation of this manifold movement, therefore, by adopting the notion of the 'Way' which captures the dimension of movement underlying revelation and faith. From its earliest beginnings, even before the word 'Christian' was coined, the Christian religion was called 'the Way', thus indicating the early Christians' understanding of how much their faith was a dynamic response to God's great initiative of love.[4] The following points are simply a focus for the necessarily personal and communal study of the sections indicated.

Ways towards God (27-49)

The first chapter of section one of Part One is entitled 'Man's capacity for God', and with this expression we are being told that we do not have just an intellectual capacity for knowing God (the Catechism affirms both classical and personalist ways of knowing God), but rather that we are made in such as way as to receive God into ourselves. We are created by God in his image and likeness in order to enter into communion with him with our whole existence. Every man, woman and child is made in such as way as to be a 'you' for God. Therefore, our capacity for this is already a sign of a vocation, a calling. We all know in some way that we are related to, or directed towards some participation in an Infinite Being. Various cultural expressions of this are found in human history and, indeed, the Church's dialogue with other religions presupposes it.

The Catechism reminds us that 'without revelation' we can say that God exists more than what he is. The last word in our search for God is silence before the Mystery. In saying this, the Catechism highlights that God is not made in our image and likeness, but the other way round. This tells us all something about the risk of reducing the God we believe in and whose existence we affirm to our own measure in thought, word and deed.

We must always let God be God. This is true on a daily basis for each of us. Cardinal Vlk of Prague tells of how, in the 1950s at the beginning of the communist rule in his country, they used to look to the western democracies, more particularly to American forces, to human forces, to save them. God, however, did not act as they imagined. God brought them to understand slowly, very slowly, as a Church, that his way, the path of the future, was different from the one they had thought. They had to wait for his way.[5] The theme of revelation and faith teaches us that we do not make God; we discover his self-revelation. So let us consider the manifold movement which unfolds throughout God's revelation and our response.

God's Way towards us: God of the Way (50-64; 68-72)

The silence of expectancy is our last word in our journey or 'exodus' towards God. The Catechism indicates how the God we seek is, in fact, always searching for us. God has 'opened up', as it were, to reveal himself to us, to reveal his own life. By this very fact alone, we see that God is a God of love. God speaks. God acts. In God's initiative we see his love. We see who God is in God's Way towards us. God is not only on the Way to us, but he is the God of the Way. God is self-exceeding, self-giving, and loving in disclosing himself to us.

In outlining the stages of how God reveals himself, a novelty can be noted in the Catechism which links up with the last section on our capacity for God. Speaking of revelation, the Catechism points to the various covenants which characterise salvation history. Covenants are these pacts, these promises entered into whereby God binds himself in a relationship to be with his people in a stable protective manner.

What we see from the Catechism is that, through the notion of covenant, the notion of revelation is extended and universalised. Revelation tended to be seen as starting with Abraham, relating only to the people of Israel, leading to Jesus Christ. In the Catechism, however, we see reference to the covenants with Adam and Eve and Noah, as well as with Abraham, Moses and the prophets. In other words, in the Catechism, revelation is proposed in a more universal manner because in saying that God offered his covenant to Adam and Eve it shows that all are touched in some way by revelation.

Accordingly, our capacity for God is in some way touched by God's Way (or 'advent') towards us. Indeed, the prologue of John tells us the Word of God is the 'light of all people' (cf. Jn 1:4). The covenant with Noah represents a relationship with all the nations, because Noah is seen as representing the new humanity born after the flood. So all nations share in some seed of revelation. Then come the specific covenants with Abraham, Moses, the prophets...

The affirmation of our capacity to know that there is a God, coupled with this extension of the notion of covenant, helps us to see another motivation behind what is called the 'dialogue of salvation' which has characterised the Church since the Council, especially the various dialogues with other religions and with people of other convictions. It also explains why there is a Pope who goes to the synagogue in Rome, visits Muslims in Tunisia, and dialogues with Gorbachev in the Vatican. We are all brothers and sisters touched in some way by a ray of those rainbows which link heaven and earth.

God *is* the Way (65-66; 73)[6]

All the covenants are directed towards the great new covenant, namely, Jesus Christ who calls himself 'the Way'. With Jesus we come to a great novelty. God is not only on his way *towards us*; he is not only a God *of* the way; God *is* the way. What the Catechism brings out is that in the life, death and resurrection of Jesus Christ, the Way, we come to know God not as an isolated individual in remote solitude, but as a communion of love between the Father, Son and Holy Spirit who have taken us into their eternal dialogue of love. 'It pleased God, in his goodness and wisdom, to reveal himself and to make known the mystery of his will. His will was that we should have access to the Father, through Christ, the Word made flesh, in the Holy Spirit, and thus become sharers in the divine nature' (51). I know, from teaching Christology and Trinity, that it is always a great discovery to glimpse the Christian God as a communion of love between the three Divine Persons.

The Divine emigrant, as one writer puts it, has spoken to us of his homeland and brought it among us. It is precisely in Jesus' total giving of himself, his becoming 'nothing' (Ph 2:6-11) out of love, a giving that was completely inspired by the Holy Spirit, and which culminates in his cry of abandonment, that we come to glimpse the relationship of love which exists between the Father, Son and Holy Spirit. We begin to see the dynamic of love: God the Father sends his Son. The Son gives up his life. The Spirit is given over to us. God's own inner life, God's own way of life, is one of self-giving and self-exceeding love.

Jesus, then, is the 'single point' which recapitulates all other points of history and revelation, and re-opens them all towards the fullness that is God as a communion of love. Jesus Christ is the new starting point for all the other covenants which went before him. In this sense, Jesus is the 'Mediator and fullness' of all revelation. The universality of revelation starts, as it were, again from Jesus. That is why we find statements to the effect that the Paschal Mystery of Christ's cross and Resurrection stands at the centre of the Good News that the apostles, and the Church following them, are to proclaim to the world (571). Or again, the mystery of the Most Holy Trinity is the central mystery of Christian faith and life, the source of all the other mysteries of faith (234).[7]

Along the Way (74-141)

So far we have looked at something to do with God's way towards us, at God who is the Way. But how does this saving revelation reach me here and now? At this point we come to the historicity of revelation as indicated when we talk about the apostolic nature of the Church. As we approach the third millennium, it is perhaps one of the most urgent needs of evangelisation to proclaim Jesus alive today, and not just as some historical entity of the past. Through the power of the Holy Spirit, God's self-communication in Jesus Christ is transmitted through the Word of Scripture, Tradition and Magisterium.

The apostles were the first depositories of the revelation of Jesus Christ. Why? Because they had lived with him, had heard his words, had seen his life. The apostles' transmission (apostolic tradition) comes about in written and spoken word. The apostles or those in communion with them wrote for all time this revelation that occurred in Jesus Christ. They drew from what they communicated through words without writing, but also through the sacraments, through their way of guiding the community. That is why we say that the transmission of revelation occurs through Scripture and Tradition which pour from the same source and reaches us today as a dynamic event inviting us to journey along with the God who has entered our history.

Here we are also at the heart of a very great ecumenical issue which has divided Reformed Churches from the Catholic Church. The Catechism, following *Dei Verbum*, tries to show that there isn't the kind of opposition between Tradition and Sacred Scripture as is often thought. Even for the Catholic Church, the first place is given to the written word. The written word is to be understood and lived in the apostolic Tradition, that is, in the life of the Church as handed on from generation to generation.

A passage in small type points out that the apostolic Tradition (with a capital 'T') is to be distinguished from the various theological, disciplinary, liturgical or devotional traditions (with a small 't') of the local churches. This Tradition, this flow of the revelation of Jesus Christ, the Way, in which we all participate, is given to the people of God, to all Christians.

Among this people, the Magisterium, that is, the bishops in communion with Peter, has a specific role authentically to interpret Tradition and the written Word of God. Their 'sure charism of truth' is a trustworthy point within the faith community which comes to us from the original apostolic community.

The Catechism presents Scripture, Tradition and Magisterium as interdependent. They are like a tripod holding up Revelation. Particular emphasis, however, as denoted by the dedication of a separate article to it (101-141), is laid on the written word of God which remains a fixed point in the faith of Christians. Scripture is inspired and so its final author, expressing himself through its human authors, is the Holy Spirit.

While the Word is fundamental, the Christian religion is not a religion of the book, but of the living word, of the word lived. It is the risen Christ, as seen in the episode of the disciples on the road to Emmaus, who interprets the Word and makes it a living word. It is the Risen One who speaks the words, not the book. That means that if I don't live the Risen One, and don't have the Holy Spirit, the book remains a book. We are a people of the living word. If the books of the Gospel were to be destroyed we should almost be able to rewrite them with our lives, with the words made flesh in and through us.

Finally, in reminding us that the books of the Old Testament retain a permanent value, the Catechism also shows how the Old Covenant has never been revoked and this is important in relation to dialogue with Judaism.

The Profession of Faith: journeying the Mystery (142-184)

Jesus Christ is the Way. The Son of God did not just come on earth, go past us and then beyond us. Jesus Christ shares his life with us and calls us along the Way that he is. This brings us to the interaction between the personal and communitarian dimensions of faith which provides the heading for section one of Part One of the Catechism: 'I believe – we believe'. Faith is a most personal act, since nothing is more personal than your relationship with God. No one can substitute for you in your relationship with God any more than anyone else can walk with your feet or think with your mind. I recall the experience of a young person in his late teens after the Shankill Road bombing. When he was in his early teens he had been very committed to trying to live the Gospel together with others, but his commitment had waned over time. The day of the bombing he said to himself: 'It's no good for me to go blaming others; I have to take some step', and so he decided to get more involved in his parish and try to live his faith in earnest. It was a uniquely personal step for him.

The Catechism talks of faith in terms of obedience, a word understood in a biblical sense of a humble listening to the word of God. What comes across from the Catechism is a notion of faith as a becoming empty before God so that he can generate his Son within us. The models presented are Abraham and Mary. In Augustine's words, Mary's 'let it be done' shows that Mary conceived in her mind, her spirit, before she conceived in her womb. The Word was generated in her spirit because she became empty, welcomed him, and had a faith that grew until her desolation at the cross. For each one of us, the 'let it be done' of faith is a personal act; it involves entrusting oneself to God who reveals in Christ by means of the Holy Spirit. It is a trinitarian reality. I welcome the Trinity who opens out to me, since it is the Spirit within me that makes me adhere to Christ, and Christ bears me to the bosom of the Father.

While faith is a most personal act, we know that Jesus Christ draws people *together* along the Way that he himself is: self-giving; crossing over to the other; love. We are drawn not just to be together, but to exist *towards* one another, to live for one another just as the three divine Persons love one another. That's why the New Commandment becomes the Way of Christ in history. It's why the Church is not some 'added extra' to our faith. It is why Jesus' two great commandments are so intimately linked and form the basis of the part of the Catechism on the Christian moral life.

The more I say 'I believe' and the more this 'I believe' grows within me, the more I learn to say 'we believe'. My 'I' of faith becomes the 'we' of the Church. And this 'we' of the Church is, in reality, the 'I' of Christ spread out through space and time.[8] St Paul writes: 'For in Christ Jesus, you are all children of God through faith. For as many of you as were baptised in Christ have put on Christ. There is neither Jew nor Greek, there is neither slave nor free, there is neither male nor female; for you are all one in Christ Jesus' (Ga 3:26-28). To say 'we believe' is to say we are all one in Christ Jesus. It is why the Church is our common mother (personified in Mary) because she generates, educates and sustains us in the faith.

Faith, therefore, is our living within the specific novelty of Christian faith, namely, Christ, the Risen One is our midst, opening up for us a share in a new existence in the Mystery of God who has come among us. One author has written: 'If God is Love, as he himself has revealed and shown himself to us, the Mystery is not God's hiding from humankind, but rather God's gift of himself to us in God's way'.[9] God's Way has become our 'living-space'. We journey together in God's Way, sharing in what Balthasar calls a 'Trinitarian logic' which must be experienced in order to know it and direct ourselves along it.[10]

That is why our Profession of Faith is not meant to be simply a recitation of a collection of items of a compendium. The Profession of Faith expresses the trinitarian logic which has shaped who we are, shapes how we can be and act, think and speak, and will shape eternally the fulfilment of history in Paradise. Every Sunday, therefore, as we profess our faith, we 'journey' the Mystery of God's Way and it throws light on our daily journey at work, in the office, at home, at school. In other words, faith is a whole vision of the world from God's point of view, to be discovered and lived out day by day. Our knowledge of God is at once both 'a looking and a journeying'.[11] At this point, let's look for a moment at our profession of faith and see how its trinitarian logic can shape our journey.

The first main section of the Creed centres on *God the Father*. It speaks about creation (and the Catechism greatly emphasises the importance of this doctrine). God takes the first step towards me, towards you, towards our world. Christian faith points us completely towards the Father so that we can see things from his perspective, the perspective of the unoriginated origin of Love. Faith in God the Father Creator also tells me that I too can be a source of love in history. I too can be a co-creator. How? Revelation has told us that God, the Creator, saw all that he had made and saw it was very good, and so our faith vision prompts us to see the positive in each person and appreciate it. It also prompts us to take the initiative in love.

In a certain sense, when we live like the Father, we too create and make others exist by the love we have for them, loving as they need to be loved, facilitating the development of possibilities that would otherwise remain dormant in them. An experience that comes to mind here is that of a young man, Eddie, who had a progressive illness, muscular dystrophy, which left him paralysed in all his limbs and was eventually to kill him. Having discovered a way to transform his suffering into a source of life, both for himself and for other people, this 'handicapped' person really participated in God's fatherhood, 'co-creating' others into a fullness of life. Eddie's influence on Kevin is a case in point. In his early twenties Kevin had become a seasoned alcoholic, a pill-popper, and was engaging in sexual relationships with prostitutes. In meeting Eddie, and experiencing his concrete love despite all of Eddie's apparent limitations – restricted movements and difficulty in speech – Kevin came to realise that he wasn't a bad person trying to become good, but a broken person trying to become whole. Eddie was a 'father', 'co-creating' Kevin into a new life throughout Kevin's time in the detox unit and its subsequent limbo. Very much in the background, Eddie was a support and model. Kevin subsequently got himself a job, got married and both he and his wife now have three lovely children.[12]

The second major section of the Profession of Faith concerns the *Son*. It speaks of the Incarnation and Redemption. The Son receives all he is from the Father through the Spirit. He has made himself one with our human condition, given his life for us and is risen from the dead. This tells me that the Son reveals himself as divine not only in loving/giving but also in letting himself be loved, not only by giving but also by receiving. The poverty which receives is a condition of love also. We too are capable of letting ourselves be loved. This section indicates that we can be protagonists of love by making ourselves one with our neighbour and 'giving', but also by receiving. I recall the world Youth Day in Czestachowa in 1991 when over a million young people from around the world, but especially Europe, were gathered together. Some bishops had accompanied the young people and joined in as fellow-pilgrims. I recall the comment of some non-practising young people who, in noticing how some of the bishops were simply with them, sharing their sandwiches and being with them in simple ways, discovered a whole new love for the Church.

The third section of the Profession of Faith is about the *Holy Spirit*. It speaks of sanctification and the universality of God's love. In the Trinity the Spirit is the eternal bond of the unity between the Father and the Son and also their openness. Our faith vision tells us that our love can never be closed in on itself.

Sometimes, in meeting children who are going to be confirmed I tell them one of the most moving experiences I heard of during the Bosnian war. It is that of a family who were separated during a particularly bad period of fighting. When eventually the teenage children were allowed to return to their village, they met their distraught mother. Her husband lay dead beside her. Soon the suspected murderer was brought to her by a group of neighbours who wanted her merely to concur in accusing him – they would 'look after' the suspected culprit. All awaited the mother's reply. But, to her children's amazement, she refused to give any indication which would result in the accused man being killed. She explained that they had all been neighbours before the war. They had all played together as children. She had always spoken of forgiveness; now was her time to put it into practice. When I tell about this experience I ask the children: 'Who was that "voice" within her which prompted her to love and forgive?' As St Augustine tells us, the Holy Spirit is our 'interior teacher'.

The journey today

The Catechism proposes the faith. As one commentator said after its publication: 'The Catechism is now in our hands',[13] but anyone involved in evangelisation, catechesis or ministry is faced with questions about the new phenomenon of unbelief, the new agenda of unbelief.[14] A Catechism is probably not the place to go into a treatment of that and it doesn't. Vatican II had looked at this in what has been called one of the most important declarations of the Council, a milestone in the history of the Church in this century, namely, the pastoral Constitution on the Church in the Modern World, *Gaudium et spes* (19-21).[15] A Pontifical Council for dialogue with culture exists. But, does the Catechism have anything to tell us about this vast area of concern today for evangelisation, catechesis, and preaching?

Firstly, a word about the phenomenon of unbelief, or at least, the 'exile' of God from people's day-to-day horizon. It is occurring precisely where there is a whole history which has been Gospel-influenced, namely, the western world. I have always found helpful a reading of the present situation given by John Paul II. He comments that the whole crisis of faith experienced today is not something which comes to us from outside the Church and Christianity, as some difficulty or external obstacle in the work of evangelisation which has to be overcome. Rather, he says, it is internal to Christianity and to the Church. In order words, the crisis of faith is something within the historical journey of faith.[16] He throws light on what he means by pointing to the mystical experience of, for example, someone like John of the Cross. He compares the crisis we are going through with a dark night which has acquired an epochal dimension of collective proportions.[17]

Taking this notion of a 'dark night', the period we are going through is like an epochal purification of our notion of God and our living out of that understanding of God. Bruno Forte asks a probing question which faces us all in our teaching, preaching and evangelisation: Is the God of Christians a Christian God?[18] Rahner, Balthasar and others point to the shocking observation that what we claim to be the central doctrine of our faith, the Trinity (CCC, 234), impinges hardly at all on our understanding and living of the faith.[19]

As I mentioned, one of the major achievements of the Credal section of the Catechism is the consistent presentation of the *trinitarian* structure of our faith. There is a need to present the trinitarian relational nature of the Christian God who is One. This will certainly involve a renewed presentation of the Christian God. Significantly, in Vatican II, Scripture, Tradition and Magisterium are seen in a Trinitarian type of relationship. The Church is understood to be a people gathered into one in the unity of the Father, Son and Holy Spirit.[20] The government of the Church too is conceived in the Council in the image of God who is One and Triune.[21]

The Catechism helps in providing and enabling a clear presentation of the trinitarian structure of our faith. Important and all as a clear presentation is, Paul VI's well-known observation in *Evangelii nuntiandi* (n.41), still holds true, and perhaps even more so today. He pointed to the importance of being living Gospels when he said: 'Modern men and women listen more willingly to witnesses than to teachers, and if they do listen to teachers, it is because they are witnesses.' The world will not believe if it does not see. Jesus himself asked for witnesses so that others would believe: By this will all know you are my disciples if you love one another (Jn 13:35); be one so that the world will believe (Jn 17:21).

One of the novelties found in the Catechism is precisely this feature of pointing to witnesses. They are the living interpretations of the Gospel, of Christian truth, throughout the centuries. We are introduced to our great 'contemporaries in the faith' as Archbishop Schönborn calls them: Augustine, Francis of Assisi, Catherine of Siena, Joan of Arc, Teresa of Avila, John Henry Newman, Elizabeth of the Trinity. Archbishop Schönborn comments that the Catechism gives particular importance to the words of the saints. Mostly they are placed at the end of a section, as a kind of extension, as the last, and in a certain sense, therefore, the most authoritative word.[22]

Balthasar once wrote that if the miracles of absolution and consecration bring about, again and again, an ever new presence of the events of Good Friday and Easter within the Church, why should it not be the same with the constant repetition of the theological existence of the Lord in the life of his faithful and saints?[23] The Catechism indicates that the Christian faith lived out can be a point of access for others to experience Jesus Christ anew.

The reference to witnesses also says something about the importance of sharing one's experience of faith. When I find myself with a parish group where inevitably the concern of parents about the lack of faith in their sons and daughters arises, I like to recall the experience of a woman who once explained to me what she does. She simply shares what, for example, going to confession is for her. With a love which is detached from wanting results, she explains why she goes, how she approaches the sacrament, and what it means to her for her life.

The fact that the Catechism contains so many Scripture citations suggests it wants to tell us that the whole of our faith can be found in some way in the Word. So, today, perhaps the Catechism is indicating a way in terms of sharing the Word, sharing our experiences of the Gospel lived, which opens up the horizons within which faith grows. This is the dialogue of life undertaken, for instance, in the Pope's recent encyclical letter on ecumenism.[24] But could it not also be a way for evangelisation, teaching and preaching? Recently, after preaching on the Sunday Gospel which emphasised the theme of hope, a woman came up to tell me of her delight. It seems that many years ago someone had once explained to her from experience that hope is very important for the Christian life, in that 'as long as we have life, we can always start again'. I could see that the experience communicated to her had remained with her as an inspiration for the rest of her life.

In talking to children preparing for their first confession and first communion, I like to tell them of an episode I witnessed myself. One day I was walking with a married couple and their child when we passed an ice-cream van. The small child declared to all that he wanted an ice-cream (and I was in considerable sympathy myself with that idea!). But his parents said he couldn't because he had just eaten a large dinner with sweet included. The child got into a tantrum and began to cry and stamp his feet. His father, obviously referring to St Paul's notion of the 'old man' said simply to him: 'Colm, that is the old man in you; let's see the new man'. To my great surprise, the child stopped screaming and turned towards his parents and gave a lovely smile. Obviously his parents had communicated this to him and the small child understood there is a difference between the old and new man within each of us. From the reaction I get when I tell this experience to the children preparing for their first confession, I have seen how sharing experiences of the Gospel lived opens up doctrines of faith for others.

There is another feature which I would also like to highlight in terms of the inculturation of our faith today. The Constitution on Divine Revelation states that the Church has already received and welcomed in Jesus Christ the full and definitive word of God, but, at the same time, with the help of the Holy Spirit, the Church is always advancing towards the plentitude of divine truth, until eventually the words of God are fulfilled in her (*Dei Verbum*, 8). During the Council, the Louvain theologian, Gérard Philips, emphasised that the novelty and importance of this expression lies precisely in affirming that there is an interdependence between our knowledge and possession of revelation.[25]

Each new era produces new Spirit-inspired inculturations of the Gospel which open up realms of the Christian mystery which have always existed but which we possess in a totally new manner. Looking back over our history, we can say that each new era has been blessed by God with charisms which lift up the Gospel in a new and vibrant manner, providing a whole new way of looking at, understanding and thus possessing more fully the 'deposit' of which the Church is custodian and dispenser.

Cardinal Ratzinger has pointed to examples: Athanasius is not thinkable without Abbot Anthony's new experience of Christ, nor are Bonaventure and the Franciscan theology (and indeed a whole current of renewal in the Church) in the thirteenth century without the enormous new re-actualisation in the figure of Francis of Assisi.[26] By emphasising so much the lived experience and wisdom of the saints and mystics, the Catechism is giving us a key for evangelisation today, namely, the role of the charisms in the Church of our day which can lift up our faith in a new way.

But what are the modern charisms and spiritualities highlighting? Do they provide hermeneutical keys which can open up this Catechism for today? Stefano de Fiores has written a book about modern spiritualities in the Church, in which he outlines key features of contemporary spirituality.[27] Amongst other things he notes a greater emphasis on the more central elements of our faith: God, Jesus and his new commandment, the Cross, Mary as disciple.... In a similar vein, the German theologian, Eugen Biser, in writing that we have reached a spiritual 'turning-point' which opens up a new possibility for the Christian proclamation,[28] contends that the characteristics of the turning-point can be expressed in two biblical icons of central elements of our faith.

The first icon is that of Christ crucified who cries out in his abandonment on the cross. Our era has indeed been described as a 'landscape of crying'. Biser remarks that: 'The cry – often fairly repressed – becomes a visible figure there where modern literature, philosophy, and psychology, as in particular in Karl Jaspers and Carl Gustav Jung, concentrate on the figure of Job and feel their problems are presented in this figure'.[29] This cry finds its echo and response in the cry of Christ on the Cross 'who, in his abandonment, not to be consoled by any visible help but only by addressing himself to God, gave to those who could not be helped in any manner other than that which only he could give: himself'.[30]

The other icon is that of Emmaus, of the disciples who discover the presence of the Lord in their midst, in that burning of their hearts, in their listening to the word and in the breaking of the eucharistic bread, in which the risen Christ grasps and draws their existence towards its fullness, which indicates that faith – writes Biser – 'becomes perceptible there where preachers make the effort to translate the written testimonies into a living language. This takes place where, in the consciousness of the Christian community, those words are realised: 'where two or three are gathered in my name, I am in the midst of them' (Mt 18:20)'.[31]

Drawing upon Rahner's image of the 'winter time of the Church', Biser concludes that 'beneath the snow-covered fields life is preparing for a new awakening.'[32] Nietzsche spoke of us moving into the adult age of faith. While Nietzsche spoke of a faith which became dogma, and which then was transformed into morality and ultimately ended up self-dissolving, Biser underlines instead that, perhaps, the Christian faith is about to enter into a new state of its existence, a mystical state. It is only a faith which is deepened from a mystical point of view which can reach humankind in its actual identity crisis and in its existential crisis'.[33] He sees faith as having a future because 'in the measure it has learned to "go out of itself" it has gained an unprecedented capacity to empathise but equally the frankness to express and declare itself'.[34] While proclamatory in nature, the Catechism also points to the place of mysticism in deepening our faith.

Conclusion

What I have tried to present was revelation and faith in the Catechism as reflecting the tone set by Vatican II on Divine Revelation. Our ways towards God are within the greater Way of God towards us. In fact, in the paschal mystery, the death and resurrection of Jesus Christ, we discover that God is the Way in which we move and live and having our being (Acts 17:28). So our faith response is a dynamic participation in a trinitarian logic of love. The icons of Jesus Crucified and Abandoned and Jesus Risen in the midst of his people opening up our sharing in the triune life, link well with the affirmation by the Catechism of the centrality of the paschal mystery and the doctrine of the Trinity in the presentation of the faith.

5

THE SACRAMENTAL LIFE IN THE CATECHISM

Seán Collins OFM

'There is no such thing as a kiss.' This statement generally makes them sit up, in undergraduate liturgy classes. When I then add, 'There are only people who engage in osculatory activity', they get the point. We have reduced baptism, eucharist, and so on to being things, when in fact they are people behaving in a certain way. (Marriage was so blatantly about people that it proved difficult to lasso it into the hylomorphic corral – look at the contortions involved in providing it with matter and form!)

Isolation and analysis, the procedure which proved so fruitful in classical scientific method, lent a spurious and totally misplaced aura of scientific rigour to the study of the sacraments. This perhaps explains why it was retained even though its ability to illuminate the most important aspects of the sacraments, such as discipleship, community and empowerment, was negligible. (Liturgical celebration too has been bedevilled by this pseudo-scientific delusion.) The realisation that sacraments are not chemical compounds and do not behave as such is hugely liberating because it means that we can restore them to the area of human interaction where they belong, and which is far more fun than controlled experimenting – compare the repeated hissing of the words of consecration by scrupulous priests in former times with the atmosphere of praise and delight in which we are invited to celebrate the eucharist today.

How people relate to each other, and thus to themselves, and how human enrichment and expansion happen, functions in a way that is the opposite of the 'isolate and analyse' process. It happens through making connections, multiple links at every level, through absorption and amalgamation ranging through past and present and providing aspiration and motivation towards the future. This is precisely the dynamic of sacramental activity.

Context is everything

I am reminded in this connection of an aphorism frequently used by Professor Margaret Heavey to her undergraduate students in the Classics Department of UCG thirty years ago: 'Context is everything, in life as in letters'. She was trying to raise our sights above the mechanics of rendering words and phrases and lead us into a sympathetic experience of the concerns of the writer. Though her own erudition was prodigious and her standards exacting, she had no patience with the aridity of uncontextualised scholarship – the kind pilloried by Yeats in 'The Scholars':

> Bald heads forgetful of their sins,
> Old, learned, respectable bald heads
> Edit and annotate the lines
> That young men, tossing on their beds,
> Rhymed out in love's despair
> To flatter beauty's ignorant ear.
>
> All shuffle there; all cough in ink;
> All wear the carpet with their shoes;
> All think what other people think;
> All know the man their neighbour knows.
> Lord, what would they say
> Did their Catullus walk that way?

It wouldn't be difficult to find a parallel with an amount of theological scholarship, and singularly easy in traditional liturgical and sacramental theology, where the text was often taken to constitute the entire *locus theologicus* and the context lost sight of.

The great strength of the presentation of the sacraments in the Catechism is, I would contend, its solid contextualization of sacramental life. It anchors it in three ways – in the trinitarian economy of salvation, in the mission of Jesus Christ and in the life of faith and conversion of the Christian community. This is far more significant, and has greater potential for a renewed catechesis, than the treatment of individual sacraments which is comparatively bland and concerning which I shall simply highlight a few points.

The sacrament turn-off

When sacraments are presented without any anchoring in life and simply as a closed system for keeping on the right side of a God who is interested only in totting up brownie points on a scale called 'grace', many people are alienated. They are in good company. Saint Francis of Assisi never found difficulty in praising God for the glories of creation, but balked initially at the darker side of life. He famously kissed a leper and thus overcame his distaste for disease and deprivation. But the narrowness of 'churchy' things and their apparent denial of life repelled him. Here was a subtler and, I suspect, ultimately more radical challenge. He used to see in the churches of Assisi an old woman, swathed in black and afflicted with a deformity which bent her to the ground. He became obsessed with the idea that if he got involved with religion he would end up like her. It cost him a lot to overcome this hurdle, and he did so only when he realised that (in his own phrase) God is the great almsgiver who lavishes gifts on everyone and does not apply a means test of merit or exact the forfeiture of joy from beneficiaries.

Patrick Kavanagh's early poem, 'Worship', captures the same reaction to a deadening and life-negating experience of sacraments:

To your high altar I once came
Proudly, even brazenly, and I said:
Open your tabernacles, I too am flame
Ablaze on the hills of Being. Let the dead
Chant the low prayer beneath a candled shrine,
O cut for me life's bread, for me pour wine!

In presenting a theory and praxis of the sacraments we need to be in touch with the distaste – even disgust – felt by not a few people at the comfortable pieties of a domesticated God and self-serving sacraments. The young Dietrich Bonhoeffer once delighted Karl Barth by quoting Luther to the effect that 'the curse of a godless man can sound more pleasant in God's ears than the Hallelujah of the pious'. Any sacramental catechesis which hopes to commend itself to believers today must digest the truth contained in this statement, and must be situated within the broad sweep of God's loving plan for all humankind – rather than constituting an exclusive and quasi-magic set of secret codes and passwords in the possession of the chosen few and denied to the vast majority who are heading for perdition.

The Catechism uses the overarching notion of 'blessing' to achieve this contextualisation, and situates the sacraments in such a way that they are neither esoteric nor arbitrary, and this, I think, is the most inspired and stimulating aspect of its presentation.

All God's activity is blessing

The concept of 'blessing' embraces 'the whole of God's work... from the beginning until the end of time' (1079). It unites creation and redemption, and sees God's purpose of salvation as one and unchanging, 'from the liturgical poem of the first creation to the canticles of the heavenly Jerusalem' (ibid.). From the human side, 'blessing' means the acknowledgement of God's bounty and grateful acceptance of it (1078). 'Blessings' are thus not spiritual as opposed to material gifts: all of life is blessing.

The sacramental theology of the Orthodox theologian Alexander Schmemann begins from this very starting-point, and perhaps a quotation from Schmemann can highlight the significance of the Catechism's approach:

> Nowhere in the Bible do we find the dichotomies which for us are the self-evident framework of all approaches to religion. In the Bible the food that man eats, the world of which he must partake in order to live, is given to him by God, and is given as communion with God. The world as man's food is not something 'material' and limited to material functions, thus being different from, and opposed to, the specifically spiritual functions by which man is related to God. All that exists is God's gift to man, and it all exists to make God known to man, to make man's life communion with God. It is divine love made food, made life for man. God blesses everything he creates, and, in biblical language, this means that he makes all creation the sign and means of his presence and wisdom, love and revelation. 'O taste and see how gracious the Lord is...'[1]

Sacramentality is therefore a continuum, and the radical originality of the work of Christ is safeguarded not by hiving him off into a special salvation-enclave for believers, but by placing him at the head of the most general providence too. When the Catechism makes what might seem to be exclusive claims for the Church and the liturgy (e.g. 'In the Church's liturgy the divine blessing is fully revealed and communicated [1082]), we must remember that it is Christ, rather than any ecclesiastical ordinance, who is the centre of divine blessing and human response. This avoids the appearance (which is very real for many) of saying that God has given up on creation and abandoned it as beyond repair, and has now reopened for business in smaller premises called the Church, purveying first-aid kits called sacraments.

The paschal mystery

The Catechism links Christ's work in the sacraments with the notion of the paschal mystery. This can be a fruitful line of approach, provided we remember that it's the experience and life of Jesus that is the given, not the term 'paschal mystery', which is just a shorthand way of referring to the experience. The paschal mystery is not some kind of procedure Jesus performed, but his total movement, in his humanity, towards the Father. What we call the sacraments are the things we do, as a community of believers in him and because of him, to remember and be in touch with this movement of Jesus.

The Catechism's treatment of the institution of the sacraments by Christ is appropriately nuanced: 'The mysteries of Christ's life are the foundations of what he would henceforth dispense in the sacraments... The Church gradually recognised this treasure received from Christ and... has determined its dispensation' (1115 and 1117). The sacraments are 'powers that come forth' from the Body of Christ (1116). The object of this power is the transformation of the celebrating community into Christ in every aspect of its life: 'the fruit of the sacramental life is that the Spirit of adoption makes the faithful partakers in the divine nature by uniting them in a living union with the only Son, the Saviour' (1129).

It is thus clear that sacraments have no relevance outside the ambit of faith. They are not general vehicles of divine benevolence but patterns of gathering, remembering and commitment. These patterns, in so far as they elicit responses from the human psyche, employ the same kinds of psychological mechanisms and processes commonly elicited in similar situations (of national celebration, family bonding, commemoration of heroes and founding figures, etc.); in so far as they are focused on one whose reality 'cannot remain only in the past... and so transcends all times while being made present in them all' (1985), they are able to put us in immediate and living communion with Christ. While being thus specific, and not intended as levers for modifying the circumstances of life in general, the sacraments do not separate believers from the general run of humankind. The reason for this, as the Catechism sees it, is that the general blessings of life, health, family, friends, and so forth, are bestowed on all (independently of faith) through the Word by which they are created – the same Word which, made flesh, unites believers in faith to itself so that all blessings are received more knowingly, embraced more fully and returned to God more thankfully, through and with the Word made flesh, Jesus Christ.

This outline of a Christian anthropology can be developed very fruitfully in catechetical terms, with inductive and deductive approaches complementing each other without undue tension.

The Holy Spirit in sacramental life

The outline of the role of the Spirit in liturgy and sacraments (1091-1109) is effectively presented, and will further help in stripping the sacraments of the magic veneer with which they are sometimes invested. 'The desire and work of the Spirit in the heart of the Church', says the Catechism (1091), 'is that we may live from the life of the risen Christ'. The Catechism outlines, with parallels from scripture and the liturgy, how the Spirit prepares us for the mystery of Christ, recalls it, makes it present to us and unites us to the life and mission of Christ.

The Spirit is 'the Church's living memory' (1099), so that anamnesis is an expression of the unity and continuity at every moment of the wonderful works of God (already brought out in the 'blessing' concept), rather than just a vague recollection of something from the dim and distant past. (The opposite of anamnesis would be amnesia, the chief result of which is loss of identity – since people who cannot remember or recognise anyone are bereft of relationships and so can't know who they are.) The epiclesis is an invocation of the unifying and transforming Spirit for the fulfilment of God's plan in each sacramental celebration, and the drawing of every believer into the dynamic of the 'Passover' in Christ towards union with God. 'Communion with the Holy Trinity and fraternal communion are inseparably the fruit of the Spirit in the liturgy' (1108). The Eastern liturgies call the Holy Spirit '*Koinonopoietes*', maker of communion. The Spirit is the deep tug of all things towards primal unity.

Specifics on the sacraments

Every attempt to categorise the sacraments is defective. They present a certain parallel to the stages of natural life (1210) – but this can be seriously misleading if pushed too far (as in Confirmation *vis-à-vis* baptism), as the Catechism itself admits (1308). I'm not sure how helpful people will find the division adopted by the Catechism in 1211. 'Sacraments of Initiation' is traditional and clear, and justified by our ritual books – but to treat eucharist as a sacrament of initiation is hardly enough. 'Sacraments of healing' for reconciliation and anointing of the sick is fine too – but then surely the eucharist is a sacrament of healing also. 'Sacraments at the service of communion and the mission of the faithful' is cumbersome and begs too many questions. Luckily, the actual treatment of the sacraments doesn't seem to depend too much on this division; perhaps it is attempted simply because this was generally done in textbooks. It could well be dropped.

In general, the use of the liturgical celebrations themselves as the source of reflection is to be commended (though the treatment of baptism veers between consideration of infant and adult baptism). The exposition rarely contains fresh elements – perhaps because the Praenotanda for the various liturgical books (those which were published before this kind of introductory matter became the norm have been equipped with it in newer Latin editions – e.g. ordination) were already an attempt at liturgical catechesis in advance of systematic and official catechesis in other areas, and these Praenotanda have been heavily drawn on by the Catechism.

I don't think that, by and large, the material on individual sacraments lends itself as it stands to catechesis. It gives the impression of being geared towards organisers of ritual and presiders (the Praenotanda, which began as a sort of commentary on the rubrics, are still struggling inside that strait-jacket), and reads like the old manuals. But having said that, I would agree that it provides a foundation on which to construct a practical catechesis – which is what the Catechism claims to do. (I suppose in any case that this is an area fortunate enough to have a wealth of catechetical material available.)

The Catechism's treatment of the individual sacraments

To the definition of baptism given in Canon Law (Can 849) is added the idea that through this sacrament people 'are made sharers in [the Church's] mission' (CCC 1213). This reinforces the presentation of the sacraments as a dynamic enlistment of believers in the transformation of society rather than Green Shield stamps offering personal and private benefits. Initiation is a journey in stages, and the order of these stages is what is different in the case of infants and in that of adults (1229). The point is made in paragraph 1254 that for all the baptised, faith must grow after baptism. There is a nuanced and sensitive treatment of the necessity for baptism and the fate of infants who die before baptism in paragraphs 1257-1261.

The treatment of confirmation reflects the current ambiguity in its understanding and practice. Paragraph 1285 begins by saying that the unity of initiation must be safeguarded, but paragraphs 1290-1292 outline the difference in traditions about this sacrament. The breathtakingly simplified presentation of the New Testament evidence in paragraph 1288, which follows that of Paul VI in the Apostolic Constitution which established the essential rite for the sacrament in 1971, is geared to justifying the present practice rather than to elucidating the picture in the early Church.

The treatment of the Blessed Eucharist is extensive, but the legacy of Counter-Reformation emphases is more pervasively present than may be necessary or desirable in a catechetical text. The transforming power of the eucharist as a shared covenant celebration could have been emphasised more. There is, admittedly, a section entitled 'The Fruits of Holy Communion' which deals with transformation, but its style (as well as its title) is individualistic, and apart from paragraph 1397 ('The Eucharist commits us to the poor') there is not much emphasis on social responsibility flowing from the Eucharist. The statement that 'it is in keeping with the very meaning of the Eucharist that the faithful, if they have the required dispositions, receive communion each time they participate in the Mass' (1388) is theologically more cogent than the current legislation (the authentic interpretation of Canon 917 given by the Commission for interpreting the Code of Canon Law on 26 June 1984) which allows reception of Holy Communion twice a day. The key question of course is what would be a genuine reason for participating in more than one Mass in the day.

The treatment of the sacrament of penance and reconciliation, while acknowledging that the manner in which it has been celebrated 'has varied considerably' (1447), in practice follows the method of analysing the acts of the penitent and those of the confessor which was used in the Praenotanda to the Rite of Penance. Some emphasis on conversion, the call to the whole Church to be a sign and instrument of forgiveness and reconciliation (1442), the table fellowship of Jesus as the model of reconciliation, and the revitalising effect of reconciliation on the whole Church (1469), does not suffice to dissipate the feeling that we are dealing primarily with a mechanism for effecting moral improvement rather than a liturgical celebration of the reconciling love of God. The Catechism explicitly states: 'Like all the sacraments, Penance is a liturgical action' (1480). This however is not the dominant message conveyed.

The treatment of anointing distinguishes between the charism of healing and the sacrament of anointing, and conveys the nature of the sacrament rather well, I feel. The section on holy orders, even though it quotes extensively from the liturgical texts (or perhaps because of this, since ordination texts will naturally reflect the social structures of their time more than other sacramental texts) conveys a sense of disembodied authority and power more surely than that of a service of the Christian people. One feels that the most effective catechesis on orders will situate the sacrament (as do most of the agreed ecumenical statements on ministry) in the context of the fidelity of the Church to Christ and Christ's constant empowering of the Church in its mission. Marriage is dealt with in a way which, while it is uncompromising in proposing the ideal, is realistic and compassionate towards difficulty and failure. But the values of marriage are probably best conveyed in stories.

Conclusion

In the recent film *Smoke*, Harvey Keitel is a tobacconist who, at 8.00 precisely each morning, takes a photograph of his shop from across the road. The film brings together the stories of people whose lives intersect by chance and whose relationships wax and wane. The collection of still photographs, precise but uncontextualised, is a control on things: satisfying in its way, but mechanical. The weaving of lives is as imprecise as smoke hovering in the air, but it is where laughter and tears are, and the pulse of promise.

6

THE MORAL VISION OF THE CATECHISM

Janet Smith

There is little question that promulgation of the Universal Catechism is one of the greatest events of this century – and perhaps for several centuries. It is a great privilege and honour to be here to comment on the moral vision of the Catechism and to be in such distinguished company. I hardly feel myself worthy of the great honour of sharing the podium with such distinguished Churchmen and scholars, but as a philosopher I am accustomed to being the handmaiden of theology and am pleased to render what humble service I can.

An important feature of the moral vision of the Catechism is revealed initially by its title: 'Life in Christ'. Indeed, all of Christian morality can be summed up in those words, for the moral life for the Christian is quite simply to 'imitate Christ'. So what more needs to be said? Why did the authors of the Catechism create so much work for themselves – and so much reading for us – by devoting the longest portion of the Catechism, nearly three hundred pages in the English edition, to the subject of morality?

Reality is complicated and rich and although Christ himself is the fullness of revelation, we, not being angels, need to work our way step by step through the many layers of meaning in life. No truth is revealed whole and simple to the human mind. Morality is a very complicated portion of reality because it involves not only eternal truths but also the individual particular; it involves human character and choice and the daily mess of life.

Thus it is appropriate that the human person have more help in the living of the good life than the true statement 'imitate Christ'. The human person needs many aids, many sources of moral truth. The Catechism identifies the major sources of moral truth; it speaks of the guidance of the Holy Spirit, of grace, of the beatitudes, of natural law, of human and Christian virtues, and of the Church itself. It teaches extensively about the commandments. These are all traditional themes in the Church's moral vision. The presentation of them in the Catechism, however, not only reflects the role of these themes in the tradition but also mirrors developments in the Catholic moral vision.

Here I would like to focus on two elements of the moral vision of the Catechism that are distinctively modern. First, I will look at the what use the Church makes of what is known as 'rights language', which means talking about morality in the terms of 'rights'. This is a language which supplements the Church's moral vision in some important ways but also poses problems for the Church. In the second and shorter portion of the paper I shall look at the emerging importance of conscience in the Church's moral vision.

Rights language

One considerable challenge for the Church in modern times is finding a way of conveying its moral teaching to an age that most manifestly does not share its moral presuppositions. The Church holds many views very contrary to the modern age; for instance, it holds that there are moral absolutes; it holds that suffering can be a redemptive good; it teaches that we should readily sacrifice possession of the goods of this world in preference to securing the goods of Heaven; it understands freedom not as doing whatever one wants, but as liberation from sin and the right to do what is good. Moreover, the Christian understands that the supernatural is always penetrating this world to help souls attach themselves to what is good and holy. It is often difficult for Christians to divest themselves of their modern presuppositions and adopt the vision of the Church. Here I wish to identify one particular modern presupposition and to use it as a foil to portray the much richer moral vision of the Church.

Many have observed that the modern world is so pluralistic in its moral thinking that there is no common moral discourse. One mode of moral discourse that seems to have a kind of universal currency is the language of human rights. Universal declarations of human rights seem to provide a backdrop against which cross-cultural discussions of morality and politics can proceed. Since the final decade of the last century, since Pope Leo XIII, and very much in the last decades of this century, rights language has played an almost dominant role in Church encyclicals dealing with moral and political matters.

There are two likely reasons for the prominence of rights language in Church documents. First, as mentioned, rights language is the coin of the day as far as moral discourse is concerned: if one is going to try to make a case of morality in the modern age, it is nearly impossible to do so without recourse to rights language.

Second, rights language carries with it a salutary dimension that combats a dangerous feature of the modern ethos and that is relativism. Whereas relativism dominates modern moral judgments, rights language, with its reference to inalienable rights, carries with it the sense that there is a universal and absolute set of moral demands, true at all times and places.

Catholic thinkers like John Courtney Murray and Jacques Maritain have applauded the Church's adoption of rights language since they believe it compatible with the natural law tradition of the Church. Yet, it has long been argued by others that the use of this language poses some problems for the Church. They observe that rights language grows out of the political thought of such Enlightenment thinkers as Hobbes and Locke whose view of man and God was in considerable opposition to that of the Church.

There is confusion about what a 'right' is. Some rights, often called 'negative rights', describe what is known as a 'zone of non-interference'. To say, for instance, that one has a 'right to life' or a 'right to privacy' means that there are very few justifications for taking another's life and that no one should violate another's privacy.

Other rights, known as 'positive' rights, make claims on others to provide something to the needy. Children are said to have a right to food, shelter, clothing, and education from their parents. It is not always clear whether a right is negative or positive or, in the case of a positive rights, who has the obligation or duty to supply the need. For instance, it is not immediately clear whether the right to a job or to health care is a negative or positive right, or who has the obligation to provide jobs and health care.

What we understand to be the source of rights also makes a great deal of difference to how we understand rights – how we understand what constitutes a right and how absolute and universal the rights are. Does the state confer rights upon us? Are they God-given? We could ask these questions differently; are rights given to us in virtue of our nature – are there fundamental human rights – or are rights simply a legal invention? What is the good that they serve? Human liberty? Human dignity? And finally, what are our rights? Do we have a right to freedom of speech? To free practice of religion? To abortion? Are there limits to these rights?

A full consideration of these questions is definitely beyond the scope of this talk, but they begin to suggest some of the problems with 'rights language'. A book entitled *Rights Talk* by Mary Ann Glendon, the Harvard lawyer who headed the Vatican delegation to Beijing, illuminates even further some of the problems with 'rights language'. It is quite ironic that, as one of the fiercest critics of rights talk, in Beijing she found herself drawing a great deal on rights language to defend women, children, and culture against horrendous violations of their fundamental human dignity. Yet, this situation would hardly have surprised her, since she has herself documented well that those who wish to speak of morality in the modern age are quite necessarily dependent upon rights language. This passage represents well Glendon's critique of 'rights talk'.

> Our rights talk, in its absoluteness, promotes unrealistic expectations, heightens social conflict, and inhibits dialogue that might lead toward consensus, accommodation, or at least the discovery of common ground. In its silence concerning responsibilities, it seems to condone acceptance of the benefits of living in a democratic social welfare state, without accepting the corresponding personal and civic obligations. In its relentless individualism, it fosters a climate that is inhospitable to society's losers, and that systematically disadvantages caretakers and dependents, young and old. In its neglect of civic society, it undermines the principle seedbeds of civic and personal virtue.[1]

Glendon makes many claims here. She claims that rights talk does not allow for nuances – that any right quickly comes to be seen as absolute and without limitation. Elsewhere she notes that rights seem to proliferate and quickly assume a status of absoluteness; for instance, the 'right to privacy' has begun to dominate many legal decisions in the United States – and, as is well known, is the basis for the legalisation of abortion and euthanasia. We soon find ourselves claiming we have a right to whatever it is that we want and claiming that others should provide it for us.

Glendon also claims that rights talk eclipses all talk of responsibility. She observes that young people are able to recite a litany of the rights that are secured by a free society but are not able to list what obligations and responsibilities members of a free society might have. She maintains that rights talk reduces each of us to an autonomous centre of rights independent of relationships and of the community. We become so concerned with securing our own rights that we exhibit little interest in the well-being of others. In fact, others are seen as potential rivals for the goods to which we have rights.

Modern rights talk asserts that the foremost right is liberty and apart from harming others, we believe our liberty to pursue our own concept of the good should be unfettered. In the modern view, rights secure our liberties; the ultimate goal is for each of us to do what we want, when we want – as long as we do no harm to others. Indeed, in a US Supreme Court Case, *Planned Parenthood* vs. *Casey*, it was stated that 'At the heart of liberty is the right to define one's own concept of existence, of meaning, of the universe, and of the mystery of human life' (112 S. Ct. 2807 (1992)). This claim was made in support of abortion and has since been used in support of euthanasia.

One of Mary Ann Glendon's most salient observations is that rights language impoverishes our moral discourse. It reduces all moral claims to claims of justice. Entire other spheres of moral discourse are forgotten. For instance, we no longer speak in terms of virtue (though there are currently powerful attempts in the US to reinsert virtue language into our moral discourse) or in terms of doing God's will, or in terms of duty, or natural law, or keeping the commandments. My students are always astonished when I speak of a moral obligation to take care of our health – they balk at this claim unless it can be framed in terms of what we owe others. That health is a human good that we have an obligation to seek or preserve seems a foreign concept to them. If no injustice is done, if no rights are violated, they can not see that something immoral has been done. Having lost the language of these other sources of morality, we have also, it seems, lost the moral vision that undergirds them.

To understand how rights talk impoverishes our moral discourse, let us evaluate a scenario and see how different would be the terms of the discussion of the moral dimensions of the situation from the point of view of one who reasons in terms of rights and from the point of view of one who shares the Church's moral vision.

The scenario is this: a young unmarried woman engages in an act of sexual intercourse; she becomes pregnant; she ponders an abortion but decides to carry the child to term; she goes on welfare but also sues the father for child support; she places the child in day care so that she can pursue a career.

The individual who reasons in terms of rights might say that the woman has a right to have sexual intercourse when and with whom she likes; she has a right to an effective contraceptive which the medical profession has yet really to provide her; she has a right to an abortion which outweighs the foetus's right to life. (She also has a right to the opinion that the foetus has no right to life.) She has a right to public support in order to raise her child; she also has a right to child support from the father of the child. She has a right to self-fulfilment so she has the right to place her child in day care. Since no rights have been violated according to this evaluation, it is difficult to see how any disapproval of her action could be expressed. Those who reason in terms of rights may sense that all is not morally laudable here, but after all, she is just doing what she has a right to do, she is doing what she is free to do.

Rights language could be used to express disapproval of this woman's action, but we must make very clear that it would be a different rights language. The 'rights' we invoked to justify her action are in service of individual liberty. Reference to rights to register disapproval are not those designed to maximise freedom but are rights that are rooted in the dignity of the human person, a dignity bestowed upon the human person by God. From this perspective, it could be said that people have no right to have sexual intercourse outside of marriage, that they have no right to use contraception or to have an abortion; the child can be said to have a right to be conceived by parents who are married to each other (as *Donum vitae* states) and, of course, to have a right to life. It could be said that the parents have no right to charitable support for their misdeeds and that they have no right to pursue their own selfish interests at the expense of the well-being of their child. Moderns who disapprove of the actions portrayed would likely speak this way, would likely use rights language to express their disapproval. They would, however, be speaking a different 'rights language' – a 'rights language' that understands rights to be protective of human dignity, not to be a means to maximise human freedom. I will return to the question of the foundation of rights in a moment.

Before we consider the proper use of rights language, let us note that one who shares the Church's moral vision could evaluate this scenario without any use of rights language. Disapproval of the woman's action could be expressed in a multitude of ways. In having sexual intercourse outside of marriage the woman is not acting in accord with human dignity; she is violating the meaning and purpose of sexual intercourse for she is not using her sexual powers to express her spousal love for another and she is not being responsible towards any child she might conceive. In so acting she is breaking the natural law. She is also violating the laws of scripture and the Church that teach that sexual intercourse outside of marriage is a grave offence against God. She is violating the meaning of sexual intercourse by using contraception for she is not expressing the full meaning of complete self-giving that the sexual act is meant to express. Both the male and the female involved in the act of sexual intercourse outside of marriage have failed to act in accord with the dictates of love; they have used and exploited each other (even if they felt love for each other) and have not brought their child into the world in a loving fashion.

The woman does not have the virtue of moderation or temperance in respect to her sexual desires since she does not order these desires to their proper good. If she had decided to have an abortion she would be doing greater damage to herself than to the unborn child. If she knows the nature of her act, she would be committing a mortal sin and endangering her immortal soul. She would be forming vices such as injustice and perhaps cowardice in her soul. The community may be charitable to her in giving her welfare to support her child but can the woman and her child be said to have a right to welfare? The couple has harmed the child and the community by bringing a child into existence outside of the support of a loving marriage.

The father (who would share fully in the evil of the action) certainly ought to assume financial and emotional responsibility for the child. Both parents ought to do everything they can to ensure that the child does not suffer from their poor decisions – and by poor decisions I mean immoral actions. The woman and the man should put the well-being of the child above their own self-fulfiling career and life interests.

Both individuals should have recourse to the sacrament of confession and the Eucharist for the grace to amend their ways and to fulfil their responsibilities. Had they consulted their consciences before they acted and attempted to form their consciences in accord with Church teaching, they would have realised that sexual intercourse outside of marriage is wrong and as free and responsible moral agents would have voluntarily postponed sexual satisfaction until they made a commitment to each other and to the children their actions may produce. They should have prayed to Christ and relied upon his grace and love to strengthen them so they could resist their unruly passions and could act in accord with their responsibilities. In so far as they overcome these passions, and act in accord with their responsibilities, in accord with the dictates of human dignity, love of each other, and the love of God, they would be becoming perfect as their heavenly Father is perfect and would look forward to living for eternity with God himself.

Note that the evaluation in accord with the Church's moral vision can be done without any reference to rights and that it is much more complicated than the evaluation in terms of rights.

Rights language focuses on a fairly narrow range of ethical concerns – the just interactions between individuals or between individuals and the state. In addition, the Church's moral vision encompasses human dignity, natural law, virtue, grace, love, charity, the commandments, prayer, the sacraments, conscience, the passions, obligations to others and to God, sin and the eternal destiny of man. These are all themes of the Catechism. Such concerns can easily be lost in the moral vision governed by rights.

Perhaps the difference between a moral vision governed by rights language and the moral vision of the Church can best be seen through contrasting what it means to be a creature bearing rights and a creature bearing duties. Our age is slow to recognise duties and responsibilities. In fact, it tends to find in the words 'duty' and 'responsibility' negative connotations that suggest a curtailment of freedom, whereas rights are connected with freedom. A creature bearing rights is a creature full of needs and demands that often seem to conflict with the needs and demands of others. A creature bearing duties is interconnected with others as one who must actively seek the good of others, and who, in doing so, is also achieving goods for one's self, if only the very important good of performing one's duties.

The Christian moral vision sees the human person as indebted from the moment of conception and throughout life. He owes God and his parents for his coming into existence and for his continued existence. He owes countless others for making his life and his enjoyment of life possible. Each human person is a creature much indebted to God and others. He is obliged to live a life of self-giving, if only to make some small repayment for what he has received. His focus should not be upon himself and his needs, and demands, and rights, but on doing good for others. Those who perform their duties achieve true freedom, the freedom from selfishness and vice. Thus while rights language can serve the important function of protecting human dignity from assaults against it, the language of duty advances the ennobling, the human person and the advancement of true freedom.

We must realise, then, that when the Church uses 'rights language' is uses a 'rights language' that differs considerably from modern 'rights talk'. As was seen above, the Church is careful to note that it understands rights to be grounded in human dignity, which encompasses more than our status as free creatures. Such a grounding is essential for it prevents the irresponsible proliferation of rights that are grounded only in our needs or desires. It combats the lethal modern tendency to enshrine inauthentic exercises of liberty into rights (more about this in a moment).

The clearest stating of the foundation of rights is perhaps found in a passage from *Donum vitae*, quoted in the Catechism (2273):

> ... human rights depend neither on single individuals nor on parents; nor do they represent a concession made by society and the state; they belong to human nature and are inherent in the person by virtue of the creative act from which the person took his origin. (DV III)

Here rights are linked to human nature and to the Creator who formed that nature. In fact the Catechism links rights talk not only to human dignity but also to the commandments and to natural law as well:

> The natural law, present in the heart of each man and established by reason, is universal in its precepts and its authority extends to all men. It expresses the dignity of the person and determines the basis for his fundamental rights and duties... (1956)
>
> The Ten Commandments belong to God's revelation. At the same time they teach us the true humanity of man. They bring to light the essential duties, and therefore, indirectly, the fundamental rights inherent in the nature of the human person. (2070)

Here we can see that the Church tethers rights language to the traditional moral terminology of the Church; such statements make it impossible, for instance, that one could have a 'right' to do something at odds with human nature and dignity or to do something in violation of the commandments.

In recent documents the Church has been sharp in its warnings against the modern age's overvaluing of freedom and its erroneous understanding of the concept. In an age of relativism and scepticism rights language, rather than serving to protect fundamental human goods, begins to be used to protect violations of fundamental human goods. We find in *Evangelium vitae* a marvellous dissection of the dangers of modern rights language. It speaks powerfully about how the laudable modern interest in ensuring that the fundamental rights of all are respected has, through a distorted understanding of freedom, led us to begin to transform what should properly be termed crimes into fundamental human rights. At one time abortion was considered a heinous crime, then it was argued that women should have the right to choose abortion, then access to abortion was spoken of as a fundamental right, and in some areas of the globe, notably China, abortion is now used as an instrument of the state; women who have had one child are forced to undergo abortion. In *Evangelium vitae* the Church powerfully describes this process. In the US, right-to-die forces are winning through the same shift from crime, to fundamental human right, and I suspect, before long to obligation.

We have focused here primarily on the dangers of 'rights language'. We noted early in the talk that 'rights language' does serve useful purposes, among them that of advancing the view that some elements of morality are universal and absolute. The association of rights language with freedom and liberty is also important and salutary, even though the understanding of freedom and liberty to which it is attached is excessive or distorted. The Church is rightfully eager to ally itself with the advancement and protection of human freedom.

Now I wish to speak briefly about another very modern concern that achieves some importance and prominence in the Catechism. It is in its teaching on conscience that the Church clarifies its understanding of authentic human freedom. The growing importance of freedom in the Church's moral vision – and the difference between the Church's understanding of freedom and the modern view of freedom – can perhaps be seen with some clarity by comparing the CCC with the Roman Catechism.

Council of Trent: Cosmology versus Christology

The last official catechism of the Catholic Church, the Roman Catechism (RC), was issued in 1566. Such a great distance between catechisms perhaps serves to magnify unfairly differences that have gradually taken place over centuries. Comparing a Renaissance city to a modern one would reveal such differences as to cause some to think one had perhaps moved to a different universe. Yet the beauty of centuries-old structures, their adaptability to modern use and, indeed, their frequent superiority to modern structures suggests that we can hardly say that the past is without relevance to the present; nor can we make the boast of unrelenting progress that we might like to. A change in treatment of a topic does not, of course, suggest a change in teaching; it most likely suggests rather the differing concerns of the time in which the topics are addressed. The RC was written to counter the Protestant Reformation and properly reflected the concerns of that time. The Catechism has been written during a time of considerable confusion within the Church about Church teaching and in an age saturated with the values of modern secularism.

The section in the RC that covers morality deals exclusively with the ten commandments. The Catechism, on the other hand, places a discussion of the Ten Commandments as a second section in the part entitled 'Life in Christ'. The first section of this part, entitled 'Man's Vocation: Life in the Spirit', covers many topics such as man's freedom, the morality of the passions, the conscience, virtues and sin. A second chapter in the first part is entitled 'The Human Community', and a third chapter deals with law and grace. Only then follows a treatment of the ten commandments. The absence of many of the topics of the Catechism in the RC does not suggest, of course, that the Church did not draw upon these sources of morality in the past. A more comprehensive treatment of the sources of morality may be present in the Catechism because there has arisen in the intervening centuries greater dispute about what constitute the sources of morality.

One can, though, discern a theme threaded through the moral portion of the Catechism that seems to have a prominence one could not quite imagine in the RC. The Catechism picks up the christological and personalistic emphasis of the Vatican II which had moved some distance from the cosmological and natural law emphasis of the past. To oversimplify matters, one could say that the Church has shifted from an emphasis on God the Father as lawgiver who has written his will into the laws of nature, to an emphasis on Christ as our model of perfection and human dignity as the grounding of morality in the Catechism. Whereas the RC stressed God as the author of nature and the author of all moral laws, the Catechism stresses that all moral law is in accord with the dignity of the human person. These are emphases that began to emerge in the documents of Vatican II and come to a fuller flower in the Catechism.

The Catechism does not reject or abandon a view of the cosmos as ordered by God or of natural law as a guide to morality but goes well beyond them in its presentation of morality. Hence in the Catechism we find the emergence of the 'dignity of the human person' as a focal point of moral teaching. And I would like to note further that the dignity of the human person is seen as rooted not so much in his status as a rational creature whose mind is able to grasp reality but in his status as a free and self-determining creature who must shape himself in accord with the truth. Such key themes of personalism permeate the moral vision of the Catechism. A personalist cast imbues all discussion of morality; that is, there is a constant reference to man's dignity as manifested in his power to determine himself freely in accord with the truth.

The moral section of the Catechism begins with this passage:

> The dignity of the human person is rooted in his creation in the image and likeness of God (article l); it is fulfiled in his vocation to divine beatitude (article 2). It is essential to a human being freely to direct himself to this fulfilment (article 3). By his deliberate actions (article 4), the human person does, or does not, conform to the good promised by God and attested by moral conscience (article 5). Human beings make their own contribution to their interior growth; they make their whole sentient and spiritual lives into means of this growth (article 6). With the help of grace they grow in virtue (article 7), avoid sin, and if they sin they entrust themselves as did the prodigal son to the mercy of our Father in heaven (article 8). In this way they attain to the perfection of charity. (1700)[2]

In this passage we can see several of the main concepts that inform a personalist approach to ethics: man as made in the image and likeness of God, man as determining himself by his deliberate and free actions, a concern with the interior life, the need of conforming our actions to the good that is made known to us by our conscience, and the goal being attainment of perfect charity. These themes play a major role in both the Catechism and in *Veritatis splendor*.[3] These concepts, of course, are also central to natural law ethics and have been a constant part of Church teaching. The simple fact that the passages cited in support of the teachings of the first portion of the moral section of the Catechism are all from non-modern sources indicates the timelessness of these themes. But these themes have been knit together in a certain fashion that is new and that is a response to developments within the Church and within the modern culture.

Let us emphasise the phrase 'It is essential to a human being freely to direct himself to [beatitude].' The emphasis on self-determination that is emerging in Church documents reflects the concerns of Pope John Paul II in his philosophical work, which in turn are a response to modern philosophic concerns. Again, while Pope John Paul II is fully aware of the undue emphasis that our age puts on human freedom, he also recognises the interest in human freedom as a positive development of the modern age (see VS 31). Rather than abandoning such categories because of their blatant misuse, he strives to rescue and reorder them.

There is a surprising passage in *Veritatis splendor* that indicates how thoroughly modern the concern with self-determination is. I haven't done a thorough word search, but I suspect the word 'autonomy' has made few appearances in Church documents.[4] The word is one allied closely with the philosophy of Immanuel Kant. In its etymological roots it means 'self-rule'; in Kant it is used to describe the necessity that man be a self-legislating entity; that he not be heteronomous or one who is ruled by another – and for Kant, even being ruled by God is unacceptable heteronomous submission. Autonomy would seem to be very much at odds with Christianity for humans are to do God's will and obey God's law rather than to be wilful and to be their own sources of what is lawful. Kant, of course, was not a relativist; indeed he wished to formulate all moral dicta in terms of universal absolutes. Relativism, however, quite naturally grew out of Kant's metaphysical scepticism, and his rejection of any heteronomous source of moral norms. So both the Kantian understanding of autonomy, which roots moral obligation in the rational nature of the human person, and a more modern notion of autonomy which is identical with relativism, makes the concept of autonomy an unlikely candidate for being a part of the Church's moral vision.

Yet, the Church's understanding of conscience in some very important ways amounts to an advocacy of autonomy. Certainly we are not to be the source of moral norms; we are to recognise that God is the source. God, however, wrote the first principles of practical reasoning on man's consciousness and directed man to devise laws for his governance in accord with these principles that are a part of his nature. Man, then, in being a law unto himself is not a law apart from God.

The Catechism, in fact, quite directly though very briefly addresses the concern of autonomy:[5]

> Atheism is often based on a false conception of human autonomy, exaggerated to the point of refusing any dependence on God. Yet, 'to acknowledge God is in no way to oppose the dignity of man, since such dignity is grounded and brought to perfection in God....' 'For the Church knows full well that her message is in harmony with the most secret desires of the human heart.' (2126)

In the Church's understanding, it is only when one is acting in accord with the most secret desires of the human heart that one is acting truly autonomously, and since God placed those desires there, there is no conflict between following the most secret desires of one's heart, following God, and being fully autonomous.

The Church denies that true autonomy risks putting the moral agent at odds with God; it also denies that there can be a conflict between the conscience and the Church; the Catechism states: 'No opposition between individual conscience or reason on the one hand, and the moral law or the Church's teaching authority on the other can be admitted.' (2039)

The dignity of the human person lies in his ability to understand that the good that he is to do freely is indeed a good for him. For a human to do good out of fear or coercion is not to do good in a human and meritorious way. The dignity of the human person lies in the ability to do what is good, freely. He is to make the good his own good. He is personally to appropriate what is good. He is to form his conscience to be so in accord with the good that when he is acting out of obedience to the good he is actually acting in accord with the good that he dictates to himself. Such a co-operation between God and the human person leads *Veritatis splendor* to suggest that we ought to speak neither of autonomy or heteronomy but of a participated theonomy – man is not under God's law but participates in God's law.

What is ultimately good for the human person is a proper relationship with God. Man is to worship God freely. Thus the Church places such an enormous emphasis on the importance of conscience because conscience is properly allied not with radical autonomy but with the freedom to worship. In a letter on the eve of the Madrid Conference on European Security and Co-operation (1 September 1980), Pope John Paul II stated:

> ... freedom of conscience and of religion... is a primary and inalienable right of the human person; what is more, in so far as it touches the innermost sphere of the spirit, one can even say that it upholds the justification, deeply rooted in each individual, of all other liberties. Of course, such freedom can only be exercised in a responsible way, that is, in accordance with ethical principles...

Several themes of this paper come together in this passage. Pope John Paul II speaks of freedom of conscience and of religion being the primary and inalienable right of the human person and the foundation of all other liberties. It is because he has a conscience that man should be free and that freedom, thus, must be exercised responsibly, that is to say, in accordance with ethical principles.

The above discussion of 'rights language' and 'conscience' provides just the slightest of glimpses into the riches of the moral vision of the Catechism. What I have attempted to do here is to show how responsive the Catechism is to modern concerns while also suggesting that it is altogether faithful to the inherited moral vision of the Church. While I have focused on rights and on conscience I hope I have left no one with the impression that Christian morality is primarily about rights or man's wrestling with his conscience in order to formulate correct moral norms. Christianity is about the desire and attempt to do what is good out of love for the person of Christ, who is the Way, the Truth, and the Life. It is not so much about following the dictates of conscience as it is about following the promptings of the Holy Spirit. As the Catechism states: 'Life in the Holy Spirit fulfils the vocation of man.' (1699) Those who seek holiness through receiving the sacraments, will develop a special relationship with Christ and the Holy Spirit and will find themselves drawn to live lives of loving service. And, ultimately, that is the moral vision of the Catechism.

7

THE EDUCATION OF CONSCIENCE
A LIFELONG TASK

Teresa Iglesias

INTRODUCTION

The education of conscience: a central pastoral task

The 'formation of conscience'(1783-85)[1] must be considered a central task from a pastoral and catechetical approach to the Catechism. For the ultimate purpose of our catechetical or pastoral activity must be 'the true advancement of the human person in his or her whole truth, in his or her freedom and dignity'.[2] Moral and spiritual growth, till we reach the perfection of love and happiness, has been recognised throughout history as a true goal of any human life. Conscience is at the core of this 'truth of the person', of his or her dignity, of his or her aspiration toward reaching for perfection in freedom (1776,1954,1956).

It is through the process of recognition and response to the reality of our very being that we become persons of conscience. This holds for everyone, whether Christian believers or otherwise.[3] For every one is a moral being, everyone has a conscience – as much as everyone has lungs to breathe with. Truly, 'the education of the moral conscience, which makes every human being capable of judging and of discerning the proper ways to achieve self-realisation according to his or her original truth... becomes a pressing requirement that cannot be renounced'.[4] Thus, achieving self-realisation is a journey of personal moral growth, a *journey of conscience*. Human personal existence is such a journey and hence a lifelong task.

It is in these terms of 'a lifelong task' that the Catechism characterises the education of conscience (1784), and this is my concern here. I will approach it in two parts. First I will attempt to set the notion of conscience in context by focusing on the significance of the 'Treatise of Conscience' in the overall structure of the Catechism. Then I will deal with the nature of conscience as portrayed in the Catechism. This understanding will lead us, I hope, to appreciate better what it is to live in accordance with conscience, responding to conscience. I will end by touching briefly upon some challenges which, as faith-educators or morals-educators, conscience presents to us. As an introduction to my discussion let me focus on the importance of viewing the Catechism as a whole.

Viewing the Catechism as a whole

When we were little and studied our catechisms we learnt off by heart, among other things, the following: (i) the Creed; (ii) the Sacraments; (iii) the Ten Commandments; (iv) The Our Father. These are, in brief, the 'Four Pillars' (13) upon which the new Catechism stands, and the 'four parts' into which it is divided. Once they are pointed out to anyone with a basic Christian formation, he or she will have a general idea of the contents of the Catechism and what it is all about. The Catechism summarises this structure and its purpose when it says:

> [Christ's faithful are called]… to proclaim the Good News everywhere in the world… by professing the faith, by living it in fraternal sharing, and by celebrating it in liturgy and prayer. (3)

The Catechism refers to its contents as '*an organic presentation* of the Catholic faith in its entirety…', and as 'a unified whole… [to] allow the reader to view each theme in its relationship with the entirety of the faith'(18). Thus the faith is presented in its unity, in its entirety, as one; for we have 'One faith, one baptism, one Lord…'.[5] The words 'organic whole' suggest the metaphor of a living organism, a living reality, a living being; the image of the 'pillars' suggests that of a construction, a building which is to be compared to that conceptual structure which the Catechism presents.

Another approach to the overall content of the Catechism can be suggested. 'The faith in its entirety' could be viewed as the expression of 'a life story', a narrative of faith, a telling of a conversation and of a sharing of lives between God and human beings, a story of 'God with us'; a story which has a beginning, a climax, and an end – at the point of time in which we narrate the story, and in view of what we foresee thereafter. The act of telling one's own life story, at a particular time, gives it *unity*, for life is then interpreted and seen as a whole, with a significance and a foretaste of the future. In fact, only in retrospect can life, and so faith life, be seen in its unity, as a whole. Moreover, the Christian faith, historically, is incarnated in personal life stories and events. It is *about persons*. It is not a system of ideas, and has not been handed down to us primarily as a system of ideas. The person and his or her story is at its centre. The history of salvation is a story of persons.

The central *characters* in this story are God himself (the family of divine persons, God the creator, God the redeemer, God the sanctifier), who addresses me, you, and every other fellow human being, and the human family as a whole. The plot of the story, telling of lives as lived in divine-human inter-relationship, centres around love, understood as mutual self-revelation, mutual self-quest, self-entrustment and self-sharing; the struggle and quarrels into which human beings are inclined to enter, both with God, with themselves and with others, are also part of the story.

I think this approach to the re-presentation of the faith as portrayed in the Catechism is worth suggesting because in the narrative the personal is paramount, *the person becomes the centre*, life takes priority over ideas, principles and doctrines, which are always meant to serve the person. The telling of a life story focuses on people, on concrete events and facts, on the reality of their lives as actually lived. It is a 'personal approach', leading to people, more than an 'intellectual approach' leading to ideas, to a system of doctrine.

What I want to indicate with this suggestion is that, in catechetical terms, the personal approach in the presentation of the faith and the nature of the moral life, is more true to our existential reality and more readily reaches the human mind and heart. (If this approach were to be rigorously adopted in doctrine and in ethics, i.e. *making the reality of the person truly the centre*, much of our phraseology would have to be revised and changed from our abstract 'reified' terms to concrete talk about people and their existential dimensions.) In other words, it is my view that the Catechism must be seen as primarily concerned with living persons. It is not only an orthodoxy. It is the content of personal life – both divine and human – that primarily matters. Persons, 'the good of the person' and 'the goods of the person',[6] are thus the pervading reality with which the Catechism is concerned. Clearly the Catechism considers that living faith or 'faith-life' is the personal reality which doctrine, 'faith belief', serves.[7] And this distinction between faith life and faith belief is worth noting, given that persistent tendency among many of our contemporaries to consider the object of religion to be its doctrines and rules rather than *life* itself, i.e. the life of persons who entrust themselves in faith to Christ. As the Catechism puts it, what matters is 'Faith putting down roots in personal life,... faith shining forth in personal conduct' (23). This is the ultimate purpose of any catechetical activity.

*   *   *

1. THE TREATISE ON CONSCIENCE WITHIN THE CATECHISM

(a) A 'new' treatise

It is within the overall context of the centrality of 'the good of the person', of personal moral life, and of a personal relationship with God – the centrality of the life of faith – that conscience should be viewed within the Catechism. The treatise on conscience is a very short one, but of great significance. It must be noted that *for the first time* a treatise devoted to conscience has been included in a Church Catechism, so there must be very good reasons for this. I will suggest some of them below.

The treatise comprises about four pages, paragraph numbers 1776-1802. It is placed within Part III, 'Life in Christ', concerned with Christian moral life. This part has two main sections; Section One is concerned with the different *constitutive elements of the moral life*, and Section Two with its practice as *love of God and neighbour* as expressed in the Commandments. The constituents of the moral life are divided into three chapters. The first chapter is entitled 'The Dignity of the Human Person', the second 'The Human Community' and the third 'God's salvation: Law and Grace'. Conscience is treated within the first chapter. There is a natural relation between these three chapters which are all concerned with the nature of the dignity of the human person and his or her ultimate fulfilment. This is the anthropological key to the Catechism. I will refer further to it below. The *recognition* of the dignity of the nature of the human being and his or her ultimate realisation are to be grounded on the fact that the human being is a *moral being*, self-directive in himself or herself, and as created and related to God – and so a being whose existence is fulfiled in love and communion with God. It is this moral inner dimension of the human person that holds sovereignty over all other dimensions. Conscience, in the Catechism, is central to this ontological view of the human being as a moral-religious being, of a unitary life and nature, a life which is at once corporeal and spiritual.

Thus it may be contended that conscience is at the heart of the Catechism because conscience is at the heart of the human person (177). Yet, although conscience is central to personal moral life, is not the whole of the moral life. The moral activity of the person, which is always realised in concrete choice and action, is not totally reducible in its various dimensions to the reality and experience of conscience, but it does not exist without it. In other words, the *workings of conscience*, as the Catechism indicates, must be understood in relation to other fundamental moral realities (and hence, notions), all interconnected. That is, conscience is part of a 'package deal', not a single item that can be picked up – if I may use analogy of the supermarket – without bringing with it its full contents; and the package contains the elements of the moral life understood in terms of:

(i) *The nature of the human person* in his or her dignity grounded in a personal bonding with God – as origin and destiny (see 3.1.1).[8]

(ii) *Beatitude*, or happiness, as the call and ultimate goal of the person (3.1.2).

(iii) *Freedom*, which makes the person a moral subject (3.1.3).

(iv) *The acts of the person*, as moral acts (good or evil) when 'freely chosen in consequence of a judgement of conscience' (3.1.4).

(v) *The feelings*, sentiments or 'passions' that are constitutive of the human experience and contribute to the moral quality of human action (3.1.5).

(vi) *The virtues*, those settled habits, brought about by choice (and affected by environment) which spontaneously dispose the subject to act for the good (3.1.7).

(vii) *The choice of evil or sin* (3.1.8).

(viii) *Law and grace*, both that 'inner' and 'outer' rule of conduct expressing God's loving providence over us (3.3.1).

Those familiar with older classic treatises on the moral life know why conscience was not prominent in them; it was usually included or 'absorbed' in the treatment of virtues, in particular prudence.[9] So it is important to realise that a treatise on conscience, even if short, is given a new and significant place in the Catechism. This is a welcome development. The treatise can be read in the light of the more thorough exposition of conscience given in *Veritatis splendor*.[10] In fact, this encyclical could be regarded in itself as an expanded treatise on conscience; its relationship to the truth about what is good, to freedom, to the unity of human nature, to law and to grace. Thus the encyclical confirms the significance of the Catechism's treatise on conscience, and opens ways for further developments in its explicitation and formulations. I will use it in this manner in my exposition.

(b) Reasons for the 'new treatise'

Let me now indicate some reasons why I consider that the treatise on conscience has been introduced into the Catechism as central in our understanding of personal moral life today. This may enable us to appreciate better its basic importance in the journey of our personal moral growth, the *journey of conscience*.

(i) The dignity of the human person

In recent times, particularly since Vatican II, the conceptual development related to personal moral life within the Catholic Church has come to be focused around *the idea of the dignity of the human person*, (see *Gaudium et spes*, chapter one)[11]. As I have already indicated the Catechism is based on this development. The newly sharpened awareness of who the human being is, in his or her uniqueness, individuality, freedom, moral autonomy and solidarity, and personal relationship with God, has of necessity come to be directly connected with our notion(s) of personal moral conscience (33). Although we cannot say that our task of recognising 'the truth of the human person' is either accomplished or adequately formulated today, particularly in the metaphysical dimension, it must be said, nevertheless, that our Christian sense of the worth of the person or of *'the good of the person, who must always be affirmed for his own sake'*[12] is deeper today. This realisation is intrinsically related to our deeper sense of the dignity and meaning of personal freedom. I think that the centrality of the dignity of *each* human being, and the religious, metaphysical and ethical presuppositions of this reality within the Catholic Church today cannot be overemphasised:

> Indeed, the Church wishes to serve this single end: that each person may be able to find Christ, in order that Christ may walk with each person the path of life.[13]

In human terms this claim amounts to the socio-ethical requirement that the Church proclaims, namely,

> ...the human person... is and ought to be the principle, the subject and the end of every social organisation.[14]

The Catechism also states:

> ... the common good presupposes respect for the person as such. In the name of the common good, public authorities are bound to respect the fundamental and inalienable rights of the human person. Society should permit each of its members to fulfil his [or her] vocation. In particular the common good resides in the conditions for the exercise of the natural freedoms indispensable for the development of the human vocation, such as the right to act according to a sound norm of conscience and to safeguard... privacy, and rightful freedom also in matters of religion (1907).[15]

> The person represents the ultimate end of society, which is ordered to him [or her]: What is at stake is the dignity of the human person, whose defence and promotion have been entrusted to us by the Creator, and to whom the men and women of every moment of history are strictly and responsibly in debt (1929).[16]

(ii) The awareness of 'conscience' in secular culture

The new awareness of the all-importance of the individual human person is a secular reality as well. The Church acknowledges it as one of the achievements of our culture:

> This heightened sense of the dignity of the human person and of his or her uniqueness, and *the respect due to the journey of conscience*, certainly represents one of the positive achievements of modern culture.[17]

In our time this achievement is particularly related to the recognition of human equality and of individual freedom, finding political expression in a democratic organisation of social life. The primacy of the individuality and freedom of the person has come to be advocated in various formulations of human rights. The defence (or negation) of this reality is also at the centre of the fundamental moral, political and social conflicts in our time. In some concrete cases these conflicts are even formulated in terms of the word 'conscience' (whatever the diversity of the meaning of the word). For example, societies such as Amnesty International advocate and defend the rights of 'prisoners of conscience' world-wide. Very many laws now have clauses respecting (or negating) 'objectors of conscience'. There is no doubt that our culture is sensitive to respecting (or negating) conscience. Thus, the Catechism, by addressing the reality of conscience, recognises and vindicates this sensitivity inherent in our contemporary mode of understanding ourselves.

(iii) The development of the idea of conscience

The notion of conscience, as it was first used in the ancient Greek world, was explicitly introduced in the New Testament by Saint Paul.[18] Through his usage and interpretation of the ordinary meaning of the Greek term in his time, it has become a notion incorporated into Christianity and its self-interpretation. The notion has undergone its own peculiar historical development within Christian thought and life. Although the historical sources of the notion of conscience – Greek, Pauline, Stoic, Scholastic, modern and contemporary – can all be traced in the pages of the Catechism, the attempt there is not to present us with a finalised synthesis of this development; rather it is to impart to us the essentials of the idea of conscience, a 'new' depth and significance implicit in the 'old' notion, and to encourage us to continue in the task. In other words, the Catechism attests to a conceptual development by giving conscience a central place within the moral treatise and by enshrining it within the foundational idea of 'the dignity of the human person'. This, in my view, must be gratefully acknowledged.

(iv) J.H.Newman: a testimony to a life of conscience

Another reason, in my view, for conscience being in the Catechism must also be welcomed. We are reminded in *Veritatis splendor* that a doctrinal decision of the Church's Magisterium

> ...is preceded and accompanied by the work of interpretation and formulation characteristic of the reason of individual believers and of theological reflection.[19]

In modern times, I dare say, no Christian person has affected both the concept and the life of conscience as John Henry Newman has done. The Catechism vindicates this impact by making one of Newman's sayings on conscience the centre-piece of the treatise. Newman's testimony is in keeping with the biblical, philosophical and ecclesial understanding of the notion of conscience. The saying sums up a whole treatise on conscience.

> Conscience is a law of the mind; yet [Christians] would not grant that it is nothing more; I mean that it was not a dictate, nor conveyed the notion of responsibility, of duty, of a threat and of a promise... [Conscience] is a messenger of Him, whom both in nature and in grace, speaks to us behind a veil, and teaches and rules us by his representatives. Conscience is the aboriginal Vicar of Christ (1778).

Newman's understanding of conscience is more than a theoretical achievement; it grounds and expresses the whole of Newman's 'life story', his life journey, which indeed was a journey of conscience. He is a *witness* and *exemplar* of what it is to be a person of conscience and to lead a life following conscience – which is to lead a life in the Spirit of God. This exemplary impact and weight of a Christian person's life experience (which also grants a new depth to the overall human experience) gives new depth to the meaning of the Christian understanding of 'conscience'. The Catechism acknowledges this fact and includes it in the great river of the faith tradition of understanding itself. It is a recognition that conceptual history, or as Newman himself put it, 'the development of ideas', in the Church and in the world, is altered, enriched, moved on, by the *exemplary impact* of the personal achievement of some of its great members[20].

2. THE NATURE OF CONSCIENCE AS PORTRAYED IN THE CATECHISM

(a) Basic truths 'presupposed' by conscience

To understand the meaning of conscience in Catholic terms requires a recognition of certain truths which pervade the reality and meaning of conscience. These are truths concerning the relationship between God and each human being, and hence express the view of the human being as a moral and religious being as indicated above. This view runs through the whole of the Catechism. Let me point out four of these basic truths:

(i)   There is a *one-to-one personal relationship between God* and each human being.
(ii) The human being possesses a life of *self-governance in freedom*.
(iii) The human being is ultimately *accountable only to God*.
(iv) The human being is directly *guided by God from within*, by nature, and by 'grace' *through the indwelling of the Holy Spirit*.

*(i) There is a **one-to-one personal relationship** between God and each human being*

God creates each one of us, calls each one into being individually, for communion with him as the supreme good. This divine origin and destiny are the terms in which each one's life (as inserted in the life of the human community as a whole) is to be understood (27). One's own life story is primarily a story of relationship with God; the story which each person creates in response to God's call and presence, and in terms of which our relationship to others gain their ultimate meaning. God has granted each human being 'direct access' to him, an I-Thou relationship, a sharing of intimacy by having granted to each person the gift of his divine life in his Spirit. Each of us counts for God. Each is precious in the eyes of God. Each is of supreme importance for God. It is in this call to communion with God that the dignity of each person ultimately lies. This basic truth is at the heart of all Scripture and central to Christ's own life and ministry. Many believers have come to express the experience of this reality in incisive words. Newman is one of them:

> Only this I know full well now [he writes in year 1864] and did not know then, that the Catholic Church allows no image of any sort, material or immaterial, no dogmatic symbol, no rite, no sacrament, no Saint, not even the Blessed Virgin herself, to come between the soul and its Creator. It is face to face, *'solus cum solo'*, in all matters between man and his God. He alone creates; He alone has redeemed; before His awful eyes we go in death; in the vision of Him is our eternal beatitude.[21]

*(ii) The human being possesses a life of **self-governance** in freedom*

By freedom the human being can initiate and control his own actions (1730). God has left each human being to be the master of his or her own counsel (Sir 15:14). The human being 'has been entrusted to his own care and responsibility' so that the attainment of his perfection is a process of 'personally building up that perfection in himself'.[22] Of his or her own accord the human being is to seek and cleave to his Creator and freely attain his perfection (1743,VS 39). This self-governance enables each of us to realise our own destiny in a personal unique way, guided from within, from the core of our own heart, responding to the very nature of what and who we are. 'The rightful autonomy of the practical reason means that man possesses in himself his own law, received from the Creator'.[23]

(iii) The human being is ultimately only accountable to God

The only origin and destiny of the human being is God; the human being as a self-governed creature freely fulfils his or her destiny by responding for or against the call to goodness and truth – God's own call – which pervades the totality of one's own life and each moral choice and action. The human being has this natural power of responding, the 'response-ability' to the call of his or her own God-given nature and destiny in every claim made by reality. And hence he or she is ultimately accountable to him who makes the call – God alone.

(iv) The human being is **directly guided by God from within** by nature and by 'grace' through the indwelling of the Holy Spirit

The greatest gift of Christ **to each one** is a share in divine life when receiving the Holy Spirit at baptism. The Spirit 'divinises us' so that human inner life is no longer of human powers alone; divine powers are constitutive of it as well, both individually and as a Church community. This is what permits us 'to live in the Spirit', which is described in the Catechism as the vocation of the human being (1699). By the power of the Spirit – we acknowledge by faith – the human person is self-governed in a divine way, within a community of faith and love which is Church. Having received the Spirit within this community, and thus becoming members of it, the whole Christian personal task becomes a task of responding to our new mode of being and the design God has for each one; it is the task of responsibility for each individual Christian to respond to that imperative power of the Spirit and act on it. The power of free assent belongs uniquely to each one of us.

To point to this specifically Catholic context required for the understanding of conscience does not distance ourselves from that natural context in which the experience of conscience is present outside Christianity. It is rather incorporated in it; for 'in nature and in grace' conscience is the messenger of Christ.[24] 'Obedience to our conscience, in all things, great and small, is the way to know the truth'.[25] Where the distance occurs is in relation to that other view of conscience which can be described as 'purely secular' and uprooted from its religious content or possibility. I will refer to this meaning later. Let me now outline the nature of conscience in its main features, taking the Catechism as a guide.

(b) Eight propositions on the nature of conscience

There are two basic questions related to the nature of conscience: What is conscience? How do we live in accordance with conscience? These are questions very much concerned with the understanding of ourselves, of what and who we are as moral-religious beings, as already indicated. The answers to these two questions are interrelated, for once we understand the nature of conscience we come to recognise the requirements inherent in living as 'persons of conscience' (1782). The Catechism deals with these questions in four parts in the treatise of conscience (see Appendix to this article on pp. 240ff).

The manner in which the notion of conscience is portrayed in the Catechism may be viewed in the light of the following propositions:

1.   Conscience is a person's *most secret core* and sanctuary: (1776, 1777, 17795).

2.   Conscience is an *inner critic*; 'the verdict of conscience' (1771, 1781).

3.   Conscience is an *inner guide*; 'a judgement of practical reason' (1777, 1778, 1780).

4.   Conscience is *fallible* (1786, 1792, 1797, 1799).

5.   Conscience is inviolable when certain (1790, 1793, 1800).

6.   Conscience *requires virtue*, in particular the virtue of prudence (1780, 1788, 1806).

7.   Conscience is *formed by the Word of God* (1792, 1802).

8.   Conscience is *transformed* by the indwelling of the Spirit (2074).

Propositions 1-6 can be regarded as expressing a meaning of conscience as present to us 'in nature', i.e. they describe an understanding of the reality of conscience as it is attained by ordinary human experience, and by the reflection and formulation of that experience, as many writers and moralists have done.[26] Propositions 7 and 8 are eminently Christian. Proposition 8 is not explicitly formulated in the 'Treatise of Conscience' in the Catechism but it is clearly implicit there and in what is said in other parts.

(i) Conscience is the person's most secret core and sanctuary

'The secret core' refers to the inner-life dimension of the human person. He or she is recognised as a subject through the consciousness and experience of this inner life, this interiority. The human being is the only being with this kind of interior life. That is why communication and communion between persons is possible. We cannot have a true conversation, say, with a computer because it has nothing to tell us about itself. It has no interior life. The characteristic biblical term for this interiority and inner life of the person is 'the heart' (see 368; and e.g., 1431, 1432). At 'the heart' is where all fundamental human questions are dealt with. The Catechism says: 'Conscience...[is] present at the heart of the person...' (1777). Clearly, conscience is a matter of the heart, or I may add, of the intelligence of the heart, of our deepest convictions and inner affective and moral movements. This connection between conscience and the heart is crucial for its understanding. By placing it 'at the heart of the person' the Catechism recognises it as constitutive of the person's interior life in its affective, intellectual, moral and religious dimensions, all of which are integrative parts of the heart, that inner 'place' where personal subjectivity is found. The *state of the heart*, we may say, is the state of conscience. Thus, conscience is our secret core, the inner centre only accessible to oneself by a movement of inward-turning, of attentive gaze; it is also where we stand inwardly in relation to ourselves and to God who is present to us in this interiority. To want to force entrance into this core, to control it, to govern it from outside, is to violate it. The heart is that self's inward centre of self-possession and self-governance by which we are 'secretly' present to ourselves and to no one else, unless we want to reveal and share this core with another self out of free communicative love.

Conscience is also a 'sanctuary' since the human heart is not only accessible to us but is accessible to God as well. 'God sees the heart', 'speaks to the heart', and does so from within. In the heart the human being is 'alone with God whose voice echoes in his depth' (1776). That is why conscience is also referred to as 'the voice of God'

> ...conscience does not close man within an insurmountable and impenetrable solitude, but opens him to the call, to the voice of God. In this, and not in anything else, lies the entire mystery and the dignity of the moral conscience: in being the place, the sacred place where God speaks to man.[27]

God relates to each person individually. God is there in the human heart as a *presence* and as a *voice*. Thus, conscience regarded as God's place is an inner sanctuary. There God can be heard, God can be listened to – for God indeed speaks there– and has to be responded to, or be denied a response. So conscience is at the centre of that inner dialogue between God and the human being. This presence is given a 'new' reality by the supreme gift of Christ, the Spirit dwelling in our hearts.

(ii) Conscience is an inner critic: 'the verdict of conscience'

The most ancient meaning of conscience, the Greek *suneidesis*, meaning 'knowing with oneself', and the Latin term *conscientia*, did not always carry with it an ethical sense.[28] But by the time the notion was introduced into the New Testament by Saint Paul, it had come to be understood in some of its usages as the inner moral critic. The experience of conscience – in its various manifestations – has been taken as constitutive of what and who we are, of human nature, as part of our inner moral self-guidance, or, as some of the ancient writers put it, 'a divine element in us'.[29] Conscience is experienced and manifested to the subject as an inner witness (1777-81):

> Conscience is the *only* witness, since what takes place in the heart of the person is hidden from the eyes of everyone outside. Conscience makes its witness known only to the person himself. And in turn only the person himself knows what his own response is to the voice of conscience.[30]

What conscience witnesses is *how the person stands in relation to the good*, in his or her attitudes and acts; it witnesses '...the universal truth of the good, at the same time as the evil [or good] of this particular choice' (1781). Thus, the primary object of conscience is the recognition and evaluation of *the doing of the good*. Conscience, we may say, is the 'caretaker of the good'. When good is done conscience is at peace, quiet, but when evil is done it rises, emerges, 'wakes up', makes its voice heard. Conscience is primarily the critic of wrongdoing, as the *critic* of self-violation. Conscience, thus, is a *judging witness*, or 'a court',[31] a discerning power which approves or denounces concerning the good, not in general terms regarding that recognition of the good as 'the law written in the heart', but regarding the good to be carried out *here and now*. Conscience '...judges particular choices, approving those that are good and denouncing those that are evil' (1777; Rm 1:32).

The particular *effects of this judgment,* or verdict, is either approval with inner peace, or denunciation or condemnation in remorse. The voice of conscience is then recognised inwardly as an acute 'intelligent feeling', an inner movement of *remorse,* and of *guilt* when it ascertains that evil has been done.[32] The universality of the experience of remorse in human beings testifies to this power of inner judgement about the good by conscience. It also testifies to our unitary nature, to the intelligence of the heart, where feelings and judgements are manifested in a single experience: the 'pricking' of conscience which is not a mere intellectual experience; it deeply involves feelings. A critic also assumes responsibility for the task denounced and how to retrieve its damage. That is why the movement of remorse and guilt calls for recognition and, if attended to, effective repentance (1453).

(iii). Conscience is an inner guide: 'a practical judgement'

Clearly a critic criticises, or responds to violation according to criteria, i.e. according to a recognition of what is good and cannot be violated. It is this inner demand for the 'knowing of the good' that makes conscience to be understood as a 'law of the mind' (of the practical mind), a knowing and discerning of what is good both at the general level of principles (the Scholastics used the word synderesis for this intellectual habitual recognition of a universal and objective norm of morality), and at the concrete level of individual action requiring insight and *practical judgement* (described as the proximate norm of personal morality). The particular or specific sphere of the discernment of the good with which conscience is concerned is the concrete good to be chosen in individual action, always a particular action, a here and now choice. For this reason conscience has come to be identified as a practical judgement, or a judgement of practical reason (1777-780), which is a judgement concerned with an action done (or to be done), a judgement enshrined in the act of choosing and doing this or that. This judgement is also described as 'prudent judgement' (1780), that judgement to be made on the spot when necessity arises.

Veritatis splendor[33] develops the idea of conscience as a practical judgement, and acknowledges the fact that, from a pastoral point of view, individuals (non-scholars) may not know in detail the theological formulations of our understanding of the workings of conscience; yet the most fundamental requirement of a good conscience which is accessible to all is this:

> It is 'the heart' converted to the Lord and to the love of what is good which is really the source of true judgements of conscience.[34]

(iv) Conscience is fallible

It is possible for a person to be certain that something should be done here and now because he or she considers it to be good, even though in fact it is not. For it is the case that in human judgements the possibility of error is always present. Conscience, as the judgement of an action, is not exempt from the possibility of error. This is a claim that if accepted makes us committed to the truth that since conscience can be false (although certain) it is not infallible about the truth concerning the good to be done. We can also be doubtful in conscience, or sustain ambiguities about what is good or about what should be done; we can also undergo conflicts of conscience whereby two goods which appear to be necessary to be done also appear difficult to choose. Right conscience is both true and certain. The fallibility of conscience is ordinary human fallibility, with which we all are acquainted. Acknowledgement of this human condition or limitation makes us guarded, humble, listening, seeking always what is true and good. The results of our attentive gaze on reality and the dispositions that permit recognition of things as they are, are basic to right conscience. Yet, since conscience is fallible it cannot be regarded as the maker, the authority, and guarantor of its own truth. Rather, as already indicated, it bears witness to a truth that is recognised rather than created by conscience. Conscience then is anchored and 'serves' the truth about the person's good. Inherent to conscience is a spontaneous discriminatory sense of the concrete, in a similar manner in which other senses and intellectual powers discriminate their objects, carrying with it the obligation or duty to act in this or that particular way of doing the good.

The secular view: conscience is infallible

It is in this idea of the 'fallibility' of conscience that the Christian understanding of it parts company from the secular one. The Catechism mentions 'a mistaken view of the autonomy of conscience' (1792); mistaken because it negates 'the truth of the person', as recognised by the Christian understanding upon which the notion of conscience is grounded.

Conscience in our secular environment is generally understood as a set of personal moral convictions sincerely and strongly held. Thus, to follow our conscience is to act in accordance with these convictions. If we are consistent in action with our own views, we are persons of integrity, morally authentic. Even in the face of great moral opposition from others the person is called to express them or act in accordance with them with courage. So to be consistent is to be authentic, and to be authentic, in face of opposition, is also to be courageous. To be consistent and courageous is to be moral. But the content of conviction, the *grounds* as to why this or that conviction should be held or not, are not taken to be constitutive grounds of conscience, but a matter of personal choice as much as the decision the individual has to make about how to act in the particular case. Thus, acts of conscience are not primarily judgements but decisions made on autonomous grounds[35]. Conscience then is ultimately grounded in the individual will which claims to 'make the good by choice', and not as a response to the recognition of who and what we are; thus, in this perspective the will is 'free floating', not anchored in human nature, or on 'the truth about the good of the person'; the claim is that there is no such truth, for there is no such nature, but only the sovereignty of human will and choice.

In this perspective the primacy of personal moral conscience is upheld together with its inviolability and infallibility. For there is no other criterion for the truths of conscience but *itself*. Because conscience is both inviolable and infallible, 'every view must be respected' and 'every one is right', and 'every one is entitled to his or her own opinion' and 'who am I to tell others that he or she is wrong?' If the ruling principle in one's life is only one's personal conviction adopted 'by choice', then one's autonomy is construed as independent of that obediential attitude required by a recognition of reality as given in what we are; it is this recognition that leads us to see that we cannot constitute reality to 'our liking' by free choice without distorting the kind of beings we are. In other words, the issue of what meaning of conscience is to be upheld is the issue of whether the subject's will is the ultimate rule of morality, or alternatively the rule comes from the recognition of that reality which makes claims upon us, and to which we have the freedom and responsibility to respond.

The modern secular view of conscience can be traced back to its connections with rationalism and the idea of private judgement. So it has been with us for quite some time. A writing of the late eighteenth century (1798), illustrates this point well:

> Dreadful consequences are derivable to society... [from the use of]... a plausible word wrested from its proper

sense. It has been imagined that provided men follow the direction of their own 'consciences' they are justified in whatever mode of conduct they may adopt,... as the term 'conscience' is now too generally understood... in other words to say that because men are persuaded a thing is right therefore it cannot be wrong. 'Conscience' – or should it rather be called 'private persuasion' – [is] therefore considered as the private judgement of the party on the legality or illegality of his own conduct. When men therefore talk of 'liberty of conscience' they would do well to consider whether it is not, as the phrase is now generally understood, rather a liberty of their own making than a portion of that liberty with which Christ has made them free.[36]

A word has 'its proper sense' only within a conceptual moral framework, i.e. a particular conception of the human being and of existence as a whole. That is what gives a word 'life'. Words belong to 'forms of life',[37] to our forms of existing as linguistic beings, which are always forms of self-understanding. In our culture there are forms of self-understanding, of interpreting one's own reality, which are incompatible with the recognition of that reality as enshrined in a vision of the person in Christian life.[38] When moral frameworks embedded in 'forms of life' are active side by side, as are the secular and the Christian in our times, words common to both frameworks, like 'conscience', may share certain common shades of meanings. Yet the contextual setting will differ so as to make them say different things. This gives rise to the conceptual crises and 'confusion' to which we are all constantly exposed, and which require sensitive and intelligent discrimination. Clearly, the secular idea of the primacy of conscience as the ruling principle of one's own personal moral life and of its inviolability, are also held by the Christian and the 'natural' view of conscience. But the idea that conscience cannot be mistaken, that it is infallible, is not. Hence the two meanings are radically different.

Yet, it must be said that even in secular terms the idea of an infallible conscience, as a private conviction which is inviolable, cannot be sustained and it is fact it is not sustained in many spheres of public life. For example, murder, fraud, trading of human beings, etc., are not, and could not be accepted as justified on grounds of conscience. Hence it is conscience that must be obediential to the real, to what is good for human beings, and not the other way around, whereby conscience is said to 'create' the good.

(v) Conscience is inviolable when certain

A practical judgement may be both true and certain, although it can also be certain but not true. That is, the agent judging the act acknowledges with certainty that something good is true when in fact it is not. As noted above, error is always a possibility in our judgements. Yet we can only follow what we know to be the truth. That is why the Catechism states:

> A human being must always obey the certain judgement of his conscience. If he were deliberately to act against it, he would condemn himself (1790).

Thus, conscience, when certain, must always be followed and respected. We cannot act against our own better judgement concerning what is the good to be done. That is why an erroneous or false conscience (when the agent is not morally responsible for the error) retains its dignity, and hence its claim for respect and inviolability. In these circumstances 'the evil committed by the person cannot be imputed to him' (1793). Nevertheless here there is always a call to overcome the possibility of error; the sustained disposition to seek and follow what is true and good will then find fulfilment in what is really true and good, and not in what appears to be so. Here the **preconditions of mind and character required for adequate recognition of the real good and not of the apparent good**, are at stake. For it is obvious to us all that a human being may neglect the state of his or her conscience, the state of his or her heart and mind, without any concern for seeking what is true and good, whether as regards general truths and the concrete acts to be performed. Then conscience, like any other uncultivated human power and sensibility, becomes 'blind' to its true object, and loses its discerning ability.[39]

(vi) Conscience requires virtue

With the recognition that something is truly good (and that one is not in error about it) comes also the recognition of a dictate that this good must be done, a recognition of duty. Yet the person still may not do it, may not follow the dictate of conscience. Hence another element is required in order to act in accordance with conscience, in order to act well; this is the power of virtue, that quality of soul – or character – which disposes us to choose and act well. St Augustine describes virtue as 'the good use of our freedom to choose' and 'an orderedness of love'. By virtue we make ourselves and what we do *good*. The Catechism describes virtue at paragraph 1804, indicating that virtues of mind and heart are required in order both to attain and to follow right conscience. The words of St John's Gospel proclaim this truth: 'He who does what is true comes to the light' (Jn 3:21).

It is the virtue of prudence which immediately guides the judgement of conscience (1806). Prudence, because it is a *habit*, a firmly inbuilt disposition, a natural spontaneous way of acting well, cannot go wrong, or cannot be misused precisely by being a disposition, while the judgement of conscience can. That is why prudence always 'renders good the person and his acts'. It is 'the virtue that disposes practical reason to discern our true good in every circumstance and to choose the right means of achieving it' (1806). 'Good sense and good judgement' are other usual expressions for naming this virtue.[40] It is necessary for our living well and choosing well to have a vision of what we call general principles concerning the good (the Catechism presents them in the Ten Commandments) but living well is always realised in concrete action, here and now; thus action, by being concrete, requires that discriminatory power of the concrete; this is what the judgement of conscience guided by prudence attains. As a well-experienced physician puts it:

> To judge if the circumstances are correct here and now, is the work of prudence or of practical wisdom or of discernment – a virtue not teachable in medical school and not replaceable by computer programmes. It is the cardinal virtue of experienced and seasoned practical human beings.[41]

> As it has also been noted, with the virtue of prudence we can deal with concrete issues as they stand without attempting to resolve them wholly into abstract evidences within the security of law.[42]

To sum up. The idea of conscience cannot be detached from the idea of virtue and of the virtuous person. For the settled disposition of seeking what is true and doing what is good is a basic requirement of right conscience, of discerning the good, of choosing it and of doing it. This good, God's design for each one, is uniquely personal and has to be discerned continuously throughout life, as a lifelong task. Only virtuous persons, i.e. virtuous parents and educators, can adequately communicate to children the reality of living by conscience.

(vii) Conscience is formed by the Word of God

'The Word of God is a light for our path' (1785). The Word of God as present in Scripture has to enter the heart and mind of every believer by faith, prayer and the practice of virtue (1802). Conscience, as the inner core of our heart and mind, is moulded by this constant contact with the Word of God. It is by familiarity with the Word of God that our Christian life is nourished, and hence grows. Ignorance of Scripture is ignorance of Christ as the object of our faith. About 150 years ago, in his concern for the ills in the life of faith, Newman wrote something which is still applicable to our own time:

> The Bible is the best book of meditation which can be, because it is divine. This is why we see such multitudes in France and Italy giving up religion altogether. They have not impressed upon their hearts the life of our Lord and Saviour as given us in the Evangelists. They believe merely with the intellect, not with the heart. Argument may overset a mere assent of the reason, but not a faith founded in a personal love for the Object of our Faith.[43]

It is this divine book, the Bible, as read and interpreted within the community of the Church, that is given to each one of us to penetrate our consciences. The Church, by speaking to us either through Scripture or in its Magisterial teachings, does not conceive of personal conscience as 'subservient' to any external force; the truth of conscience is that the person must always be self-directed freely from within. The Christian understanding of conscience recognises and respects this primacy of interiority in personal moral life; it acknowledges and defends the judgement of conscience that has its own imperative character and its own freedom, as already indicated. This is a God-given endowment to each person which makes him or her self-sovereign in his or her actions as an autonomous free agent, and on which personal dignity is founded. At all times the human being is called to act as guided from within by the powers of his heart and mind. Yet, the human being is not alone; for his or her self-direction each one counts on God's presence both as the inner guide and intimate friend, and as the external guide in the words and community of the Church which is God's instrument serving personal conscience:

> ... in the Church and her Magisterium Christians have a great help for the formation of conscience... The Church

puts herself always and only at the *service of conscience*, helping it to avoid being tossed to and fro by every kind of doctrine proposed by human deceit (cf. Ep 4:14), and helping it not to swerve from the truth about the good of the person, but rather, especially in more difficult questions, try to attain the truth with certainty and to abide by it.[44]

(viii) Conscience is transformed by the indwelling of the Spirit

That the Spirit of Christ dwells in our hearts is a central reality of our faith. Christians are called to live according to *the realities of their faith*, which are not experiential but nonetheless truly real. The Spirit of Christ living in us is such a wonderful reality. Given to us at Baptism as 'a real personal visitation', it is a sharing with us of his own divine life; 'regenerating' our beings enables us to seek the divine realities by 'the very instinct of our new nature'.[45] By baptism the 'natural conscience' becomes a 'graced conscience'. How do we let the presence of the Spirit in our inner core affect our own personal consciences? This is a question which we can put to ourselves; it discloses to each one of us a reality by which we have to lead our lives.

The Catechism does not focus directly on the relation between conscience and the indwelling of the Spirit within us. Nevertheless, the Catechism gives us the opportunity and the doctrine to do so, both for ourselves and for those over whom we may have an educating responsibility. We must travel the inner journey, the journey of conscience, the journey of the Spirit, accompanying and encouraging each other. One of the great effects of this journey with the Spirit is the creation of trust in one another, and hence the recognition that the Church is truly, and must be lived as, a *participatory Church*, a Church of dialogue of true believers who have the task to make responsible affirmations of conscience; in this community of the Spirit every true believer has a place because very one has (and cultivates) a graced conscience; every one has a say and every one has to be listened to because every one is indwelled by the Spirit and lives responding to Spirit's promptings – 'by nature or by grace'. The Catechism says:

> In the work of teaching and applying Christian morality, the Church needs the dedication of pastors, the knowledge of theologians and the contribution of all Christians, and men of good will. Faith and the practice of the Gospel provide each person with an experience of life 'in Christ' who enlightens him [or her] and makes him [or her] able to evaluate the divine and the human realities according to the Spirit of God. Thus the Holy Spirit can use the humblest to enlighten the learned and those in the highest positions. (2038)

3. CHALLENGES IN THE EDUCATION OF CONSCIENCE TODAY

Some catechists have personally told me that the idea of conscience, its importance and role in personal moral or Christian life has never constituted a part of their catechetical programmes. There may be many reasons for this which are understandable. At this juncture of the life of the Church the programmes should be designed in the new light of the Catechism.

In educating our consciences, and those of others, there are certain challenges we have to meet in our present age, challenges which are different from those of other times. Let me mention two here. One of them must be seen as a precondition required for the education of conscience. It is the requirement of interiority, which the Catechism mentions at paragraph 1779. Our culture has lost much of the sense that human beings have inner lives, with their own inner laws and claims, that must be respected and responded to, or ignored at our peril and at the cost of inner division. Every one has to live this inner dimension, and enter and travel the inner journey. And this is not a mere matter of *knowing* the inner reality, or of *skills* to detect its structure; it is an encounter with *our soul* and a responding to the calls it makes. The denial of our inner selves, its neglect, gives rise to lives lived by externals, lives which are not fully human because truncated and partial. Teresa of Avila, so well experienced in this inner journey, encourages any one to begin it, and advises us 'do not think that you are hollow inside'. When our inner self is buried (alive!) it always suffers inwardly from its neglected state; a time of acute crisis may come, e.g., in illness or when close to death, and then the 'soul-pain' will pierce our being.[46] Conscience then calls us to ourselves; it has to be attended to in order for us to reach unity and harmony. Not only we adults are called to live from within, from our consciences; we may also ask, how can the consciences of children be recognised by themselves if they are never helped to turn attention to their inner selves? If they never pray? If they never have time to observe the invisible manifested in the visible world and in themselves?

A second task is connected with what I indicated at the beginning of my discussion: the centrality of the person. 'The good of the person' is the central core of moral life. Yet in much of our current teaching or guiding of our consciences or those of others we tend to take as our core criteria the general principles, or commandments, by which we are to abide with little or no reference to the love for the person Christ and for others. Our Christian life is thus turned into a 'rule-following', a 'set of practices' or 'an orthodoxy'. Thus, the core of Christianity in what is good – the very person of Christ and his care for us and his salvation, the 'real good news' – seems to have disappeared. Many discuss what 'the Church teaching' is about this or that issue – and of course the Catechism (this wonderful gift of the Church to our times) gives us the contemporary answer to these questions. But the Person of Christ is not a Catechism, and the faith is faith in him. Let me quote some passages from *Veritatis splendor* to illustrate what I am attempting to say:

... we must not be content merely to warn the faithful about the errors and dangers of certain ethical theories. We must *first of all* show the inviting splendour of that truth which is Jesus Christ himself (83) (my emphasis).

... the Church finds its support – the 'secret' of its educative power – not so much in doctrinal statements and pastoral appeals to vigilance, as in *constantly looking to the Lord Jesus* (85).

... the consoling certainty of Christian faith, the source of its profound humanity and *extraordinary simplicity*. At times, in the discussion about new and complex moral problems, it can seem that Christian morality is in itself too demanding, difficult to understand and almost impossible to practice. This is untrue, since Christian morality consists, in the simplicity of the Gospel, in *following Jesus Christ*, in abandoning oneself to him, in letting oneself be transformed by his grace and renewed by his mercy, gifts which come to us in the living communion of his Church (119).

8

THE DECALOGUE IN THE CATECHISM

James McEvoy

The serious Christian study of the Ten Commandments immediately entails the evaluation of issues that are so central to Christian faith and life as to be inseparable from both. In the first place, in what way is the believer to read the Ten Commandments? How many commandments are there in fact: ten, plus two (i.e., the love of God and of neighbour); or ten, plus one (if it is considered that the love of God and the love of the neighbour are really the same, indivisible love); or, finally, just one, which can be expressed in a single eloquent imperative: Love!?

The Decalogue (literally, 'ten words') finds its true place in Christian belief and practice through its dialectical interaction with the other essentials of the Christian religion, such as revealed promise and providential fulfilment, Spirit and letter, the New Israel, fidelity and freedom, law and love. When wrenched from their appropriate theological setting the commandments degenerate to become a series of categorical imperatives, or even a set of rules.[1] If they are allotted the central role in moral theology, as they were by some writers of Catholic moral textbooks, or manuals, in more recent centuries, then the Ten Commandments displace the virtues, both natural and theological, producing a severe distortion of consciousness. If on the other hand the Decalogue is neglected, or is considered outmoded and expunged from revealed truth, then subjectivism in one or more of its various forms is the predictable outcome.

Theological location of the Decalogue within the Catechism

The prologue to the Catechism draws attention to the structure of the work (pp. 9-10), in the following terms:

> 13. The plan of this catechism is inspired by the great tradition of catechisms which build catechesis on four pillars: the baptismal profession of faith (the *Creed*), the sacraments of faith, the life of faith (the *Commandments*), and the prayer of the believer (*The Lord's Prayer*).

Now the *Creed*, the seven Sacraments, the Commandments within the life of faith, and *The Lord's Prayer*, taken all together as forming the basic architecture of a unified exposition of the Catholic faith, do not come out of nowhere. These same elements structured the Catechism of the Council of Trent. They can be found in various combinations and proportions throughout later medieval catechesis (in the wake of the Fourth Lateran Council, 1215), and they were already prominent among the building blocks of patristic catechesis.

Part One (The Profession of Faith) is devoted to revelation and faith (Section 1) and to the truths of faith that make up the Creeds (Section 2). Part Two (The Celebration of the Christian Mystery) expounds the sacramental economy (Section 1) and the seven sacraments (Section 2). Part Three (Life in Christ) deals with beatitude, 'the final end of man created in the image of God' (p. 10). True happiness is reached 'through right conduct freely chosen, with the help of God's law and grace' (Section 1), and 'through conduct that fulfils the twofold commandment of charity, specified in God's Ten Commandments' (Section 2) (ibid.). Part Four (Prayer in the Life of Faith) deals with the place and importance of prayer in the life of the believer (Section 1), and concludes with a commentary on the Our Father. The plan of the Catechism was deliberately fixed in order to bring out the articulation of an organic whole.

Part Three, Life in Christ (which directly concerns us here), is divided up as follows.

Section 1. **Man's Vocation: Life in the Spirit**
    Ch. 1 The Dignity of the Human Person
    Ch. 2 The Human Community
    Ch. 3 God's Salvation: Law and Grace
Section 2. **The Ten Commandments**
    Ch. 1. 'You shall love the Lord your God with all your heart, and with all your soul, and with all your mind'.
    Arts 1-3. The First, Second and Third Commandments
    Ch. 2. 'You shall love your neighbour as yourself'.
    Arts 4-10. The Fourth to Tenth Commandments

The Ten Commandments, in short, are allotted their place within the Christian life, only subsequently to the detailed consideration of human dignity and freedom; the morality of human acts; moral conscience; the virtues (human and theological); the gifts and the fruits of the Holy Spirit; the person in society; social justice; grace and justification, and the Church as teacher of the faith and guide to the moral life. The Decalogue is viewed as the explicitation of the love of God and the love of the neighbour. The renewal of moral theology which has filled the past seventy years or so, and which has plunged its roots deeply into biblical studies and historical theology, is reflected at every turn of the discussion of the commandments, and is exhibited in the very structure of the Catechism. The pioneers of the theology of love from the 1930s to the 1960s (Spicq and De Lubac, for instance) would have been able to identify in this feature of the work the full fruit borne in the Church by their labours.

The chapters devoted to the commandments of love are easy to read and not very lengthy (pp. 445-524). The exposition is accompanied by summaries to help its assimilation. Rather than give a detailed commentary on the text, it seems preferable here to place before the reader aspects of the theology of the Decalogue, with a view to deepening the appreciation of its significance when viewed from the Catholic perspective. This can be done in several stages, beginning with a reflection on the place of the Decalogue within revelation.

The place of the Decalogue within Revelation

The Ten Commandments are known in two forms, a longer (Exodus 20:2-17)) and a shorter (Deuteronomy 5:6-21). Both are quoted in full at the opening of the Catechism exposition, the first words of which invoke Jesus' answer to the young man who asked, 'Teacher, what must I do to have eternal life?' (Mt 19:16-19). In reply, Jesus first recalled the necessity to recognise God as the 'One who is good' and the source of all good. Then he added, 'If you would enter life, keep the commmandments', and he cited from the precepts concerning the love of neighbour: 'You shall not kill, You shall not commit adultery, You shall not steal, You shall not bear false witness, honour your father and mother.' Jesus then summarised these commandments positively: 'You shall love your neighbour as yourself' (2052).

The evangelical precepts are inseparable from the commandments, which they do not abolish or replace. The call to follow Christ in poverty and chastity is continuous with the keeping of the commandments. Through the precepts we are invited to rediscover the commandments 'in the person of their master who is their perfect fulfilment' (2053).

Acknowledging the commandments in the Sermon on the Mount, Jesus showed the power of the Spirit at work in the letter: 'You have heard that it was said to the men of old, "You shall not kill"... But I say to you that everyone who is angry with his brother shall be liable to judgment' (Mt 5:22) (2054). Jesus offered his own summary of the law: 'You shall love the Lord your God with all your heart, and with all your soul, and with all your mind. This is the greatest and first commandment. And a second is like it: You shall love your neighbour as yourself. On these two commandments hang all the Law and the prophets' (Mt 22:37-40; cf. Dt 6:5; Lev 19:18) (2055).

Considering the Decalogue in Sacred Scripture (2066ff.), the Catechism locates it firmly within the revelation of God to Moses: 'The ten words belong to God's revelation of himself and his glory... In making himself known, God reveals himself to his people.' (2059). The Decalogue must first be understood in the context of the exodus, 'God's great liberating event at the centre of the Old Covenant.' His liberating power appears from the fact that in the Old Testament the Decalogue was never handed on without first recalling the covenant. At this point we meet the first of a number of quotations from early Church writers, invoked by the authors of the Catechism: Origen maintains,

> Since there was a passing from the paradise of freedom to the slavery of this world, in punishment for sin, the first phrase of the Decalogue, the first word of God's commandments, bears on freedom: 'I am the Lord your God, who brought you out of the land of Egypt, out of the house of slavery.'[2]

In the biblical account, 'all the obligations are stated in the first person ("I am the Lord") and addressed by God to another personal subject ("you")' (2063). The singular personal pronoun designates the recipient, as God addresses each person in particular, at the same time as he reveals his will to the whole people. At this point a striking quotation from St Irenaeus is included in the exposition:

> 'The Lord prescribed love towards God and taught justice towards neighbour, so that man would be neither unjust, nor unworthy of God. Thus, through the Decalogue, God prepared man to become his friend and to live in harmony with his neighbour.... The words of the Decalogue remain likewise for us Christians. Far from being abolished, they have received amplification and development from the fact of the coming of the Lord in the flesh.'[3]

These introductory considerations serve to locate the commandments firmly within the biblical revelation of the Old Testament, while at the same time adopting the New Testament perspective, wherein the commandments are not abolished but perfected, in the person of Jesus Christ.[4] The inseparability of covenant and law in the Old Testament finds its parallel and fulfilment in the New, which instructs believers to live the commandments out of 'this *twofold yet single* commandment of love for God and the neighbour.' (2063, my emphasis).

The spirit and the letter, or the old and the new law

It has been observed that Christianity is unique among the world's religions in being born with a Bible in its own cradle. The Bible in question was not as yet canonically circumscribed, but it was sufficiently well defined to be referred to in current formulas such as 'the law and the prophets', 'Moses and the prophets', or simply 'the Scripture/the Scriptures'. With Jesus himself, and consequently with the disciples, we encounter a way of reading the Jewish Bible that opens up a new sense of what was written there. The text is not altered in its substance (although admittedly the particular use of Old Testament texts by writers of the New Testament is not always a simple affair of straightforward quotation), but the new sense arises from its being related to the person of Jesus, as the Christ, the fulfilment of the promise made 'in accordance with the Scriptures'. Perhaps more than in former times, exegetes of today recognise that for the Apostles and the first believers in Christ the Jewish Bible was the great, indeed the only, work of reference available. Without appealing to it the Apostles would simply not have been able to find any expression for their faith.[5]

Of course, the exegesis of the commandments is, as it turns out on subsequent reflection, only the particular case (even though a most important one) of the general issue that has confronted Christianity ever since Apostolic times: how best can the follower of Jesus, who believes him to be the Messiah, make use of the Jewish Bible in order to explore the mission of Christ within God's providence of history?

Once the nascent Church had itself begun to produce a literature, in the form of its Gospels and the apostolic writings, the hermeneutical situation changed and became the study of the interrelationship between two sets of documents, the Jewish Bible (as interpreted by Christians) and the new Christian writings themselves. The earliest Christian dialectic consisted in exploring the differences between the old body of Jewish writings and the new corpus produced by the earliest preachers of the kerygma; differences which in turn were to be appreciated in the light of the overarching unity of the divine plan, which could only be one. Broadly speaking, the categories of promise and fulfilment (or prophecy and realisation) were taken from the Gospel according to Matthew. St Paul supplied the contrast between the letter and the Spirit, which so forcibly attracted St Augustine. Paul likewise made use of allegory (a feature of the contemporary Greek literary scene) to express the relationship between two covenants, their differences and their interrelationship. The Fathers and other seminal Christian writers, such as Clement and Origen, did not start from nothing when developing their distinction between the literal and the spiritual senses of the Scriptures; they rather looked to the New Testament books for precious methodological hints as to how to read the Jewish Scriptures in their bearing upon Christ.[6]

Jesus had spoken of a 'new covenant' given in his blood. The inner logic of the New Covenant idea conceives the Christian community as a New Israel and raises a vast metaphorical edifice upon the people of the Old Covenant and its institutions (Temple, sacrifice, priesthood, Holy City, circumcision, etc.). St Paul added to his idea of the two covenants another which was to prove equally seminal for the Christian reading of the Old Testament in the light of the Christ-event: 'The letter kills but the Spirit gives life' (2 Cor 3:6). Paul meant that the Spirit of God living in the heart of the believer breathes new life into the letter of the law, allowing it to be read, and lived, 'in Christ', and in freedom from fear and alienation. The spirit in which the letter of the Law of Moses, in particular, was to be both understood and lived was, in short, the Holy Spirit; St Paul speaks of 'the love of God which is shed in our hearts by the Holy Spirit, who is given to us' (Rm 5:5). In the same letter he brings his understanding of Christian, Spirit-filled love to bear on the commandments regarding the neighbour:

> The commandments: 'You shall not commit adultery, You shall not kill, You shall not steal, You shall not covet', and any other commandment, are summed up in this sentence: 'You shall love your neighbour as yourself'. Love does no wrong to a neighbour; therefore love is the fulfiling of the law (Rm 13:9-10).

In St Paul's eyes spiritual freedom is identical with the love that is the fruit of the Spirit's dwelling in the believer (Ga 5:22). Liberty is love and love is liberty, and these equivalents stand in the closest relationship to the spiritual sense of the Scriptures which is opened up by the Christ-centred reading of them.

New Covenant – New 'Law'

In the Gospel according to St John (13:34) reference is made by Jesus to the 'New Law' which he gives to his disciples, that they should love one another. Thus it was that the language of law and commandment entered into the Christian vocabulary in the Greek (*entole*) and Latin (*mandatum*) languages. It requires only a little reflection on our part to realise that this transfer was inevitable, since it belongs to that wider logic which is to be found at work throughout the New Testament, and which can be summarised in the words of St Paul concerning the 'true Israel' (Ga 6:16). We find the words, 'New Covenant, in my blood', on Jesus' lips in the Synoptic Gospels (Mt 26:28; Mk 14:24; Lk

22:20). In the Sermon on the Mount, Matthew presents Jesus as the new lawgiver. Jesus extends the commandments of the Old Covenant in a new and original way. As the *berith* was ratified by scattering the blood of animal victims over the assembled people (Ex 24:8), so there is a new victim whose blood is shed for all. A new priest offers the universal sacrifice, with himself as the new paschal lamb-victim (Rv 6:10); and that priesthood of Christ himself is shared in by all the people (1 P 2:9). Sacrifice was performed in the Temple, where Yahweh dwelt, hence there must be a new temple for God to live in, and for spiritual offering to be made; it is the one built of living stones upon the foundation of the Twelve Apostles, with Christ as the corner-stone. There will be a New Jerusalem (Gal 4:26; Hb 12:21; Rv 21-22), and within it, at its summit, a new Zion. In short, each and every institution of the people which derived from the covenant of Sinai is given a spiritual or mystical transposition. The New Testament thus raises itself like a vast metaphor upon Israel and its institutions, understood in a literal sense.

The relevance of this transposition of meaning for the commandments and the notion of law is apparent: the 'law' of the New Covenant can be a law only in a metaphorical or analogical sense. In his argument against Faustus the Manichee, St Augustine insisted that 'letter' and 'law' have different meanings deriving from their double situation, in Judaism, and in Christianity:

> Thus, the letter with the spirit and the law with grace are not called letter and law in the same sense as when they of themselves killed, and made sin abound.... This same law, given by Moses, has become grace and truth through Jesus Christ since the spirit joined the letter, in order that the justice of the law should begin to be accomplished, which up to then had only made men guilty by rebellion.[7]

Since the law of Christianity is a 'law of love', it is in one sense not a law at all. But because it does not abolish the moral law of the Old Dispensation, on the other hand, it does somehow contain commandments and prohibitions within itself. The notion of a 'law of love' is not, however, paradoxical in itself; rather it is dialectical, since each of the terms of the expression enters into the other within the consciousness of the Church and of the believer, to form a new and original mode of thought and life.

The Catholic dialectic of law and love

If the Spirit of God casts out fear, sets free, blows where it will, then what place can commandments and prohibitions have within the Christian consciousness? This antithesis of freedom and commandment preoccupied many of the Christian Fathers of both Latin and Greek expression, probably because it is one of those tensions which will always resurface within Christianity itself, given its very nature as a Gospel of love and freedom.

If Christian writers had all at every stage listened attentively to the New Testament teaching on the life of faith, no opposition of law to love would ever have arisen. In the Gospels and in the letters of St Paul, love is the spirit which animates the living of the moral law. It can surprise and disconcert the modern reader to find that the Apostolic Fathers scarcely mentioned the Decalogue. While knowing and fully accepting the books of the Old Testament, and basing their moral teaching on that of Christ, the fulfilment of the promise, these early writers scarcely spoke of the commandments. The explanation usually given is no doubt correct: from the end of the first century the Church was engaged in separating itself out more and more from the Synagogue. Its writers were naturally struck, more than we are today, by the novelty of the gospel message and tended to underline all that distinguished it from Judaism. The Sermon on the Mount appeared to them in the light of a rejoinder to the Mosaic Law (together with the rabbinic commentaries), rather than its continuation. St Justin Martyr may stand for more than simply a personal viewpoint in this regard, when he asserts:

> For us, Christ has been given to us, the eternal and final law, a secure pact, after whom there are no more laws, or precepts or commandments.[8]

The early writers do indeed speak of precepts, and regularly quote one or other of the divine commandments, but they do not conceive Christian morality in terms of the Decalogue. Three principles instead command their moral thought: the dignity of being a child of God conferred on the one baptised; Christ's dwelling in him or her; and the Holy Spirit, who is the principle of holiness and inspiration of the moral life.[9] With St Irenaeus there is already quite a pronounced tendency to identify the Decalogue with the natural law known to the Gentiles;[10] the commandments survive the collapse of the Torah, where they were mixed up with the ceremonial code. All are obliged to observe them, since they were placed by the Creator within the human heart.

With the passage of time, however, Christian polemics against the Jews lost much of their earlier importance, in particular regarding law and commandment. Manichaeanism offered a new challenge, one which was in this regard the opposite of Judaism: the Jewish Bible was entirely rejected by them, and the Ten Commandments, together with the Torah as a whole, were attributed to the work of an irrational, evil god. When we find St Augustine revalorising the commandments and integrating them into Christian morality, it is evident that he is combating the adherents of Mani.

By the end of the fourth century the consensus of Christian writers was that the ritual and ceremonial aspects of the Torah had ceased to have any value with the coming of Christ, whereas the Decalogue remained normative. Augustine expresses the commonly-held view when he claims:

> What then are these laws of God, written by God himself in hearts, if not the very presence of the Holy Spirit who is the finger of God?[11] By the fact of his presence in us he

sheds charity in our hearts [Rm 5:5], and this charity is nothing other than the fulfilment of the law and the end of the precept.

If we leave aside the ceremonial precepts and the terrestrial promises of the Old Testament, we nevertheless retain the moral precepts, but we understand them in a new spirit, turning towards the spiritual good:

> Now, indeed, what is promised is the good of the heart, the good of the spirit, the good of the soul, that is, the spiritual good. That is the meaning of these words: 'I will write my laws in their mind and I will imprint them in their heart'.[12]

St John Chrysostom may be allowed to speak for the Greek East, just as St Augustine has been taken in the foregoing to represent the Latins. Does the moral law not still continue to be in some sense a binding, mandatory regime governing the action of Christians? The Patriarch of Constantinople wisely places the issue firmly upon the plane of consciousness. For the person living in faith and responsive to the Spirit of God the moral norms do not constitute an alienating imposition to be enforced by a superior and ever-watchful Power. In a real sense there is for such a believer no law any more; to put it in another way, there is for him no consciousness of the moral norms as a set of injunctions and embargoes which interfere with his liberty, or as a sort of boundary of which the individual must be continually and anxiously aware, lest he be tempted to stray over to the wrong side of it. The fascination with transgression and wrong-doing, as St Paul had clearly seen, inevitably begins to spell the fall from true freedom. Chrysostom prolongs the Apostle's thought, as follows:

> 'For, brethren, ye have been called unto liberty; only use not liberty for an occasion to the flesh' (Gal 5:13).
>
> ...This passage has reference to doctrine in the controversy with the Manichees. What is the meaning of, Use not liberty for an occasion to the flesh? Christ hath delivered

us, he says, from the yoke of bondage. He hath left us free
to act as we will, not that we may use our liberty for evil,
but that we may have ground for receiving a higher reward,
advancing to a higher philosophy. Lest any one should
suspect, from his calling the Law over and over again a
yoke of bondage, and grace a deliverance from the curse,
that his object in enjoining an abandonment of the Law
was that one might live lawlessly, he corrects this notion,
and states his object to be, not that our course of life might
be lawless, but that our philosophy might surpass the Law.
For the bonds of the Law are broken, and I say this not
that our standard may be lowered but that it may be
exalted. For both he who commits fornication, and he who
leads a virgin life, pass the bounds of the Law, but not in
the same direction; the one sinks lower, the other rises
higher; the one transgresses the law, the other excels it.
Thus Paul says that Christ hath removed the yoke from
you, not that ye may kick and be wanton, but that though
without the yoke ye may proceed at a well-measured
pace.[13]

Chrysostom's is an example of patristic spiritual
interpretation at its very best. He has the Decalogue in view, but
he looks to the spirit, not the letter, since in the precise sense
which he intends the Law is simply not a factor within the living,
spiritual consciousness of the just man.

St Augustine and the theology of the Decalogue

No figure in western Christian theology has had a greater or more
long-lasting influence on the theology of love and the
commandments than the Bishop of Hippo. The very order in
which the Latins ever after him were to enumerate the
commandments was due to his intervention.[14]

The numbering of the Ten Commandments betrays a
variation which is of Jewish origin. According to the Talmud,

Philo, and the Fathers of the Church before Augustine (e.g. Gregory of Nazianzen and Jerome), the verses are to be divided up as follows:

1. adoration of the one God (Ex 20:3)
2. prohibition of idols (v.4-6)
3. do not take the name of the Lord in vain (v.7)
4. work on six days but rest on the sabbath, a rest for Yahweh (v. 8-11)
5. honour father and mother (v.12)
6. do not kill (v. 13)
7. do not commit adultery (v. 14)
8. do not steal (v. 15)
9. do not bear false witness (v. 16)
10. do not covet the wife or goods of another (v. 17).

Now Augustine was to exercise a lasting influence by linking 1 and 2 in the old enumeration, thus assimilating polytheism to idolatry under a single prohibition, and in making the final commandment double, thereby according due respect to the status of woman. In doing so he opened up the way to a new, bipartite classification of the Decalogue. In the enumeration which preceded him the First Table of five elements prescribed the proper religious attitude to the God who gives life and to the parents who transmit it, in a way that no doubt reflects an Israelite mentality. The redivision of the two tablets into three commands relative to God and seven relative to the neighbour, Augustinian in origin, was to become part of the common wisdom of Latin Christianity, and was to be retained by the Lutherans.

St Augustine was also responsible for a theology of the Decalogue which was in its own way to become part of the patrimony of medieval Christianity, and to exercise an influence which continued up to and even beyond the Council of Trent. His originality emerges by way of contrast with the meagre treatment of the commandments in the sub-apostolic Church and up to his own time. It was with Augustine that the commandments entered the instruction of both catechumens and the faithful in general, and found a modest but secure place in the articulation of Catholic doctrine. Perhaps it was his opposition to Manichaeanism which more than anything else inspired his upgrading of the Decalogue. He displayed the commandments in his sermons and elsewhere as the natural law written by the creator in the heart of man, and expressly repeated to the chosen people. This legislation was taken up again, purified and completed, in the New Law which, adding to it a higher ideal as well as further precepts, proposed it as the foundation for practical morality.

In a sermon entitled *De Decem Chordis* ('On the Ten Strings'), St Augustine succeeded in bequeathing to the Church one of those inspired images which mark him out as a great poet of prayer.[15] Referring to verses of Ps 91,

> It is good to give thanks to the Lord
> to make music to your name, O Most High,
> to proclaim your love in the morning
> and your truth in the watches of the night,
> on the ten-stringed lyre and the lute,
> with the murmuring sound of the harp
> (1-3; cf Ps 143:10),

Augustine made an accommodation of the sense to fit his theology of love and command: the ten strings give no sound by themselves; only when they are touched by the finger of the musician do they make melody and harmony, and begin to enchant the ear. The image of love's divine music played on its ten-stringed instrument was to be frequently allegorised in medieval commentaries on the Psalms, but its simplicity did not admit of any improvement; anyone who had heard a harp played required no allegorical ornamentation in order to grasp Augustine's vivid meaning.

Scholastic theology and the Decalogue

The theological study of the Decalogue, begun by the Fathers, held a prominent place in the renewal of Catholic thought which took place in the course of the twelfth and thirteenth centuries. From about 1100 onwards systematic treatises began to appear, which gathered authorities and questions within some chosen, overarching framework. The Ten Commandments and the doctrine of love quickly came into prominence. They were to retain their place in syntheses of theology down to the Council of Trent. This school of theology in turn gave rise to a rich and widespread movement of pastoral theology, aimed essentially at preachers and confessors.[16] The series of Lateran Councils between 1179 and 1215 lent official encouragement to the growth of treatises on the virtues and vices, the articles of faith, the Ten Commandments, the Our Father and the sacraments, in particular the sacrament of penance. Within a generation of its inception this pastoral theology began to appear in the vernacular languages, which were being read by increasing numbers of literate laity. The discussion of love and the commandments, in both scholastic and pastoral genres, continued to reflect the pervasive influence of St Augustine.

From the innumerable studies of the commandments which circulated during these two centuries (by Hugh of St Victor, Peter Abelard, Peter Lombard, William of Auvergne, Jean de la Rochelle and Alexander of Hales, St Bonaventure, and John Duns Scotus (to mention only eminent names), two will be selected here, namely those by Robert Grosseteste, Bishop of Lincoln, and St Thomas Aquinas.

Robert Grosseteste, *On the Ten Commandments*

About the year 1230 Grosseteste, the great luminary of the early years of Oxford University, composed the first free-standing treatise on the commandments to appear since Philo.[17] A few central features indicative of his approach will be outlined in what follows, in order to illustrate the basic continuity of doctrine which prevailed between the patristic and the scholastic theology of love and the commandments, despite the considerable differences in literary form and in the political-ecclesiastical setting.

One of the variants of the title of Grosseteste's treatise reads, 'On Love and the Ten Commandments'. Nothing more apt could be found to express the theme of the work. How is the plurality of precepts to be understood and lived as a unity, in the light of the *mandatum novum* of love which is Christianity's unique law? This is, clearly, the perspective from which the central problem is addressed. From it Grosseteste unfolds his understanding of *amor ordinatus*, or ordered love, for which he is greatly indebted to the author of the adage, *dilige, et quod vis fac* – the 'Doctor of Love', as St Augustine was admiringly called in medieval times.[18]

The wisdom of God, the author explains, has subsumed the multiplicity of precepts into one mandate, indeed into one word: *ama!* love! This word must, he insists, be understood dialectically, as ordered love: love nothing that must not be loved; do not fail to love anything that should be loved, but love each thing as much as it ought to be loved by you, and in the way it ought to be loved. If you find that as a pilgrim still on the way you are unable to do this, then at least retain the invincible love of this love, and love your loving each single thing just as, and as much as, it should be loved by you. For if you love that love, then in a way you have that love as it were in its very root, though not as yet unfolded into the branches of the tree. Grosseteste develops the allegory of love as a tree. Love sprouts from a single root. It bifurcates into the twofold commandment, and then from these two shoots there ramify ten branches, three from one shoot and seven from the other. Like twigs from branches grow the almost innumerable moral precepts to be found in Scripture. The study of the commandments in their organic relationship to their unique root and double shoots is to command all our attention, for that, the writer concludes, is the Scripture in a privileged sense, written by the Spirit of God (who is the finger of God [Ex 8:19]), for our salvation.

The first Commandment prohibits idolatry. Grosseteste gives it an entirely spiritual sense:

> From the love of God, then, there grows like a first branch the First Commandment of the Decalogue: 'Thou shalt not have strange gods before me.' For he who loves God above all clings lovingly to him as the supreme good and believes that he alone is the supreme good. For if he believed something other to be a good equal to or greater than that which he loves supremely, then that thing loved supremely would not be God, since 'God is that reality, a greater than which cannot be thought',[19] and is indeed greater than can be thought... If he believed in, and thus thought, a good equal to or greater than that which he loves supremely, then that thing loved supremely would not be God, and so he would not love God... Since God is by definition the supreme good, what the supreme good is for each man, in his belief or his love or his worship or his reverence – in all of these at once or in several of them – is God.

Works on the commandments inevitably reflect the political and social context within which they were written.[20] The feudal setting of medieval social life is perhaps most evident in the lengthy discussion of the Eighth Commandment, since the basis of public peace and order depended upon fealty, oaths and the sense of honour. The numerous *exempla* in the work, which are aimed at preachers, also have a feudal character. The following is an instance; it is attached to the Fourth Commandment:

> Let us imagine an earthly king seated upon the throne of the kingdom, and a servant of his expelling him from the throne and heaping ordure from the streets and the squares

upon it, as an insult. That such a deed merits the most severe punishment is patent to all. But how much more severely will they be punished, who place something before God in their love–before the high king, the high priest and the high judge!

In his commentary on Galatians, written around the same time, Grosseteste turns his attention to law and love, showing himself to be a discerning reader of both St Augustine and St John Chrysostom:

> *But if you are led by the Spirit, you are not under the law.* [Gal 5:18]. That is, if you follow the guidance of the higher reason that is conformed to the Holy Spirit, you are not under the law, i.e. you do not follow the law through fear of punishment, but being with the law you follow it through love of justice. [Or,] you do not require the written law as the giver of instructions. For he who by virtue of true loving choice (*dilectio*) follows the guidance of the Spirit, wishes to each one his best good and no evil, indeed he actually hates that evil should come to anyone else. Hence true love, spontaneously and without the Scripture commanding, avoids killing, adultery and theft; indeed it does, performs or thinks simply nothing evil. On the contrary, it honours parents, and renders to each one what is his own. In this way it is not under the law, since it does not require the law; for whatever the law lays down concerning good behaviour or forbids regarding evil behaviour, that is just what love would do of its own accord and without the precept or prohibition of the law. That is why the Apostle says elsewhere, The law is not imposed on the just man [1 Tim 1:19]. For in what way is it imposed upon one who would fulfil it, even if it were not there?[21]

In Grosseteste's eyes, the spiritual comprehension of the Ten Commandments places one above them when considered as laws or prohibitions, but without of course evacuating their sense and import. The Commandments remain, but they cannot be an alienating and constricting pressure within the consciousness of the man who is filled with the Spirit of God.

Virtue and precept in St Thomas Aquinas

St Thomas expounded the Decalogue in his treatise on the Old and the New Law.[22] It may fairly be said that the entirety of Church teaching, from the New Testament down to his own times, found its reflection there. This treatise has frequently been made the object of detailed analysis and commentary, something which cannot be attempted here.[23] Instead, only a brief philosophical contrast will be drawn between thomistic and modern approaches to morality, but without receiving any of the development that the problematic would require.

More than any of his predecessors, Thomas had an explicit and sharply thematic consciousness of the organicity of theology. This was made possible by his intellectual situation, and specifically through the expanded resources of learning it made available to him. (The university setting may have had something to do with it also). Where, in the final analysis, did he decide to locate the commandments within the warp and woof of theology? The answer must be sought in the relationship he set out to establish among three terms: freedom, the virtues and the commandments.

Unlike the majority of manuals of moral theology belonging to a later age of Catholic theology, St Thomas did not choose to build his moral thought around the commandments but made the virtues, both human and theological (for 'grace builds upon nature'), the central axis of his thinking.[24] To the virtues he joined in the first place the gifts of the Holy Spirit, and only after that (systematically speaking) the precepts and the commandments. It was on the basis of the plan and general design of his moral thought, and even of his theology considered as a whole, that he was led to insert freedom, the virtues, law and the precepts in their respective places. The general layout, furthermore, modifies the substance and content of each of these elements, relating each one organically to the body of truth.[25]

The predominant tendency of moral theologians during the modern period (between the Renaissance and the twentieth century) was to derive duty or obligation directly from the command of the divine lawgiver, and to analyse the role of conscience in presenting the law to the moral subject. Morality was essentially the work of practical reason seeking to determine in a particular case (*casus*, casuistry) how the obligation in question was to be met, granted the dispositions and circumstances of the subject. The role attributed to free will was that of choosing between contraries: to do or not to do, to say yes or to say no to the precept (or maxim) formulated by conscience. Voluntarism, with its notion of a liberty of indifference, characterised the conception of both the divine will of the legislator and the human will; law and obligation were the most salient connection between these two wills. Morality was considered real to the extent that there was obligation. Human liberty was viewed as a reality only in so far as sin was an ever-present possibility. The moral life was in consequence regarded as a multitude of successive but separate acts, each one of which exemplified the power of free will to choose at any moment between contraries. In this scheme the virtues could play only a subsidiary role, as either handy nominalistic classifiers of acts, or else habits (by definition, good habits) of obedience to commands. They lacked any of the dynamism accorded to them in a teleological moral theory that envisages the continuous unfolding of human life on its way towards perfection.

In the eyes of St Thomas, morality has its source in the spiritual nature of man created in the image of God. Within human nature there are natural inclinations to the good, to truth, and to life in society. These tendencies inspire our freedom and are its source. The inclinations towards the good and to truth incite us to act better and better. They are open to infinity, since neither goodness nor truth can be restricted to any particular level of human attainment, or to any genus of being, or even to finite being as such. Between the inclinations and the final goal of existence (happiness, and the vision of God), there exists a 'tension of aspiration'[26] which gives rise to moral progress, and puts into each action a finality that links it intrinsically with one's other actions, and indeed with the whole of life. Finality is the directing and unifying force of our acts, placing them within time and duration. Now the virtues (the outcome of reason acting upon the 'material' of feelings and attractions), have the function of developing and applying these natural inclinations to particular acts, as well as of ordering them to the progressive perfection of the subject in acting. Aquinas' moral theology is not specifically concerned with drawing some fine borderline between what is permitted and what is forbidden. His central preoccupation is with discerning the quality of the action, and shaping the best action in the given conditions of the acting subject. The virtues play the principal role in morality by strengthening the natural inclinations, thus making us able to produce in action the mature fruit of the moral life. The principal virtue is charity, whose inner law is the aspiration to the perfection of love. It is at this point that the gifts of the Holy Spirit come in, to complete the virtues; these gifts help one towards acting perfectly, in dependence upon the Spirit of God.

Within this framework the commandments are at the service of the virtues. In their negative formulations, in particular, they define the principal preconditions of virtuous action. (For instance, 'Thou shalt not kill', is a presupposition of the virtue of justice, since justice presupposes that the other is alive). The precepts provide some protection against illusions and temptations. They function also as ethical signals. The person who is (morally speaking) forced to become conscious of a particular commandment is receiving thereby a clear signal that he or she risks falling from the exercise of liberty into unfreedom, or indeed has already done so. The prohibition, in particular, comes into its own only as a moral indicator of failing aspiration, a signpost on a road that would lead downwards towards moral perdition. The commandments are, indeed, like all law, an ordinance of reason, but they are brought into relationship with freedom only by being related, somewhat negatively, to the virtues.

The difference between the thomistic and the typically modern accounts of freedom can perhaps be highlighted by the following consideration: for the most characteristic theological moralists of the modern period, the traditional claims that we are free only to do the good, and that we are free only while pursuing and doing the good, are strictly paradoxical; whereas of course they belonged to the moral common sense of Platonists, Aristotelians, Augustinians and Thomists.

The Reformation and Trent

Martin Luther's interpretation of the Letter to the Romans, in particular, stressed the opposition between Law and Grace. The Ten Commandments belong to law, within that portion of the history of salvation that preceded the redemptive grace won by Christ's saving death. In the life-of the individual, law and its commandments have likewise a kind of priority: they serve to reinforce the sense of sin. The function of the commandments is thus to destroy self-sufficiency and break down human pride, leaving the sinner conscious of his moral inadequacy and hence disposed to trust more and more in the saving power of the grace of Christ. Protestant theology may be said to have undergone a lasting influence of this approach.[27]

The Council of Trent reaffirmed, as against the reformer's theology of *simul justus et peccator*, the Catholic teaching according to which the justified man is capable of observing the commandments, with the aid of actual grace. The Roman Catechism which followed it restated the irreducible place to be accorded to the commandments, along with the Creed, the sacraments and the teaching on prayer (the 'Our Father'), as the fundamental pivots of Catholicism. In much subsequent Catholic moral theology the Ten Commandments were used as the framework for the whole of moral teaching. Casuistry was invoked in order to enable the discerning conscience, and in a particular way that of the penitent and the confessor, to discriminate between what is forbidden by the commandments and what is permitted. The more positive teaching on love was not entirely forgotten, but it tended to be linked more intrinsically to the evangelical counsels of perfection, and thus to be associated rather closely with religious profession and life, and hence dealt with in ascetical treatises and spiritual works of devotion.

'Life in Christ'

Part Three of the Catechism, 'Life in Christ', reflects with fidelity and discernment the progress of Catholic moral theology during the second half of the twentieth century. Biblical studies, together with the recovery of the best of patristic and scholastic thought, were prominent among the rejuvenating factors. In expounding the commandments the authors of the Catechism have tapped into the renewed account of Christian living which has so far resulted from biblical studies and historical theology. An attractive feature is the anthology of quotations from, especially, the sub-apostolic writers and the Fathers, which have been included in the text, and which place the reader before distilled encapsulations of the Catholic tradition. The reader is likewise reminded of the relationship of the Catechism to the Second Vatican Council by the heavy reliance of this section (as well as of the others) upon the documents of the Council. (In the section on the commandments and love, *Gaudium et spes* is the most frequently-quoted of the documents). Above all, the structure of Part Three of the Catechism relates the commandments to the virtues (human and theological), the gifts and fruits of the Holy Spirit, and to grace, all of which are discussed (in III.1) before the commandments are approached. This feature markedly affiliates the Catechism to the thought of St Thomas Aquinas. It signifies at the same time a fundamental change of direction from the manualist tradition of the modern period.

The treatise on love and the commandments presents a moral teaching on fundamentals that is at the opposite remove from fundamentalism. The balanced theology of love and precept is required, and will be given a wide welcome, in an age of market-led moral relativism, of a kind that has infected the attitudes of numbers of theologians, even in Catholic faculties and institutions. In the Catechism the Church has forged a valuable instrument for knowing the Catholic faith and handing it on, in its wholeness and organicity. The Catholic Church owed it to the contemporary world, within which it is an international agency, to state its own beliefs and principles. But more than that, it owed it to its own faithful: parents, pastors, catechists and missionaries, to supply them with a unified, up-to-date expression of the faith professed by baptised and believing Catholics.

9

THE GOSPEL OF CHRISTIAN PRAYER ACCORDING TO THE CATECHISM OF THE CATHOLIC CHURCH

Bede McGregor OP

'Contacts with the religions of Asia, especially Hinduism and Buddhism, which are noted for their contemplative spirit, for their methods of meditation and for their asceticism, can greatly contribute to the inculturation of the Gospel in that continent. A wise exchange between Catholics and the followers of other traditions can help to discern points of contact in spirituality and in the expression of religious beliefs, while not ignoring the differences. Such discernment is all the more pressing where people have lost their own traditions and are seeking other sources of spiritual support and enrichment. The growth of the so-called new or alternative religious movements is a sign of how widespread this tendency is' (Pope John Paul II).

In this paper I will not attempt to give a commentary on or even a summary of the whole of Part Four of the Catechism on Christian prayer; I will offer a few reflections on some paragraphs of this part of the Catechism from a very particular angle. But I hope this will give some idea of the essential character and spirit of its teaching. Basically, I will attempt to underline the specific and unique nature of Christian prayer in the context of other forms of prayer and meditation found in other religious traditions and contemporary new religious movements. Christian prayer is a gospel that all peoples have a right to hear about from Christians, it is a gift from God that meets the deepest needs of every human heart. We must listen deeply to what our non-Christian brothers and sisters have to say about prayer and meditation but we also need to be able to render an account of the gospel of Christian prayer to them. The Catechism provides us with the material we need for this task.

Two thirds of the world's population is non-Christian and pray or meditate or try to relate in a saving way to some form of transcendence or Absolute, personal or impersonal. They want to be anchored in Someone or Something Eternal in the midst of the experience of relentless transience, suffering and inevitable death. The disciple who asked Jesus – Lord teach us to pray – speaks not only for himself but in some sense for every human person that ever existed. The search for God and the desire to be in relationship with him is rooted in our human nature in some way. The disciple asks that God himself teach us how to relate to him in our human condition. The same request is put, always and everywhere, to the Church, the sacrament of the real presence of the Risen Christ in our world today : teach us to pray. So my first objective is to try to present the specific and distinctive nature of the Good News of Christian prayer in the context of the prayer life of non-Christian peoples. It is not a question of simply trying to show the superiority of Christian prayer but to indicate its true nature as good news. We are servants of this good news and of our non-Christian brothers and sisters and believe there is no need for them to lose anything that is true and good and beautiful in their own religious traditions but they will shine forth even more clearly in the light of Christ especially in the experience of his prayer.

I also want to keep in mind one of the descriptions of mission given in the Catechism and quoted from the encyclical letter, *Redemptoris missio*: 'The entire missionary sense of John's Gospel is expressed in the ' priestly prayer': 'This is eternal life , that they know you the only true God, and Jesus Christ whom you have sent' (Jn 17:3) The ultimate purpose of mission is to enable people to share in the communion which exists between the Father and the Son. The disciples are to live in unity with one another, remaining in the Father and the Son, so that the world may know and believe. This is a very important missionary text. It makes us understand that we are missionaries above all because of what we are as a Church whose innermost life is unity in love, even before we become missionaries in word and deed (RM n.23). The priestly prayer of Jesus is one of the key texts on prayer in the Catechism; it sums up the whole economy of creation and salvation. It fulfils all the petitions of the Our Father (805). So I would maintain that catechesis on Christian prayer and the missionary activity of the Church are inseparable: they both have as their ultimate purpose the facilitation of a real meeting and communion of the human person with Jesus Christ and in him with the Father and the Holy Spirit. Mission is about meeting the human person at the level at which he opens out to God or ultimate meaning and there we offer him the gospel of Christian prayer.

My second objective is to present the missionary character of Christian prayer itself; to suggest that growth in mission awareness and commitment is an acid test of authenticity and growth in prayer. I will try to do this by reference to some phrases of the Our Father, the only other prayer of Jesus discussed in some detail by the Catechism.

Thirdly, in a tangential way, I want to suggest, throughout these reflections, how the Gospel of Christian prayer as set forth in the Catechism, is central to the task of the new evangelisation so urgently needed in our own western cultures of non-belief, or of merely residual Christian values, in an environment where the all pervasive mass media are sometimes not only indifferent but even hostile and anti-Christian in their attitudes and policies and where the way of life we experience is marked by the grave personal and social sin of the privatisation of religion, so that religious faith is given little or no place in the serious and public discussions and decisions concerning life itself, marriage and the family, and the socio-economic and political life of our people.

Finally, with Luigi Giussani, Madeleine Delbrêl, Hans Urs von Balthasar and a host of other writers at the source of a new impulse for evangelisation, I would argue that the only ultimate and real problem is the problem of faith, and the Catechism, as an integral witness to the faith of the Church, provides us with a most useful instrument for tackling this problem.

Part Four of the Catechism begins with the question: What is prayer? Before dealing with this question I want to keep before us a scriptural portrait of Christ as the man of prayer. First a verse from the Gospel according to St Mark: 'In the morning, long before dawn, he got up and left the house, and went off to a lonely place and prayed there' (Mk 1: 35). I find this a good text for expressing simply and profoundly the heart and soul of Jesus and the source of his public ministry. He prayed long and deep and often. There is no escape from this fact about Jesus. We begin to know who Jesus is and what his mission is when we try to understand what is happening in his prayer. We learn about the Father and the Holy Spirit and the salvific will of the Trinity.

Another verse that illustrates how prayer was at the deepest centre of the life of Jesus, is taken from the Gospel according to Luke: 'Then he withdrew from them, about a stone's throw away, and knelt down and prayed... and in his anguish he prayed even more earnestly, and his sweat fell to the ground like great drops of blood' (Lk 22: 41-44). When things are extremely difficult and dark and oppressive we are invited to pray more, not less. Prayer is not confined to times of inner peace and quiet and the moments when we can manage sufficient space, privacy and serenity. Sometimes the prayer of Jesus is marked by deep groans and sighs that come straight from the heart in the midst of great distress. His prayer on the Cross is not the only witness of his prayer in the midst of suffering. The tears of Christ are an unforgettable part of his prayer recorded in the Gospels and recalled so eloquently in the Epistle to the Hebrews: 'During his life on earth, he offered up prayer and entreaty, aloud and in silent tears, to the one who had the power to save him out of death, and he submitted so humbly that his prayer was heard' (Hb 5: 7). This picture of the prayer of Christ in the midst of deep anguish and pain may have special appeal to all kinds of people whose lives are marked by tragedy, psychological disorientation and various forms of prolonged illness and who cannot easily escape to some oasis for quiet, contemplative prayer either inwardly or outwardly. Part Four of the Catechism is simply an attempt to present and lead us into an experience in faith of the prayer of Christ himself. There is no Christian prayer apart from him. And sometimes, in an image taken from Scripture and used in the Catechism, prayer is a battle.

Jesus gives us the gift of his interior life, not just information about it, but the ability to live and share it with him. We are baptised into his relationship to the Father and the Holy Spirit, so that we are ontologically placed in a state of prayer. What the Father, Son and Holy Spirit do eternally at the heart of their communion with each other takes place in the human person through grace and indwelling so that we can really participate and enjoy the trinitarian life in ourselves and together. Part Four of the Catechism deals with the nature of Christian prayer as it unfolds in the course of Revelation and is accessible to us in Scripture and Tradition and taught by the great Fathers and Doctors of the Church, east and west, and the saints, men and women, and all this as mediated authentically by the gift of the teaching authority in the Church. The Catechism is simply a witness to our Christian faith, an instrument for renewing and deepening it, and a most useful tool for the whole work of evangelisation.

In a very real sense, the whole of the Catechism is about prayer. The principle *lex orandi, lex credendi, lex agendi* is an important one. Some writers seem to suggest that the basis for inter-religious dialogue and inter-religious meditation and prayer is a common human *sophia* (wisdom) beyond and below the level of relative differences in vocabulary, ritual and culture in its philosophical and religious expressions. We all share the same human nature, are all made in the image and likeness of God. We are all religious human beings – open in our nature to transcendence however wounded and obscured this openness may be by sin and a culture built on a diminished sense of the sacred. It is often argued, even by some Catholic theologians, that at the core of human nature one religion is ultimately the same as another and so also is prayer life. But the world of faith determines the ontology of prayer and meditation, and the various religious faiths are not just superficially different but absolutely, both in general and in detail despite the analogical similarities that arise from a common human nature, rites of passage, needs and aspirations.

Let us take the simple example of humility that the Catechism says is the foundation of Christian prayer (2599). Humility appears as a central part of Islamic prayer. At the first light of day, the muezzin calls out from the minaret the Adhan, the first invitation to prayer with the words: 'Come alive to prayer, come alive to good. Better than to sleep is to pray.' Then follows the frequent praise of God and various profound bows and prostrations. This ritual is repeated five times a day, every day, of a devout Muslim's life. The very word Islam means submission to the will of God in an interior attitude of humility. Humility is seared into the very soul of the Muslim by daily practice, and really good Muslims are very impressive indeed. We thank God for their witness.

But theirs is utterly different from Christian humility. In Christian prayer we begin with the astounding humility of God. He not only becomes a human being, but becomes the suffering and faithful servant of every human person in the washing of the feet and his dying and death on the Cross. God is the loving and faithful servant of each one of us and this is the meaning of his sacrificial and redemptive love. Christian humility is an attempt to respond to the infinite kenosis of God. That is an essential attitude of Christian prayer which is incomprehensible to our Muslim brothers and sisters. Our God is so weak and vulnerable, our God is a distortion in whom there is no comeliness, lacking the majesty and sovereignty of Allah. It is blasphemy to our Muslim friends to suggest we are gifted with a created sharing in the very nature of God so that we can authentically call him Father in Christ and through the power of the Holy Spirit. Nor do the eastern religions have a sense of this redemptive love of God to which we Christians respond in prayer. Where there is no Christian faith and creed there can be no Christian prayer. It is difficult to over-estimate the importance of the other parts of the catechism dealing with the Creed for understanding Christian prayer.

Revelation is the key word when it comes to unlocking the meaning and practice of Christian prayer. Decoded, this means there is no access to Christian prayer apart from revelation; it has its origin solely in God. Flesh and blood have not revealed it. God is absolutely first. God has first loved us. The primacy of the divine initiative and of grace operates particularly in Christian prayer. It is God's gift to us (2559-2561). It always and everywhere begins with God but does not stop there. The human person is invited to respond and prayer becomes the meeting of the freedom of God who first chooses us in love and the freedom of the human person whom he invites to respond in love. This is an important principle in the Catechism when it comes to discerning humanistic and secularised forms of prayer and meditation found in amorphous movements like New Age or meditation used for mainly therapeutic purposes. Christian prayer can never be a purely human, mechanical technique. Christian prayer is God's way to us before it is our way to God or to purely human goals.

The first answer the Catechism gives to the question on the nature of prayer is taken from St Thérèse of Lisieux. She says: 'For me, prayer is a surge of the heart; it is a simple look turned towards heaven, it is a cry of recognition and of love, embracing both trial and joy' (2559). I would like to dwell a moment on the words ' a cry of recognition and love'. We need first to recognise the personal, unconditional, tender, eternal love of God for us. Balthasar says that Christian faith is nothing other than allowing oneself to receive what is bestowed by that God who, in his essence, is love and surrender. Karl Rahner echoes this when he says that a Christian is someone who allows himself to be infinitely loved by God. I would add that it is not simply a recognition of the creative love of God, that we are loved into existence and sustained in existence by his love, even though this is a fundamental and precious gift. It is seeing with the eyes of faith the redemptive and indwelling love of God for us. It is God's look of forgiving love on us that sustains prayer, that gives rise to the surge of our heart and the simple and continuous looking at the mystery of this love made visible in Christ, in good times and difficult ones. Prayer is recognising that we are recognised by God. He is always looking at us with deep, personal love. Christian prayer needs to operate in this context to be authentic.

The Catechism then gives us a description of prayer from St Augustine: 'Whether we realise it or not, prayer is the encounter of God's thirst with ours. God thirsts that we may thirst for him.' Our prayer is a response to the plea of the living God; it is a response of love to the thirst of the only Son of God (2561). It is important to present this eternal thirst of God for the human heart to our non-Christian brothers and sisters. They have a right to hear that they are infinitely lovable and loved by God. He died out of love for them, they are important to him, he will never stop caring for them and they are called to meet him face to face when they die and already now in their hearts. At the centre of their being there is someone who loves them and Christian prayer is simply a response to this reality of God's indwelling. Surely the mission of the Church to proclaim these truths cannot be an infringement of human freedom and religious liberty, a form of spiritual colonialism. I have never met a non-Catholic or a non-Christian who has objected to being told of their infinite importance to God. We invite them to consider and accept God's gift of communion, and covenant with them. The 'I thirst' of Our Lord is as important for the whole of missionary spirituality as it is for providing the deepest milieu for praying.

This fundamental teaching on Christian prayer as God's gift makes one hesitate about those experiments in prayer where technique, especially a mechanical repetition of a mantra, seem to be given an undue place. We cannot engender contemplative graces simply by mental control and human effort or yogic postures and breathing exercises. Sitting in a mindless state of relaxation may possibly be therapeutic for some people but is it prayer or Christian meditation? Sometimes a kind of magical mentality creeps into certain forms of prayer and meditation where we unconsciously try to manipulate or control God and bend his will to our purposes. The truly religious attitude seeks to let God's will be done in us, to allow him to take control and guide us, a bending of our will to his will. It is openness to the divine initiative of Love. The prayer of petition, in the last analysis, is a concrete request that his will for us may be done whatever the immediate request may be; it is not a question of magic or panic or cajoling God.

The biblical accounts of prayer as God's gift, as covenant and as communion stress the divine initiative, the divine commitment, and the call to intimacy and union. Our response comes from the heart; it is the heart that prays. If our heart is far from God, the words of prayer are in vain. Or as Mahatma Gandhi says in a different context, heart without words is infinitely more precious than words without heart. Thérèse of Lisieux puts it well when she writes: 'If God has not got your heart he has nothing'. Prayer is the life of the new heart. It ought to animate us at every moment (2697). We recall Ezekiel: 'I shall give you a new heart, and put a new spirit in you. I shall remove the heart of stone from your bodies and give you a heart of flesh instead' (Ezk 36:26). Ultimately it is the human heart of Christ at the centre of our human heart that prays. However, the primacy of the will in prayer does not eliminate the role of the mind and so the Catechism quotes the classic definition of St John Damascene: 'Prayer is the raising of one's mind and heart to God'. Habitual thinking and reflection about Our Lord can surely be a way of loving him. Attention to him, of some kind, is a necessary accompaniment to the movement of the heart. Surely a mindless prayer with no effort at attentiveness will be almost as deficient as a heartless prayer. The inseparablilty of the mind and will in a truly human act sometimes seems to be neglected in certain forms of meditation influenced by eastern traditions and some kinds of 'highs' in charismatic prayer.

The revelation of prayer and the universal call to prayer

Hans Urs von Balthasar begins his little book on Christian meditation with a statement that leads us to the heart of the nature of Christian prayer and its radical distinction from all other forms of prayer or meditation. He writes: 'The decisive question is whether God has spoken to the human race – about himself, of course, and likewise about his reason for creating man and the world – or whether the Absolute remains the Silence beyond all words of the world' (*Christian Meditation,* p.7).

If God has spoken then there can hardly be anything more significant than what he has to say. No purely human insight or experience and its expression can be put on the same level as God's own personal, inner experience and its communication to us. God's self-disclosure is the rivetting core of our identity as Christians. It determines the totality of our being and mission. The Church is born out of this revelation of God; she is a community that treasures the Word of God above everything else; the entire mission of the Church in all the richness and diversity of the many vocations and ministries within her is a function of Revelation. The mission of the Church is to seek to allow God's voice be heard to the ends of the earth and not be drowned out by the noise of merely human opinions. This is particularly true of her basic mission to teach the human person how to pray in the way that God has taught her how to pray. Ultimately we cannot teach ourselves to pray. God gives us the gift of prayer. The story of Christian prayer coincides with the history of revelation and salvation. It is precisely this revelation of Christian prayer that the Catechism seeks to put before us. As God gradually reveals himself and reveals us to ourselves, prayer appears as a reciprocal call, a covenant drama. Through words and actions, this drama engages the heart. It unfolds throughout the whole history of salvation (2567).

Prayer in the Old Testament

The early chapters of Genesis give us a clear teaching on the universal call to prayer. The human person is made in the image and likeness of God and even after he sins, he remains an image of God and retains the desire for the one who calls him into existence. This search and desire for God in the very nature of the human person is an important truth for all catechesis and preaching. Whatever the appearances might be to the contrary there is an openness to God in every person. People like Luigi Giussani, following on the well-known saying of St Augustine, 'you have made us for yourself, O Lord, and our hearts are restless until they rest in you', have built a whole approach to catechetics and religious education on this supposition. The Catechism points out that all religions bear witness to the essential search for God by the human person. This is brought out by the story of Noah and the covenant God made with him. In his indefectible covenant with every living creature, God has always called people to prayer. This truth is particularly helpful in the context of inter-religious dialogue and especially inter-religious meditation and prayer. Sometimes we can forget that God always goes before us in our various ministries and we can underestimate what he has already done and is doing in the very depths of the person and the ways in which he himself is teaching them. Paul captures the spirit of the story of Genesis when he writes: 'And he did this so that all nations might seek God and, by feeling their way towards him, succeed in finding him. Yet in fact he is not far from any of us, since it is in him that we live, and move and have our being, as indeed some of your own writers have said, "we are all his children" ' (Acts 17: 25-28).

The Catechism presents a beautiful overview of the revelation of prayer in the Old Testament. It cannot be bypassed without great impoverishment of the prayer formation of the Christian. It shapes the human mind and heart of Jesus at certain levels, makes a significant formative influence on the early Church, and retains all the actuality of a divine pedagogy for us today, individually and as a community. There is an irremovable contemporaneity about the Word of God in the Old Testament. God is still speaking to us here and now in the words and images, poetry and songs, stories and history, heroes and heroines, rogues and vagabonds, victories and defeats, law and prophets, kings and queens, in the totality of the Old Testament. Every Christian needs to attend the divine school of prayer opened to us in the Psalms which constitute the masterpiece of prayer in the Old Testament. They present two inseparable qualities: the personal and the communal. They extend to all dimensions of history, recalling God's promises already fulfilled, and looking for the coming of the Messiah. Prayed and fulfiled in Christ, the Psalms are an essential and permanent element of the prayer of the Church. They are suitable for men and women of every condition and time (2596). Is it possible deeply to understand the New Testament without also plunging into the Old Testament? Both are records of Revelation and the mystery of Christ.

I omit full treatment of the Old Testament on prayer simply because of a lack of time and not a lack of conviction about its importance. However, I would like to say a word about Abraham because of his significance to Jews, Muslims and Christians, and the way he illustrates one of the most profound and always present characteristics of authentic prayer: it is an expression of faith in a personal God. The Catechism says: 'When God calls him, Abraham goes forth 'as the Lord had told him'; Abraham's heart is entirely submissive to the Word and so he obeys. Such attentiveness of the heart, whose decisions are made according to God's will, is essential to prayer, while the words used count only in relation to it. Abraham's prayer is expressed first by deeds: a man of silence, he constructs an altar at each stage of his journey. Only later does Abraham's first prayer in words appear: a veiled complaint reminding God of his promises which seem unfulfilled. Thus one aspect of the drama of prayer appears from the beginning: the test of faith in the fidelity of God (2570). All three of the great monotheistic religions refer to Abraham as the father of believers. Faith is central to prayer. Prayer is an accurate measure of our faith. Bernanos puts it well in a pointed question: 'Is it not a peculiar contradiction that people can totally believe in God and yet pray to him so little, and so badly?'

Prayer in the fullness of time

The Incarnation of the Word of God changes the whole nature of prayer. Our Muslim brothers and sisters believe that God reveals himself through the Archangel Gabriel to Muhammed and through him to the whole world. Our Jewish brothers and sisters, and we, too, believe that God spoke and speaks to us through the law and the prophets, prescriptions, precepts, promises, ordinances, commands and through the history of events and experiences. Our oriental brothers and sisters believe that the absolute is to be found at the heart of ascetical and mystical effort and experiences. Our African brothers and sisters spontaneously believe that God speaks to them through the lavish gift of creation all around them, through the basic realities of their tribal and family life, through the spirit world and their ancestors. All peoples believe that in their search for God rooted in their nature they have found him in some way – thus we have the religions of the world. But with Jesus it is utterly different and unique. In and through the humanity of Jesus God speaks directly for himself and reveals and shares his inner life. Jesus the Incarnate Son of God offers us a share in his own filial relationship to the Father in the Holy Spirit. The classic text from the letter to the Hebrews puts it succinctly: 'Often and in varied ways God spoke to our ancestors through the prophets. In these final days he has spoken to us all through his Son, whom he appointed as heir of the universe. He, the reflection of his glory, the imprint of his being... effected purification from sins and took his place at the right hand of Majesty on high. He has become so much more exalted than the angels as the name he inherited surpasses them' (1:1-4). Other religious traditions point to and in some sense prepare a way towards eternal life. Jesus is eternal life, the Way itself, the beginning and the end.

Christian prayer is Christocentric

All catechesis and particularly catechesis in prayer is radically Christocentric and this is what gives Christian prayer its specificity, its utter uniqueness. The Catechism puts it cogently: 'At the heart of catechesis we find, in essence, a Person, the Person of Jesus of Nazareth, the only Son from the Father... who suffered and died for us and who now, after rising, is living with us for ever.' To catechise is to 'reveal in the Person of Christ the whole of God's eternal design reaching fulfilment in that Person. It is to seek to understand the meaning of Christ's actions and words and the signs worked by him.' Catechesis aims at putting ' people... in communion...with Jesus Christ: only he can lead us to the love of the Father in the Spirit and make us share in the life of the Holy Trinity' (426). Angelo Scola deduces from all this a fundamental methodological principle, namely, that every catechetical proposal, every catechetical programme, must bring about by its very nature an occasion for an encounter with Christ, as well as the verification of that encounter in mission. The distinctiveness of Christian faith and prayer is to be found in the Person of Christ, in his humanity. God became man to show us how to live his filial relationship to the Father in the Holy Spirit in our humanity. So those forms of spirituality and prayer which seem to neglect some aspects of our humanity are to that extent non-Christian. It has been well said that God wants to remain man forever. So, if God thinks it worthwhile to be completely human surely we should not neglect our humanity when we seek to live the life of the Trinity in Christ through grace.

What are the full implications of saying prayer is Christocentric? The catechism says that there is no other way of Christian prayer than Christ (2664). Whether our prayer is communal or personal, vocal or interior, it has access to the Father only if we pray in the name of Jesus. The sacred humanity of Jesus is therefore the way by which the Holy Spirit teaches us to pray to God our Father. I think Mother Teresa of Calcutta puts it beautifully when she writes: 'In reality there is only one true prayer, only one substantial prayer: Christ himself. There is only one voice that rises above the earth: the voice of Christ. Prayer is oneness with Christ.

'When times come when we can't pray, it is very simple: if Jesus is in my heart, let him pray, let him talk to his Father in the silence of my heart. Since I cannot speak, he will speak; since I cannot pray, he will pray.

'That's why often we should say, "Jesus in my heart, I believe in your faithful love for me". When we have nothing to give – let us give him that nothingness. Let us ask Jesus to pray in us, for no one knows the Father better than Jesus, who sends us his

Spirit to pray in us, for we do not know how to pray as we ought.' (*Prayer*, Mother Teresa and Brother Roger, pp. 13-14) To pray, then, is simply to share in the filial openness of Christ to the Father in the love of the Holy Spirit dwelling within us.

Christian Prayer is trinitarian

The Christocentric nature of Christian prayer is trinitarian. The Catechism sums it up as follows: 'The mystery of the Most Holy Trinity is the central mystery of Christian faith and life. It is the mystery of God in himself. It is therefore the source of all the other mysteries of the faith, the light that enlightens them. It is the most fundamental and essential teaching in the hierarchy of the truths of the faith. The whole history of salvation is identical with the history of the way and the means by which the one true God, Father, Son and Holy Spirit, reveals himself to men and reconciles and unites with himself those who turn away from sin' (234). The only difference between the enjoyment of the mystery of the Trinity here on earth and in heaven is that here and now we live and enjoy this mystery in faith and in the next life in vision. Elizabeth of the Trinity puts it very simply when she says: 'If you really want to go to heaven you must learn to love Heaven in the centre of your soul'.

Christian prayer is also ecclesial and Marian

Just as Christian prayer is our praying in Jesus and with him and through him to the Father in the Holy Spirit, so is it praying in his Body the Church. We never pray alone but always with the support of a whole host of witnesses and especially together with Mary. The archangel Gabriel asked Mary to call her Son Jesus and one of her maternal roles is to teach us to pray in the name of Jesus: to do whatever he tells us. While the Catechism does not actually quote St Louis Marie de Montfort I think his teaching permeates the Catechism teaching on the Marian dimension of Christian prayer.

Let me just quote two short paragraphs out of nine from this section of the Catechism entitled 'In Communion with the holy Mother of God': 'In prayer the Holy Spirit unites us to the person of the Only Son, in his glorified humanity, through which and in which our filial prayer unites us in the Church with the Mother of Jesus' (2673). and 'Mary is the perfect Orans (pray-er), a figure of the Church. When we pray to her, we are adhering with her to the plan of the Father, who sends his Son to save all. Like the beloved disciple we welcome Jesus' mother into our homes, for she has become the mother of all the living. We can pray with and to her. The prayer of the Church is sustained by the prayer of Mary and united with it in hope' (2679).

The missionary character of Christian prayer

The clearest indication in the New Testament of how Jesus experienced and expressed his relationship with God is in the address 'Father'. Joseph Fitzmyer, the well-known biblical scholar, points out that the designation 'Father' occurs 170 times in the NT and Jesus addresses God as Father in prayer three times. 'Father' occurs four times in Mark, four in 'Q', four in 'L', three in 'M' and a hundred in John (Fitzmeyer, *According to Paul*, p.58). In John, Jesus sees his whole mission as revealing the name of the Father. He writes: 'Father.... I have finished the work you gave me to do... I have made your name known to those you took from the world to give me... Holy Father, keep those you have given me true to your name, so that they may be one like us, as you are in me and I am in you, so that the world may believe it was you who sent me' (Jn 17). Our relationship to the Father in Jesus through the gift of the Holy Spirit has the missionary purpose that the world may believe. 'If we pray the Our Father sincerely, we leave individualism behind, because the love we receive frees us from it. The 'our' at the beginning of the Lord's Prayer, like the 'us' of the last four petitions, excludes no one. If we are to say it truthfully, our divisions and oppositions have to be overcome' (2792). 'The baptised cannot pray to "our" Father without bringing before him all those for whom he gave his beloved Son. God's love has no bounds, neither should our prayer. Praying "our" Father opens to us the dimensions of his love revealed in Christ: praying with and for all who do not yet know him, so that Christ may "gather into one the children of God". God's care for all men and women and for the whole of creation has inspired all the great practitioners of prayer; it should extend our prayer to the full breadth of love whenever we dare to say "our" Father' (2793).

To assert the intrinsic missionary character of Christian prayer presupposes a particular understanding of mission. Following the teaching of *Ad gentes* of Vatican II and the Catechism in the section on the Catholicity of the Church, I would describe one understanding of mission as the actualisation of the eternal will and design of the Father for the whole of creation and the salvation of humankind in particular. Mission is seeking to do the will of the Father and implementing his plan of salvation. This is ultimately the meaning of the phrases of the Lord's Prayer: 'Hallowed be thy Name, thy Kingdom come, thy will be done on earth as it is in heaven'. 'Thy will be done' is not just the centre of the Lord's Prayer but the centre of his life as well: 'not my will but your will be done.' It is the core of Mary's spirituality too: 'be it done unto to me according to your Word'. It is at the heart of the prayer of the Church especially as she celebrates the Eucharist, the sacrament of the actual implementation of the Father's will for the salvation of the world. This missionary character must be at the core of all Christian prayer, personal or communal.

The Catechism expounds this theme so well in its commentary on the Our Father: 'We ask our Father to unite our will to his Son's, in order to fulfil his will, his plan of salvation for the life of the world. We are radically incapable of this, but united with Jesus and with the power of his Holy Spirit, we can surrender our will to him and decide to choose what his Son has always chosen: to do what is pleasing to the Father.... He commands each of the faithful who prays to do so universally, for the whole world. For he did not say "thy will be done in me or in us", but "on earth", the whole earth, so that error may be banished from it, truth take root in it, all vice be destroyed on it, virtue flourish on it, and earth no longer differ from heaven' (2825). If there is no desire to correspond to the salvific will of the Father, to have a missionary spirit, it is difficult to see how one can really make progress not only in praying the Our Father but in all other prayer too.

When I think about 'Christian Yoga', 'Christian Zen', Transcendental Meditation, Buddhist and Hindu forms of meditation, and so many other ways of prayer and meditation influenced by other religious traditions and various branches of psychology, I find the character of Christian prayer as described in the Catechism a great help in the process of discernment. I simply ask the question: is this prayer or meditation Christocentric and therefore trinitarian, is it ecclesial and Marian, is it seen as supernatural gift, is it experienced as covenant and communion, does it have a missionary character and stimulate one to pastoral and missionary outreach, does it strengthen our moral life in Christ, is it our highest priority? Is it, at least, really moving in this direction? It seems to me that we need to appreciate the distinctiveness of the good news of Christian prayer before we can appropriately engage in inter-religious meditation and prayer and the work of inculturation or inter-culturation at this level.

Prayer of intercession

The Catechism has a long article on the forms of prayer revealed in the apostolic and canonical Scriptures which remain normative for Christian prayer (2623-2649). I would like to conclude this chapter with a brief reflection on two of these which stand out with a striking uniqueness in the context of non-Christian forms of prayer and meditation. First, the prayer of intercession. Intercession is a prayer of petition which leads us to pray as Jesus did. He is the one intercessor with the Father on behalf of all, without any exception whatsoever, but especially for sinners. Jesus is 'able for all time to save those who draw near to God through him, since he always lives to make intercession for them' (Hb 7:25). Christ not only preached that we should love our enemies and pray for those who hate and persecute us – he practised it dramatically on the Cross. And, starting with Stephen in the Acts of the Apostles, the first Christian communities are described as living this form of prayer and fellowship intensely. It remains an essential characteristic of Christian prayer. Our intercessory prayer knows no boundaries, it is universal in its outreach, a form of prayer that expresses the deep solidarity of the Christian with all humankind in all its needs and aspirations. It is difficult to reconcile this kind of prayer with the prayer or meditation to be found in those religious traditions that are rooted in the Law of Karma as the great rule of the universe, a chain of necessary causality by which we receive the exact merit or demerit of all our individual actions. If we are saved we are saved through our own efforts alone. And so many of the forms of meditation that emerge from this vision of reality seem to be marked by a deep interior isolation from other people and their claims on us. It is a radical form of Pelagianism that has always been a part of human history, not least in our own generation, and even creeps stealthily into our Christian communities in various disguises.

Growth in charity should flourish in the soil of intercessory prayer. It expresses our solidarity with our non-Christian brothers and sisters and is a profound expression of an authentic missionary spirituality. It is one of the forms of prayer through which we become truly Catholic not only in name but in the most intimate depths of our lives. It is a big part of the good news of Christian prayer that non-Christians have a right to hear about. They do not object to our praying for them and they have a Christ-given place in our prayer.

Thanksgiving

One of the striking features of Our Lord's prayer is the habitual spirit of thanksgiving. How often he prays: 'I thank you Father, Lord of heaven and earth.' He thanks God before raising Lazarus from the dead, before feeding the multitudes, at the beginning of the Last Supper, for revealing himself to little ones and for always answering his prayers. Following Jesus and in union with him, thanksgiving characterises the prayer of the Church especially in the Eucharistic sacrifice and communion in which the Church becomes more fully her true self. The thanksgiving of the members of the Body participates in that of their Head (2637). St Paul lays great stress on the place of thanksgiving in Christian spirituality: 'Give thanks in all circumstances; for this is the will of God in Christ Jesus for you' (1 Tim 2:1). 'Continue steadfastly in prayer, being watchful in it with thanksgiving' (Col 4:2).

What is the content of this habitual spirit of thanksgiving? It is not only for the particular daily gifts that we are thankful but for the mighty deeds the Lord does for us. We thank him for the wonder of our being. We thank him for the gift of redemption and faith. We thank him for the gift of the sacraments. When we pray, we first thank the Lord for the gift of prayer. We thank God for his total providence for us and his never-failing presence. All that we are and everything that we possess we have received. There is nothing that we cannot be thankful for except our sin, and even then we are thankful that God can draw good even out of this worst of human evils. Thanksgiving saturates Christian prayer. I do not find this radical thanksgiving in the religious literature of any other religious tradition. Our faith reveals to us that we have more to be thankful for than others. It is this spirit of thanksgiving which provides us with one of the deepest motives for mission and the sharing of the Gospel, especially the gift of Christian prayer with the non-Christian, the lapsed Christian, with all those who struggle with faith. A spirit of thanksgiving nurtures a missionary spirituality and is pivotal if we are to be committed to the mammoth task of the new evangelisation. I conclude with the words of the psalm with which we begin the prayer of the Church every morning:

Come, ring out our joy to the Lord;
hail the God who saves us.
Let us come before Him giving thanks,
with songs let us hail the Lord (Ps 94).

THE CATECHISM IN THE IRISH CONTEXT

Bishop Donal Murray

Faith is counter-cultural
One of the obvious characteristics of traditional Irish spirituality was the ability to see God in everything. The context of Ireland today, like western culture in general, could hardly be a greater contrast. To recognise the presence of God, to hear his voice, to address him – or to put it in other words, to pray – demands an effort of resistance to values that are part of the air we breathe.

'For example', the Catechism says, 'some would have it that only that is true which can be verified by reason and science; yet prayer is a mystery that overflows both our conscious and unconscious lives. Others overly prize production and profit; thus prayer, being unproductive, is useless' (2727).

The pressure of modern life leaves little energy for prayer and contemplation. An effort of attention is required if one is to hear the voice of God. Elijah discovered that God was not in the great wind or the earthquake or the fire but in the 'still, small voice', or what the New RSV calls 'a sound of sheer silence' (I Kings 19:12). Prayer, according to the Catechism is 'both a gift of grace and a determined response on our part. It always presupposes effort' (2725). Prayer is a battle against ourselves and against the failure to listen for the voice of God. What seem like urgent priorities squeeze out what is really important:

> One of the major reasons why we are not more contemplative, why we do not pray more, and why we do not take time to smell the flowers, is that these activities do

not accomplish anything, produce anything, or practically add anything to life. We feel good about ourselves when we are doing useful things. Contemplative activity, by definition, is pragmatically useless.[1]

'Still others', the text points out, 'exalt sensuality and comfort as the criteria of the true, the good and the beautiful; whereas prayer, "the love of beauty" (*philokalia*), is caught up in the glory of the living and true God' (2727). Ronald Rolheiser says it more trenchantly when he talks about the influence on our culture of the 'yuppie' phenomenon:

> The unconscious, and in many cases the conscious, mythology that moves people today is that of success, of moving up the ladder, of being rich, of having a beautiful body, of being well-dressed, of having prestige, of luxuriating in material comfort, of achieving optimally, but in comfort, everything that is potentially obtainable within our limits.[2]

The effect of this on the ability to recognise and relate to God is simply stated: 'When we stand before reality, self-preoccupied we will see precious little of what is actually there to be seen. Moreover, even what we do see will be distorted and shaped by self-interest…. Our sense of reality shrinks accordingly….'[3]

'Finally, some see prayer as a flight from the world in reaction against activism; but in fact, Christian prayer is neither an escape from reality nor a divorce from life' (2727). There is an approach to prayer which is little more than an escape from reality. That is at least part of what was meant by describing somebody as a 'holy Joe'. In fact, the very opposite should be the truth. Prayer can lead us to face realistically the seamy aspects of reality. Prayer expands our recognition of God, challenging us to see God as the Creator and Father of people whose lives differ enormously from our own. That is one way of coming to see clearly the limitations and emptiness of some of our cultural assumptions:

> Perhaps the only way we have of not letting ourselves be

swallowed whole by our culture is to kiss the leper, to place
our lot with those who have no place within the culture,
namely the poor with their many faces: the aged, the sick,
the dying, the unborn, the handicapped, the unattractive,
the displaced, and those who are not valued by the culture.
To touch those who have no place within our culture is to
give ourselves a perspective beyond our culture.[4]

The summit and source of Christian life and Christian
prayer, the Eucharist, 'commits us to the poor. To receive in truth
the Body and Blood of Christ given up for us, we must recognise
Christ in the poorest... "... You dishonour this table when you
do not judge worthy of sharing your food someone judged
worthy to take part in this meal" (St John Chrysostom)' (1397).

These points are a kind of examination of conscience for a
culture which is marked, as Pope John Paul has expressed it, by
the silence of God. The Catechism is realistic and practical
enough to warn us that our approach to prayer can itself become
infected by pragmatism and the desire to see results: 'When we
praise God or give him thanks for his benefits in general, we are
not particularly concerned whether or not our prayer is
acceptable to him. On the other hand, we demand to see the
results of our petitions. What is the image of God that motivates
our prayer. An instrument to be used? Or the Father of our Lord
Jesus Christ?' (2735).

The challenge lies in finding the true source of self-worth,
which is more than merely pragmatic and productive, in finding
a motivating goal which is deeper than success and comfort, in
finding a way of relating to reality which is real and fully human,
which does not take refuge in illusions.

In touch with oneself

To put it another way, the reverse side of a culture where God
seems absent is that in a certain sense it tends to make us absent
from our own deeper selves. It is important for every person, the

Catechism says, to be present to him/herself: 'This requirement of interiority is all the more necessary as life often distracts us from any reflection, self-examination or introspection' (1779).

What I want to suggest here is that one of the most fundamental questions that the Catechism reflects on is a question which underlies much of the challenge and of the unease which characterise the Ireland of today – the question of identity. For perhaps the first time in history; certainly for the first time in recorded Irish history, we can see growing around us a culture in which it seems possible to speak about who we are while making no reference to our Creator or to our ultimate destiny, no reference to the origin and the purpose of human life.

I began with Part Four of the Catechism, but each of the four parts, in different ways, addresses the question of the meaning of our existence in a way that touches the challenge to faith in Ireland today.

In its treatment of the first article of the Creed, 'I believe in God, the Father Almighty, Creator of Heaven and Earth', the Catechism points out that catechesis on 'creation concerns the very foundations of human and Christian life'. It is about the response of Christian faith to the most basic human questions:

'Where do we come from?' 'Where are we going?' What is our origin?' 'What is our end?' 'Where does everything that exists come from and where is it going?' These two questions, the first about the origin and the second about the end, are inseparable. They are decisive for the meaning and orientation of our life and actions (282).

Within the last decade we have seen the collapse of the Soviet empire. All sorts of factors, no doubt, played a part in that. But one of the most fundamental certainly had to do with the question of human identity. It is not possible to understand human beings on the basis of economics or class membership alone. The human person can be understood only within the whole sphere of culture, language and history, and in the attitude that a person takes 'towards the fundamental events of life, such as birth, love, work and death'[5]:

> Different cultures are basically different ways of facing the question of the meaning of personal existence. When this question is eliminated, the culture and moral life of nations are corrupted... The true cause of these new developments [*the disintegration of the Soviet Bloc*] was the spiritual void brought about by atheism, which deprived the younger generations of a sense of direction and in many cases led them, in the irrepressible search for personal identity and for the meaning of life, to rediscover the religious roots of their national cultures, and to rediscover the person of Christ himself as the existentially adequate response to the desire in every human heart for goodness, truth and life.[6]

We would be foolish to believe that the spiritual void was confined to the countries of Eastern Europe. The west has its own void. In contemporary Ireland we may certainly detect that void; we may even detect the beginnings of a realisation that the quest for personal identity and meaning might find its goal in a rediscovery of the religious roots of our culture and of the person of Christ.

A communal vocation

This means, of course, that the answer to the question of identity is not found in some kind of isolation. Society is not an optional extra. Human persons are not isolated individuals, existing without reference to one another. Faith is a vocation to be lived in community and ultimately in the community of the whole human family. That cannot mean isolation from our culture; but neither can it mean conforming to every idea, every expectation, every current of opinion. Participating in a community does not mean becoming part of a monolith. Every member has something different to give and something new to receive. So too has every community and culture.

Only through exchange, dialogue, service, mission, through relationships, can human talents develop and a person respond to the destiny to which we are called (1879, cf. GS 2). Indeed, it is only in these ways that one can achieve the inculturation by which the Gospel takes root in new places and new times:

> Through inculturation the Church makes the Gospel incarnate in different cultures, and at the same time introduces peoples, together with their cultures into her own community. Through inculturation the Church for her part, becomes a more intelligible sign of what she is, and a more effective instrument of mission.[7]

A society is a group in which individuals look beyond themselves in two ways. In the first place, it is bound together by some principle that goes beyond the mere self-interest of individual members. Secondly, any society or grouping has to be understood in a way that looks beyond the present moment: 'it gathers up the past and prepares for the future' (1880).

Each member is, in a sense an 'heir', whose identity is enriched by belonging to the group and by all that has gone into making a particular society what it is. Each member has a certain responsibility of loyalty which requires him or her to appreciate and develop that inheritance and to contribute to advancing the goals of the society. This is of particular importance at a time when the world is changing so rapidly. There is a temptation to think of this generation as having little in common with, and little to learn from, those which have gone before us. A society must of course move on, but it must move on from where it is. We must move on, recognising the journey we have already travelled and the experience and wisdom we have inherited. Failure to see this leads to a misunderstanding of freedom and creativity. T. S. Eliot remarked that this misunderstanding is seen in 'our tendency to insist, when we praise a poet, upon those aspects of his work in which he least resembles anyone else. In these aspects or parts of his work we pretend to find what is individual, what is the peculiar essence of the man…. Whereas if we approach a poet without this prejudice we shall often find that not only the best, but the most individual parts of his work may be those in which the dead poets, his ancestors, assert their immortality most vigorously.'[8]

Intermediate groupings

Culture is an organic growth which stretches across time. It also involves a complex network in the present, which needs to be recognised in its full richness. Certain groupings such as the family and the state arise more or less necessarily from the kind of beings we are. But these are not enough. It is also vital that there should be what the Catechism calls 'voluntary associations and institutions'. A healthy society needs a rich social fabric of overlapping groups between the individual in his or her family on the one hand and the state on the other. This process of socialisation develops personal qualities, 'especially the sense of initiative and responsibility'; it can also act as a guarantee for personal rights (1882).

Pope John Paul sums up the importance of these intermediate groupings:

> These develop as real communities of persons and strengthen the social fabric, preventing society from becoming an anonymous and impersonal mass, as unfortunately often happens today. It is in interrelationships on many levels that a person lives and that society becomes more 'personalised'.[9]

Without a rich variety of smaller groupings, the family and the individual will be seen, and will see themselves, as isolated and powerless. They will find themselves trying to deal alone with the bureaucracy, the organs, the laws and the machinery of the state. Political bodies, whether national or local, will see themselves as the primary providers of health care, education, housing, the primary formulators of moral values for society and so on.

Intermediate groupings are the setting in which people develop and share their convictions, relate in a fully personal way, and together exercise their responsibilities on a human scale. Without that rich social fabric all social life is impoverished.

Ireland is, it often seems, in search of an identity. The temptation is to think that, if the identity is to be broadly-based and inclusive, it must be built on the basis of a lowest common denominator which excludes every belief and conviction on which people differ. The flaw in this is that it fails to recognise that the convictions, the ideals, the drive, the motivation that enable people to play their part in fostering the well-being of society are the fruit of a variety of family and religious backgrounds. The state cannot create those dynamisms, nor could they conceivably arise out of an attitude which fears beliefs and convictions or passes over them in silence. We cannot build a society on the shallowest parts of ourselves and then expect that society to have deep and solid foundations. That is why any perception of the state as the whole of social living is ultimately self-defeating. 'Excessive intervention by the state can threaten personal freedom and initiative' (1883).

God respects freedom; God empowers the beings he creates. Each one is entrusted with the functions it is capable of performing. This model should inspire the wisdom of those who govern human communities (1884). The principle of subsidiarity recognises that the life of smaller communities should not be interfered with nor their functions taken over, rather they should be encouraged and, where necessary, supported and co-ordinated by the larger community (1883).

Conversion

A time of flux, like the present, can sometimes see an astonishing overturning of expectations. Ideas which grow in families, churches and neighbourhoods have made what would, even a few years ago, have seemed a miraculous breakthrough into the tough world of political and violent conflict. Who would have thought it possible that loyalist paramilitaries who had engaged in horrific violence would issue a cease-fire statement expressing their 'abject and true remorse?'[10] Words like 'forgiveness', 'reconciliation' and 'hope' have become, however tentatively, part of the vocabulary of hard-headed politicians and those who had been engaged in violence in Ireland, in the Middle East and elsewhere.

The Catechism points to one 'religious' word or concept that is fundamental to our communal vocation – the word 'conversion' or 'repentance'. Alienation in society, the loss of a living sense of who we are and of what our relationships with one another can and should be, is the fruit of an inversion of ends and means; ultimate ends are made of little account or are entirely suppressed (1887).

We have organised our societies to an increasing extent as if the deep religious and moral questions could be ignored as purely private matters of no concern except to individuals.[11] This has happened because we have not sufficiently recognised that even to function well in its own terms, the state needs to acknowledge the importance of the kind of values which are expressed and which develop in intermediate groupings where people come to terms with who they are and with the values they intend to pursue.

This inversion of ends and means leads to unjust structures which can make it more difficult for individuals to live as they should; it also makes for an unhealthy society. The human person finds him or herself in self-giving to other people and to God. 'A society is alienated if its forms of social organisation, production and consumption make it more difficult to offer this gift of self and to establish this solidarity between people'.[12]

The sins of individuals give rise to social situations and institutions which are contrary to God's goodness. 'Structures of sin' are the expression and effect of personal sins. They lead their victims to do evil in their turn. In an analogous sense, they constitute a 'social sin' (1869).

The most basic response to sinful structures is to recognise the need for inner conversion of the individual. This is not an excuse for failing to face up to the need to change institutions and structures in society. On the contrary, real personal conversion 'imposes the obligation of bringing the appropriate remedies to institutions and living conditions when they are an inducement to sin, so that they conform to the norms of justice and advance the good rather than hinder it' (1888).

Of course, conversion is not simply for others. For each person the primary challenge of conversion is a challenge to him or herself. It is a challenge also to the Church: 'On her pilgrimage, the Church has also experienced the "discrepancy between the message she proclaims and the human weakness of those to whom the Gospel has been entrusted". Only by taking the "the way of penance and renewal", the "narrow way of the cross" can the People of God extend Christ's reign' (853).

A generation of decision

As we approach the millennium, that call to conversion so that we can extend Christ's reign is particularly apt in Ireland. Huge cultural changes are occurring, all of which raise the question of identity in new ways. These include increasing urbanisation, technological advances, difficulties for family life, a decline in religious practice, the loosening of community bonds and loyalties, confusion about moral values.

In facing these changes, a great deal depends on how convinced we are of our role in making our faith a living thing in our lives and in our society. Pope John Paul said clearly during his Irish visit that this is a time of decision. The truth of his statement is more pressing now than it was seventeen years ago:

> The task of this generation of Irish men and women is to transform the more complex world of modern industrial and urban life by the... Gospel spirit. Today you must keep the city and the factory for God, as you have always kept the farm and the village community for him in the past.[13]

The message of the Gospel is for every time and place. The truth of Christ can renew every age, even ours! It is just as capable of transforming the world of today as it was of transforming first-century Palestine or inspiring the Ireland of Saints and Scholars. If we are not deeply convinced of that – if we see Christianity as fighting a losing battle – then we do not fully understand the power of Christ's Good News.

The source of our obligation to witness to the Good News is quite simply the love of God which is offered to all people of every time and place (851). One of the most important aspects of that witness for us is to decide what kind of country we wish to work for. Will it be a country whose success or failure is measured by whether we find oil, by economic statistics, by how well we adapt ourselves to the western consensus on social issues? Or will we try to build a country which takes seriously its obligation to foster the dignity of every person, where no person or group is marginalised, where peace is not about getting one's own way but about ensuring that everyone belongs, where people are more important than things, where moral values are more important that economic indicators?

Who decides such things? The answer is that we do. And more often than not we decide them by omission. We decide them by doing nothing, by assuming that there is nothing we can do.

The most powerful force in society may not, in the end, be finance, nor the media, nor ideologies. It may in the end be people, in families, in groups and associations, people who are committed to beliefs and values that give them a faith that can move mountains and a hope that inspires and enthuses them.

A catechesis of the Beatitudes

The moral teaching of Jesus in the Sermon on the Mount is extraordinarily demanding. We are told to love our enemies, to give our clothing to a thief, to judge nobody, to enter by the narrow gate. But that teaching is introduced by the Beatitudes, which 'are above all promises'[14] – promises of comfort and mercy and sharing in God's Kingdom, promises that provide the foundation for unconquerable hope.

The Beatitudes are at the heart of Jesus' preaching. They take up and fulfil the promises made to Abraham 'by ordering them no longer merely to the possession of a territory, but to the Kingdom of heaven...' (1716). The promise of endless joy precedes the demands. The Beatitudes reveal 'the goal of human existence, the ultimate end of human acts: God calls us to his own beatitude' (1719). They reveal a possibility which is opened up 'exclusively by grace, by the gift of God, by his love'.[15] They reveal who we are and who we are called to be.

The promises are the fulfilment of Old Testament hope. They are also the fulfilment of an even deeper and more universal hope – the desire for happiness which is in every human heart and which God alone can satisfy (1718). Jesus Christ, 'the first and last reference point' of all moral catechesis, is the Truth who answers all the longings, hopes and aspirations of the human heart.[16]

The moral confusion and crisis[17] which marks modern life has many aspects. One of the most profound sources of the problem is a crisis of hope. There is among many people in Ireland, and elsewhere, a temptation to wonder whether anything is worth the effort of self-sacrifice, integrity and often costly commitment demanded by the highest moral standards.

People live at a frantic pace and on a superficial level. Questions about what lies beyond death are suppressed. Authentic life cannot be built on ignoring the most inescapable truth about every human being – the inevitability of death. A life which does not face the question of mortality is a life without meaning; it has avoided the question of who we are and of what life means. As a result, a sense of meaninglessness is not hard to detect in contemporary culture.

In that context, moral values and rules are no longer seen as mapping out the road to the goal for which we long in the deepest core of our being. They are seen as pointless restrictions. Immorality becomes synonymous with freedom; it is seen as a casting off of shackles. That is a frame of mind that we can recognise around us, and perhaps, if we are honest, within us.

The truth, in contrast, is that morality is founded on the desire for happiness which has been placed by God in the human heart (1718). God calls us to his own beatitude (1719). Morality is not a gloomy and restrictive imposition; it is an acceptance of the fullness of joy which is the gift of Jesus and of the peace which passes understanding. In the moral sphere it is all too easy to recognise what Pope Paul VI regarded as a serious obstacle to the communication of the Gospel – the lack of fervour: 'It is manifested in fatigue, disenchantment, compromise, lack of interest and *above all lack of joy and hope.*'[18]

Christian faith addresses the questions of meaning by proclaiming the truth that Jesus Christ has passed through death to new life. He lives now beyond the reach of death and is drawing us to himself. The Beatitudes express 'the vocation of the faithful associated with the glory of his Passion and Resurrection' (1717). The truth of Christ is so great and so awesome that, without serious reflection on the fundamental human questions of life and death, good and evil, that truth is extremely difficult to grasp or even to glimpse.

Without such a vision of the truth it is not possible to understand the real seriousness of our moral decisions. Our choices have eternal significance for ourselves and for others. Our choices accept or refuse the gift for which we were created, the endless life which the Son of God lives and offers to us. We live at every moment in the presence of God who says to us: 'Today... I am offering you life or death, blessing or curse. Choose life, then, so that you and your descendants may live, in the love of Yahweh your God, obeying his voice, holding fast to him; for in this your life consists' (Dt. 30:19,20).

The destiny which God promises us 'confronts us with

decisive moral choices' (1723). It does so by putting things in perspective. It shows us a goal so all-embracing, so capable of fulfiling the human heart, that any other benefit or ambition is of value only if it leads to the happiness which God offers us:

> It teaches us that true happiness is not found in riches or well-being, in human fame or power, or in any human achievement – however beneficial it may be – such as science, technology and art, or indeed in any creature, but in God alone, the source of every good and of all love... (1723, cf. 2548).

This is the core of who we are. This is the fundamental answer to the questions of origin and destiny.

The promise of a destiny beyond anything which we could create or imagine gives a particular tone to the Christian moral vision. A morality inspired by the Beatitudes is not a harsh external imposition but a free response to God whose paradoxical promises, 'proclaim the blessings and rewards already secured, however dimly, for Christ's disciples' (1717). That is the moral call – to accept the promise and live from it in faith (1719).

Freedom and joy

Part Three of the Catechism, which opened with St Leo the Great's reminder of the dignity of the Christian, closes with St Augustine speaking of the happiness that awaits us in the vision of God:

> God himself will be virtue's reward; he gives virtue and has promised to give himself as the best and greatest reward that could exist.... God himself will be the goal of our desires; we shall contemplate him without end, love him without surfeit, praise him without weariness (2550).

Moral living is a response to and an acceptance of God's gift of himself. Faced with such a gift, a half-hearted response, not to speak of a rejection, is utter foolishness. We are offered a gift which is everything we could ever desire; our reception of that gift is limited only by our own selfishness and pride and dishonesty. Faced with such a gift it makes no sense to approach life in a frame of mind which asks, 'What is the least I can do without committing sin?' The only appropriate question is the one asked by the rich young man: 'What else do I need to do?" (Mt 19:20).

The 'freedom' to reject that gift is an absurd and contradictory freedom because it enslaves the person who uses it. Freedom is capable of doing violence to itself and of imprisoning itself (cf. 1740):

> The more one does what is good, the freer one becomes. There is no true freedom except in the service of what is good and just. The choice to disobey and do evil is an abuse of freedom and leads to 'the slavery of sin' (1733).

There is no contradiction or tension between obeying the Commandments of God and living in freedom; the Commandments were given, after all, in the context of God freeing his people from slavery. 'Human freedom and God's law are not in opposition; on the contrary, they appeal to one another'.[19] It is God's promise and God's gift which make it worthwhile to choose and to be committed. The question of the rich young man, 'What must I do?' is a question about what gives meaning to our choices and commitments. It reflects 'the aspiration at the heart of every human decision and action.... This question is ultimately an appeal to the absolute Good which attracts and beckons us; it is the echo of a call from God who is the origin and goal of human life'.[20] The liturgy prays for those who have just been confirmed: 'Help them to fulfil your law by living in freedom as your children':[21]

> You were called to be free; do not use your freedom as an opening for self-indulgence, but be servants to one another in love, since the whole of the Law is summarised in the one commandment: *You must love your neighbour as yourself* (Ga 5:13,14).

Sacramental signs

Part Two of the Catechism, which deals with liturgy and sacraments also has something to say to the question of identity.

The meaning of sacramental signs 'is rooted in the work of creation and in human culture, specified by the events of the Old Covenant and revealed in the person and work of Christ' (1145). God speaks to us in the visible creation: 'Light and darkness, wind and fire, water and earth, the tree and its fruit speak of God and symbolise both his greatness and his nearness' (1147).

This is true not just of things like water and fire; it is true of signs and symbols taken from social living: washing and anointing, breaking the bread and sharing the cup' (1148) can be expressions of God's sanctifying presence and of our gratitude towards the Creator.

From one point of view, liturgy might be seen as the activity of the Church which is least intelligible to those who do not share the Christian faith. Indeed, even many of those who began life as Christians or who hang on to religious belief and practice by the skin of their teeth, will say that they see little point or meaning in church ceremonies. From another point of view, however, liturgy should have a certain intelligibility for everybody because it is made up from the raw material of basic human signs and symbols.

That is a challenge for us both in relation to how the liturgy is celebrated and in relation to how it is understood. Too often, it seems, the human reality which is taken up and celebrated in the liturgy has become virtually invisible. Sometimes, at a funeral or a wedding, the congregation resonates with a human experience which is at the centre of their celebration. Then one has a liturgy which is vibrant, which genuinely unites the congregation in worship – in hope, in petition, in sorrow, in thanksgiving. It is too much to expect that most liturgies would be like that, but it is none the less a pointer to what is often missing. The underlying human reality is unrecognised or weak.

Even the signs of bread, of anointing, of washing or immersion or whatever, are sometimes not easily recognisable or their human significance is not understood.

The liturgy is, among other things, a celebration of our identity and of our solidarity in that identity. But it is not just a shallow, instant identity. It celebrates who we are as heirs to the tradition, members of a community which extends through time and space. The signs are also, as the Catechism puts it, 'specified by the events of the Old Covenant'. They are 'no longer solely celebrations of cosmic cycles and social gesture, but signs of the covenant, symbols of God's mighty deeds for his people' (1150). The sacramental signs and symbols are not, therefore, entirely self-explanatory to every observer of good will.

The sacraments do not simply address the deepest meaning of our present experience; they also link us into the historical experience of God's people of both the Old and New Covenants. God's approach to us is in continuity with his revelation of himself in creation; it is also in continuity with his revelation of himself to his people down the ages. Something of the richness of that encounter is missed if we do not understand how that relationship and dialogue has been carried on through the centuries.

For a person without any appreciation of the meaning of covenant and Passover, without some understanding of the biblical resonance of bread and manna, of oil and of the laying on of hands, the sacramental signs would inevitably lack much of their meaning. More importantly, the liturgical gathering itself would lose something of its sense of continuity with the whole history of salvation. Similarly, for a person who had no appreciation of the journey which God's people has travelled down the centuries since the time of Christ, a lot of the meaning would be obscured. As one theologian expressed it: 'One would be guilty of a grave error about the very nature of the Church if one saw in the centuries of the Church's history only a deviation from the lost purity of her origins, a wearing away or a betrayal'.[22]

One hears, for instance, and can sometimes feel some sympathy with, complaints that the first reading from the Old Testament can leave a Sunday congregation cold. On the other hand, it is an expression of our deep roots in the long history of God's People. The liturgy is a reminder, more eloquent and important than we often appreciate, of 'God's mighty deeds for his people'.

The sacramental celebration is a dialogue. 'Admittedly', says the Catechism, 'the symbolic actions are already a language, but the Word of God and the response of faith have to accompany and give life to them so that the seed of the Kingdom can bear its fruit in good soil' (1153). This is not just a dialogue between this congregation and God. It is the dialogue of God with his whole people through the whole of time and space, a dialogue in which we join. It does take an effort of understanding and reflection to stretch our minds to recognise the dimensions of that dialogue, but it is an effort to know and to celebrate who we are and who we are called to be.

This is a useful corrective to an impoverished understanding of the phrase, 'We are the Church'. The 'we' who are partners in the liturgical dialogue with God are not simply the members of this congregation. We join with the Church united across thousands of miles and thousands of years. We pray together with the Pope, the bishops and all the clergy, with the whole people Christ has gathered, with the apostles, the martyrs and all the saints who have done God's will throughout the ages and with all the choirs of angels.

These signs have also acquired layers of meaning throughout Christian history. In the first instance, they have been given a new significance by Jesus himself. This is true above all of the way in which he gave new meaning to the Passover by becoming himself the Passover Lamb and by giving his own Body and Blood as the paschal meal of the New Covenant. They have acquired deeper meanings from the music and the rituals developed down the centuries. These signs have, in other words, acquired the richness that comes from having been the expression and the source of the faith and Christian life of millions of the followers of Christ in a great variety of cultural, social and personal situations for two thousand years:

> On the one hand the Gospel message cannot be purely and simply isolated from the culture in which it was first inserted [the biblical world or, more concretely, the cultural milieu in which Jesus of Nazareth lived], nor, without serious loss, from the cultures in which it has already been expressed down the centuries; it does not spring spontaneously from any cultural soil; it has always been transmitted by means of an apostolic dialogue which inevitably becomes part of a certain dialogue of cultures.[23]

The Gospel of life

At All Hallows College a few years ago, Bishop Patrick Kelly of Salford asked what it was that made the Irish such successful missionaries. Having had some experience of the fact that, in Ireland, the day might still be only getting into its stride at midnight, he concluded that it had something to do with the ability to live life to the full.

The Good News is, I have no doubt, a source of that ability to celebrate our life and who we are. The Irish context today is one of choice. We must decide what values and beliefs we wish to live by; we must choose what kind of society we wish to be. Will it be a society that is fully alive because it has deep roots, or will it be shallow and empty?

Full human life is, as St Irenaeus says, the vision of God (cf. 294). If we wish to retain that sense of life worth living to the full we need to foster the contemplative, reflective outlook which enables us genuinely to celebrate the Gospel of life.

... the outlook of those who see life in its deeper meaning, who grasp its utter gratuitousness, its beauty, its invitation to freedom and responsibility. It is the outlook of those who do not presume to take possession of reality but accept it as a gift, discovering in all things the reflection of the Creator and seeing in every person his living image.[24]

This was what Pope John Paul stressed in an address given shortly after the publication of the Catechism: 'Christianity contains the source and the 'secret' of [the] realities which constitute the perennial longing of the human heart.... The new Catechism... placed at the service of the Word of God, is meant to contribute to the joyous, ardent proclamation of that exhilarating 'secret'.[25]

It is an outlook that we in Ireland badly need to nourish and restore. We need to be people who absorb the good news which the Catechism proclaims, people who proclaim the good news joyously and ardently, people who, through absorbing and proclaiming the good news, come to a deeper understanding of our own identity.

11

THE LOCAL BISHOP AND THE CATECHISM

Archbishop Michael Neary

In the New Testament the word from which Catechism is derived, the Greek word *kateckió*, is used specifically of religious instruction on the basis of the Gospel.

Avery Dulles recognises the Catechism of the Catholic Church as the boldest challenge yet offered to the cultural relativism which currently threatens to erode the contents of Catholic faith. The Catechism responds to a deep hunger in the people of God for the bread of solid doctrine. It sets forth the whole body of Catholic teaching in an organic manner. It is a serene, comprehensive presentation of the authoritative teaching of Scripture and Catholic tradition, systematically distributed in four parts dealing respectively with the Creed, the sacraments, Christian conduct, and prayer. The Catechism is a magnificent panorama, breathtaking in its scope. Closely packed with information, it is unencumbered by professional jargon and therefore accessible to a wide public, speaking both to the head and to the heart.

The treatment of the Church, the sacraments, morality and prayer are permeated by references to Christ and the Holy Spirit. The entire Christian life is presented as a response to the gift and call of God – a response made possible by faith and the sacraments. The commandments do not appear as external impositions but as consequences which flow from membership of the people of the New Covenant (2062). The authors have faithfully carried out their mandate to produce a work that would be biblical and liturgical in tone rather than legalistic or scholastic. As Cardinal Ratzinger rightly claims, the Catechism is not ecclesiocentric; it is centred on God, who freely and lovingly turns to us by sending us his Son to be our brother and his Holy Spirit to dwell in our hearts.

The Catechism of the Catholic Church is a wonderful example of collegiality at work. It was sponsored by all the bishops with and under the Pope and endorsed in 1990. It is addressed to bishops and will be a challenge for the next millennium. Planning, I feel, should be long-term. Priests and seminarians should be encouraged to use the Catechism for a more doctrinal focus to their preaching. The Holy Father and Cardinal Ratzinger expressed the wish that the Catechism can and will serve as a 'sure point of reference'. This was both a fact and a function of the Roman Catechism in the years 1566-1966. For four hundred years the Roman Catechism played a continuing part in the renewal and reform of both catechetics and homiletics. Pope John XXIII was still recommending it in 1960. Cardinal Newman in his *Apologia* wrote 'I rarely preach a sermon but I go to this beautiful and complete catechism to get both my matter and my doctrine' (chapter 5).

One of the great tasks which lies before us with the Catechism is to persuade our people and all people of good will that here we have essential data which is necessary for the Church and will be useful for society if it is to remain civilised. On this last point it is an understatement to say that we face considerable challenges. However, we should not underestimate our strengths, and included among them must be the Catechism.

In an age which rightly prizes education, it is imperative that the education of Catholics in their faith keep pace with their secular education. An educated Christian needs a clear and coherent system of beliefs, capable of being articulated in keeping with his or her stage of personal development.

The level of theological debate in our society is not always as high as one might wish. Catholics who resort to the Creed as the background against which theological ideas ought to be evaluated are regularly dismissed as literalist and fundamentalist. The concept of a revealed religion is not very dominant today. This in its own way contributes to a cafeteria-type Catholicism where one embraces what is interesting and not very demanding but recoils from what is challenging and difficult. As a result the criteria for deciding between truth and falsehood recede and personal autonomy is substituted for moral teaching. There is a great temptation to adapt the dogma of faith to secular philosophy and language rather than see the teaching of the Church as the norm. In his Apostolic Constitution *Fidei depositum* Pope John Paul remarked: 'The catechism will contain the new and the old, because the faith is always the same yet the source of ever new light;... it should help illumine with the light of faith the new situations and problems which had not yet emerged in the past.' The Second Vatican Council had outlined a vision of the human person in the creative plan of God and addressed various aspects of that person's relationship to the modem world. Clearly all of this creates a need to review and integrate these new insights into the apostolic tradition of doctrine regarding faith and morals. This was the task for which the bishops, in union with the Holy Father, as pastors and teachers of the faith, must assume responsibility. The need for a comprehensive, integrated presentation of the faith which was faithful and systematic became ever more apparent.

The Catechism and contemporary culture

Our contemporary culture tends to be shaped by the philosophies of pragmatism, utilitarianism and social evolutionism. Pragmatism claims that the good is whatever works or is expedient. This is frequently substituted for the natural moral law and sets us on the road to moral relativism. Utilitarianism, on the other hand, is concerned with the idea of the 'greatest happiness of the greatest number'. It takes advantage of the political philosophy that the majority rules. One can see how attractive is the concept that majority rule could determine what is morally good for everyone. The result, however, would be the rejection of moral absolutes and teaching about intrinsic good and evil. Social evolutionism, on the other hand, has contributed to the resurgence of late nineteenth-century rugged individualism. The Catechism challenges these philosophies not in any contentious manner but rather in a calm and irenic way. It refrains from polemics, does nor refute or condemn adversaries, nor it is defensive in tone.

Indeed one of the central affirmations which the Catechism makes by the ordering of its material is that the faith is an integrated reality: faith, worship, morality and prayer are mutually and intimately connected. It is not possible to have a complete and wholesome Catholic life if one part is omitted or neglected. The faith is an organic whole which is professed, celebrated, lived and deepened. Thus the four pillars of the catechism – Creed, sacraments, morality and prayer, are bound together as expressions of one living faith. Cardinal Ratzinger has frequently pointed out that one of the important theological and catechetical messages of this structure is the priority of the divine initiative and the primacy of grace. This emphasis on divine revelation serves as a corrective to some widespread approaches in contemporary catechesis which endeavour to make human experience the starting-point for the catechetical process.

The challenge to intellectualism

Catechesis is an activity of the Christian community as such, people who, changed by the grace of a relationship with Christ want to live their lives as witnesses to Jesus Christ. The catechist's task therefore, is not an individual or isolated one, but one which has a very strong community dimension. Failure to recognise this results in catechesis being conceived as the communication of an abstract scientific body of knowledge for specialists rather than the verification by the people of God of the intelligence of the faith presented systematically. Just as the catechist should not be seen in isolation from the community so also the content of catechesis should not be taken abstractly.

Sometimes to attract and interest people, catechists draw themes from contemporary issues in a way that is divorced from the context and from the task of an organic education in the vision of the faith. I refer to a certain way of treating themes like ecology, peace, justice, non-violence, etc. These are valid and essential themes in themselves but must be seen as part of the whole catechetical canvas. It is necessary to recover a sense of the wholeness and interior logic of what Pope John Paul calls the 'symphony' of the faith. Nothing in the Catechism prevents the catechist from seeking points of insertion for Christian doctrine in the actual experience of men and women today. However, the catechism challenges any method that would reduce faith to personal experience. No analysis of contemporary experience can by itself disclose the contents of Christian faith such as the Trinity, the Incarnation and the Resurrection, which are known only from revelation. Present-day experience should not be allowed to block the dynamism of divine revelation.

The role of the bishop

The bishop is the sign and minister of unity both within the local church and of the local Church with the universal Church. The Roman Catholic ritual for the ordination of bishops names the bishop as steward of the mysteries of Christ, a father and brother to all in his care, guardian of the faith, builder of the Church and servant of the Gospel. The ministry of the bishop is a Trinitarian one: a personification of the Father in the Church; a fulfilment of Christ's role as teacher, priest and shepherd; an agent of the Spirit who gives life to the Church. Bishops serve the Church as a body, a college of bishops in which the apostolic college is continued. The Vatican II Decree on the Pastoral Office of the Bishop in the Church says 'Catechetical instruction is intended to make people's faith become living, conscious and active through the light of instruction' (n. 14).

According to the Vatican Council, diocesan bishops are the chief catechists of their dioceses. Their duties regarding catechetics are spelled out with remarkable clarity and brevity. There the bishop is told to see to it that children and adults in his diocese are instructed in the faith systematically and thoroughly, with appropriate pedagogical method and with no essential element of Catholic doctrine omitted. Pope John Paul II draws out the implications of this when writing in his post-synod Apostolic Exhortation on catechesis in our time (*Catechesi tradendae*). There he defines catechesis as 'an education of children, young people and adults in the faith which includes especially the teaching of Christian doctrine imparted, generally speaking, in an organic and systematic way, with a view to initiating the hearers into the fullness of Christian life' (CT 18). Pope John Paul sees the specific character of catechesis as having a twofold objective of maturing the initial faith and of educating the true disciple of Christ by means of a deeper and more systematic knowledge of the person and message of Jesus Christ (CT 19).

In the life of a bishop there are few undertakings more deserving of his time and energy than the religious formation of his people. A bishop needs to unite clergy and catechists into a team. A bishop should ignore the useless controversies and tiresome condemnations that continue to clutter catechetical discourse. A bishop has a responsibility to help God's people be prepared to make a defence to anyone who calls them to account for the hope that is in them (CT 23). The final command of Jesus in Matthew's Gospel is 'teaching them to observe all that I have commanded you' (CT 30). *Christus Dominus* of Vatican II spells out the teaching office of the bishop. 'The bishops should present the doctrine of Christ in a manner suited to the needs of the times, that is, so that it may be relevant to those difficulties and questions which are found to be especially worrying and intimidating. They should also safeguard this doctrine, teaching the faithful themselves to defend and propagate it. Bishops should also endeavour to use the various methods available nowadays for proclaiming Christian doctrine. These are first of all, preaching and catechetical instruction, which always hold pride of place (n. 13). Catechetical instruction should be very carefully imparted, not only to children and adolescents but also to young people and adults. In imparting the instruction the catechist must observe an order and method suited not only to the matter in hand but also to the character, the ability, the age and the life-style of their audience. The same Council document entrusts bishops with the responsibility of ensuring that catechists are adequately prepared for their task, that they are well-instructed in the doctrine of the Church and possess both a practical and theoretical knowledge of the laws of psychology and of educational method.

Conclusion

By rendering a clear concise proclamation of the authentic content of revelation which has come down to us from the Apostles we render a service to truth itself. In his Instruction on the Ecclesial Vocation of the Theologian Cardinal Ratzinger reminds us that the truth possesses in itself a unifying force. Jesus promised us that the truth has a liberating force, 'the truth will set you free' (Jn 8:32). It frees us from isolation, from false philosophies, and opens the way to God while uniting us to each other.

The Pope's call to integrity in catechetical content requires that we do what we can to ensure that disciples of Christ receive 'the word of faith not in mutilated, falsified or diminished form but whole and entire in all its rigour and vigour' (CT 30).

To achieve this laudable goal we must accept and implement the Catechism. This will include writing curricula for the various age groups. The Catechism itself is not catechesis but rather a means or an instrument of it. Paragraph 12 states that it 'is intended primarily for those responsible for catechesis: first of all the bishops, as teachers of the faith and pastors of the Church. It is offered to them as an instrument in fulfiling their responsibility of teaching the people of God. Through the bishops it is addressed to editors of catechisms, to priests and to catechists. It will also be useful reading for all other Christian faithful.' So it is not intended to be a substitute for the necessary development of catechisms adapted to the needs of particular groups, but a tool for communicating and learning the doctrine of the faith.

In the Apostolic Constitution, the Holy Father indicates a major and significant use of the Catechism: 'It is meant to encourage and assist in the writing of new local catechisms which take into account various situations and cultures, while carefully preserving the unity of faith and fidelity to Catholic doctrine (*Fidei depositum* 3). A major impact of the Catechism will be the effect it will have on subsequent Catholic publications. Adult education courses, based on the new text, will need to be developed especially for catechists. In the western world the Catechism comes at a providential moment. It will be a great asset in confronting the growing phenomenon of 'cultural Catholicism'. It is a clarion call to refocus clearly on the mystery of the faith in its doctrinal, moral and ascetical content as the most solid and fruitful foundation for building the faith community. The Catechism will help to provide sharper focus to our homilies particularly if it is linked to the Sunday Lectionary. To this end a guide should be prepared to help priests prepare homilies which reflect the Catechism's insights, systematically presented during the liturgical cycle (CT 48).

Serious effort must be made to catechise the faithful in the spiritual life with the aid of the section on prayer. The Catechism presents an 'organic synthesis of the essential and fundamental contents of Catholic doctrine as this pertains to faith and morals. The Prologue instructs us that catechesis has to do with making disciples, with initiating hearers into the fullness of Christian life, with the witness of an apostolic or missionary service, with the whole of the Church's life. We must seek to discover the truth, beauty and goodness of the doctrinal heritage that is ours as Catholics. We must be both informed about and formed by our knowledge of the unfathomable riches of salvation (*Fidei depositum* 3).

The essential and primordial object of catechesis is to lead people to investigate and delve deeply into the mystery of Jesus Christ in all its dimensions (Eph 3:9,18-19). In this sense the definitive goal of catechesis is to put someone not only in contact but in communion, in intimacy with Jesus Christ (John Paul II, *Catechesi tradendae* 5). As a Church, a community of believers, we need to state our fundamental beliefs as an expression of our identity. In this respect the Catechism, properly used, will contribute to a renewal of Catholic life at a challenging time in our culture when religious truth is frequently relativised into mere opinion. Authentic Catholic catechesis presupposes a sound understanding of the faith, for catechesis is the systematic presentation of the faith to the whole Christian community. The content of this catechesis must be the unchanging truths of the faith, as that faith comes to us from the Apostles. *Catechesi tradendae* (5-6) speaks of catechesis as a handing on in all its fullness what has been received, namely the mystery of Jesus Christ (1 Cor 11:23). Reading the Catechism should result in a response, 'This is our faith, this is the faith of the Church. We are proud to profess it in Christ Jesus Our Lord.'

12

HOMILY
Concluding Mass – Feast of the Ascension

Archbishop Desmond Connell

The old liturgy of Ascension Day had its own way of expressing the mystery we are celebrating. After the Gospel reading, the paschal candle, which had stood in the sanctuary since Easter eve, was extinguished to mark the end of the forty days. The smoke rising from the candle conveyed the loss of a luminous presence, the transition from a faith sustained by the visible to the purer faith of which St Peter speaks: 'Although you have not seen him, you love him; and even though you do not see him now, you believe in him and rejoice with an indescribable and glorious joy, for you are receiving the outcome of your faith, the salvation of your souls'(1 P 1:8-9).

St Leo the Great expounds the meaning of this decisive moment of salvation history in the text chosen for tomorrow's Office: 'This is the strength which is given to great minds, this is the light of truly faithful souls, that unhesitatingly they can believe what they cannot see with the eyes of the body, and direct their longings beyond the range of their sight.... The visible presence of our Redeemer passed over into sacraments; and so that faith might be more noble and firmer, sight gave way to doctrine, the authority of which was to be accepted by believing hearts enlightened with rays from above' (Sermon LXXIV, i-ii).

It is especially appropriate, therefore, that our Symposium on the Catechism of the Catholic Church should coincide with the celebration of Our Lord's Ascension.

On this day of the exaltation of the Lord we see our human

nature raised up and forever confirmed in the glory that belongs to God alone. This is the astounding fullness of the truth of the Incarnation – that the Word was made flesh, not just for the time during which he emptied himself of glory in order to accomplish our salvation, but in the definitive manner made manifest today in the mystery of his Ascension. Having come to the end of the time during which he had dwelt amongst us, he did not cast our created lowliness aside like something that had served its purpose, but assumed it fully into the glory of his Godhead so that he might be our sacrificial banquet on earth and the exemplar and cause of the everlasting fulfilment of our hope in heaven. All of creation must be astounded by this, that God should find no offence to his own inconceivable dignity in remaining forever a man marked with the signs of the death to which he submitted in mercy towards sinners. This is our joy today as we celebrate the Eucharist in commemoration of his Ascension.

'And remember, I am with you always, to the end of the age' (Mt 28:20). These paradoxical words of farewell – taking his leave yet remaining with us always – are fulfiled through the Pentecostal gift of the Holy Spirit. He who lives and reigns with the Father forever in the unity of the Holy Spirit is united to the Church as her Head. The heart of the Church, filled with the Spirit, vibrates with the living presence of Christ.

But how shall we describe this presence? It is a presence brought to focus and made tangible by memory, for the Church's memory is the gift of the indwelling Spirit. 'He will bring to your remembrance all that I have said to you'(Jn 14:26). It is not, however, a memory recalling a past that has gone, but one much more like that of which St Augustine speaks when he saw it as the active presence of transcendent reality in the depths of the soul. By this memory, sustained by the Spirit, the Church lives with Christ in a presence that is inseparable from all that he said and did, a presence that derives the uniqueness of its reality from the fact that all these things remain forever as epiphanies of his person, surpassing somehow the flux of time as the words and actions of a man who is God. No one has written more profoundly on this theme than the Venerable Columba Marmion. It is the guiding inspiration of the Second Vatican Council's vision of the liturgy.

And so the Church 'keeps all these things, pondering them in her heart'(Lk 2:19), led by the Spirit into ever-deeper familiarity with the wonderful works of God and, as St Paul says, learning 'to speak of these things in words not taught by human wisdom but taught by the Spirit, interpreting spiritual things to those who are spiritual'(1 Cor 2:14).

The Church remembers the day she spent with Christ in the persons of the two disciples who asked: 'Master, where do you live?'(Jn 1:38). She remembers Cana, Capernaum, the Mount of Beatitudes, Tabor, the lonely place where he broke the bread, the tempestuous sea. She was present in the upper room and listened to his prayer. With him she stood before Pilate, heard his sentence and followed him to the Cross. She stood in the empty tomb and learned to believe. He invited her to touch his hands and his feet, to feel the imprint of the nails, and to place her hand in his side. She stood on the Mount of the Ascension and received his blessing. She holds in her memory what he said and did, it has inspired her prayer, and she speaks of it through the ages, drawing from her treasure new things and old.

The Church's memory is the Church's faith: for all this is the Word that was made known to her, and the Christ preserved in her memory is not one merely remembered from the past, but one remembered in a presence that is touched by her faith. In the Church we abide in this memory of Christ and our faith makes contact with his presence.

By the gift of the Spirit this presence penetrates the actions of the Church, above all when, by the hands of her priests, she takes bread and wine and, remembering what he did at the Supper, obeys his command to 'do this in memory of me'(1 Cor 12:24).

Memory is the beginning of every action, of the life-giving actions accomplished not just in the presence of Christ but in a certain identity with him, or, as the Church herself expresses it, in the person of Christ. In the actions of the Church we are with Christ if our memory too is the work of that faith inspired and made active by the Spirit.

It is right, then, to give glory to God and to return him thanks for the Church's faith. It is a wondrous spectacle of surpassing beauty, purer than light, more active than life, a transforming gentleness that mirrors his strength and carries out what he sends it to do. Through that faith the world is shielded from the just anger of God. Because he loved the world and gave his Son to save it, the Church has faith by the gift of the Holy Spirit and divine retribution for sin is withheld. For that reason we pray: 'Look not on our sins, but on the faith of the Church and grant us the peace and unity of your Kingdom where you live forever and ever.' What then would become of the world if the Church could have ceased to believe?

The faith of the Church is like the fire that Christ came to cast on the earth, a purifying fire incandescent with the energy of love. It is like the sweet water of Ezekiel's vision flowing from the temple of the Body of Christ. It brings freshness and life and the fruits of the Spirit as it deepens and flows into our wasteland. It resembles the austerity of the desert and the forty-day fast in seeking the silence that allows God's voice to be heard. It rises high as the peaks – 'for the heights of the mountains are his' (Ps 94:4) – where care must be taken against headstrong attempts on the summit. 'For God resists the proud and gives his grace to the humble'(1 P 5:5).

Through the faith of the Church the Holy Spirit makes fertile the waters of baptism, the font which the Fathers have called the womb of the Church. As Mary conceived her Son in faith, not through the action of man but by the power of the Spirit, so the Church has the gift of fruitful virginity that makes her the mother of countless offspring. Unlike the people of the former covenant, they are not a race set apart from others through an inheritance confined to carnal descent: the new people receive their inheritance through faith and the Holy Spirit without restriction to nation or race. As the Jewish writer Franz Rosenzweig puts it:

'The Christian is originally, or at least by virtue of his birth, a pagan. The Jew, however, is only a Jew. Hence, the way of the Christian continually consists of freeing himself from his racial ties, whereas the life of the Jew leads him deeper and deeper into the line of his descent. Christianity is essentially a missionary activity and must spread in order to maintain its existence.'[1]

Yes, all Christians bear in their Christian origin the sign of fruitful virginity: they are born of the virgin Church who believes and is made fertile by the gift of the Spirit.

And so the faith of the Church is Catholic, making a unity of races and nations, because it is everywhere and at all times the same. As St Irenaeus says: 'The Church believes these truths, as if it had but one soul and one heart, it preaches them and hands them on as though it had but one mouth. For although there are many different languages in the world, even so the strength of tradition is one and the same. The Church founded in Germany believes exactly the same and hands on exactly the same as do the Spanish and Celtic Churches, and the ones in the East, those in Egypt and Libya and Jerusalem, the centre of the world'.[2]

The faith of the Church is apostolic. Once again in the words of St Ireneus: 'Although the Church is spread throughout the world to the ends of the earth, it receives from the apostles and their disciples the faith which it professes'.[3]

The faith of the Church has been proclaimed by the blood of the martyrs and by the lives of a multitude of saints – sometimes acknowledged by all, but more often known just to a few – bishops and priests, monks and virgins, husbands and wives, fathers and mothers, single men and women. Our own history of fidelity to the faith of the Church and of missionary evangelisation has borne its own witness in blood, in readiness for sacrifice at a time when apostasy was the price of worldly success, in a willingness to go into exile to bring others the faith. This century, made glorious in Ireland by missionary zeal, has borne witness in blood to the faith of the Church in lands oppressed by the hatred of God.

The faith of the Church inspired supreme achievements of civilisation in art, in literature, in philosophy and theology: it made ready the soil where the luxuriant growth of western science formed its roots. In reminding sovereigns – whether monarchs, dictators or democratic representatives – that they too are subject to judgment, it vindicates the cause of the poor and oppressed.

'But when the Son of Man comes, will he find any faith on earth?' (Lk 18:8). This question of Christ follows his parable of the widow who sought justice from the unjust judge. As the world grows weary of the faith of the Church there are manifest signs of a rising tide of injustice.

The faith of the Church is the indestructible support of the faith of her children. For each one of us faith is a personal response to the Word of God made with the help of his grace. We make this response in the fluctuation of our experience of life, which leads us at times through confusion and darkness as the world around us displays its indifference or challenges our security with contradictions and motives for doubt. It is important to remember that we are not on our own, that our faith is participation in the faith of the Church, that the faith of the Church is the house built on a rock to withstand the floods and the rain and the wind. It is no less important to pray often and humbly that God may sustain to the end the priceless gift he has made us.

This is not a time to lose heart. We must recover our

confidence in the faith of the Church, reminding ourselves of the marvel and beauty of what was given to us without claim or merit on our part. It is the right time to refresh ourselves once more by prayer and study in the faith of the Church. What we received was not given to us for ourselves alone; but only knowledge and love of the faith of the Church can move us to pass it on. The Catechism of the Catholic Church is the providential instrument of preparation for the opening of the new millennium.

On Ascension Day I am always reminded of St Stephen. On trial for his life, he saw the heavens opened and the Son of Man standing at the right hand of God (Acts 7:56). This seems strange. Do we not say that Jesus sits at the right hand of the Father? How then did Stephen see him standing? But Stephen was in trouble and that was no time for Jesus to be sitting down. Let us then repeat the prayer of the old liturgy. 'Christ, Son of God have mercy on us. You who sit at the right hand of the Father have mercy on us. Get up, Christ, and help us and free us for the sake of your name.'

NOTES

Introduction

1. Second Vatican Council, *Dogmatic Constitution on Divine Revelation*, 1.
2. Pope John Paul II, *Fidei depositum*, 3.
3. *Divine Revelation*, 9.
4. Pope John XXIII, Opening Speech of Second Vatican Council, as quoted in A. Flannery, ed., *Vatican Council II*, Vol.2, 434-5.
5. *Dogmatic Constitution on the Church*, 4.
6. Ibid., 9.
7. Henri de Lubac, *Catholicism: Christ and the Common Destiny of Man*, San Francisco 1988, 15.
8. *Catechism*, 23.
9. John Henry Newman, *Certain Difficulties felt by Anglicans in Catholic Teaching*, Vol II, London 1885, 248; quoted in the Catechism 1778.
10. Second Vatican Council, *Decree on the Pastoral Office of Bishops*, 14.
11. Ibid., 13.
12. Pope John Paul II, *Fidei depositum*, 2.
13. Quoting Pope St Leo the Great, Sermon LXXXIV, ii.

Chapter 2: Major Themes and Underlying Principles

1. In *Communio. International Catholic Review*, autumn 1993, p. 491.
2. Ibid., p. 491f.
3. Ibid., p. 492
4. *Discussions and Arguments*, 284.
5. *Essays Critical and Historical I*, 125-126.
6. *Lectures on the Present Position of Catholics in England*, 372-373.
7. E. d'Arcy, loc. cit., p. 497.
8. E. d'Arcy, loc. cit., p. 496.

Chapter 3: Salvation is of Christ the Lord! The Christ-centredness of the Catechism

1. 748, 426.
2. See 476.
3. See 1159f.
4. See 2129f.
5. See 2691.
6. Facing p.12.
7. 487.
8. See 'The glories of Mary for the sake of her Son', *Discourses to Mixed Congregations*, new edition (London & New York, 1892), 342f.
9. 495.
10. See 496.
11. See 499.
12. 506.
13. 502.
14. 504.
15. 505.
16. See the *Tomus Leonis* (DS 294).
17. 507.
18. Text facing p.12.
19. 773.
20. 468.
21. 475.
22. See 2600 and *passim*.
23. See 238f.
24. Hans Urs von Balthasar, *Our task: A report and a plan*, English translation by John Saward (San Francisco, 1994), p.122.
25. The incarnation of the Son of God brings a newness to human nature, not in essential principle (the *logos physeos*), but in mode of consience (*tropos hyparxeos*) (see St Maximus, *Ambigua* 42; PG 91.1341D).

26. 470.
27. *Expositio Orationis Domenicae*, PG 90.876C.
28. See 438.
29. 485.
30. 683.
31. 687.
32. 260.
33. 458-460.
34. 'For this is the way the Word became man, and the Son of God became son of man: so that man, by entering into communion with the Word and thus receiving divine sonship, might become a Son of God.' 'For the Son of God became man so that might become God' (St Athanasius). 'The only-begotten Son of God, wanting to make us sharers in his divinity, assumed our nature, so that he, made man, might make men gods' (St Thomas Aquinas 460).
35. See 1999.
36. 1997.
37. *Sacrosanctum Concilium*, n.102.
38. 515.
39. As Scheeben says, 'the humanity of the God-Man operates on the basis of the fullness of the divinity residing in it, not merely on the basis of the participation in the divine nature. Therefore its activity, although finite in itself, is of infinite dignity and value, because it is backed up by the dignity of an infinite person' (*The Mysteries of Christianity*, English translation, St Louis and London, 1946, p.330).
40. Ibid.
41. 516.
42. 517.
43. Ibid.
44. CCC.
45. 519.
46. See *Summa Theologiae*, 3a, Q48,2, ad1.

47. 520.
48. 521.
49. See 476-477.
50. The Catechism quotes St John Damascene, 'By "the Father's right hand" we understand the glory and honour of divinity, where He who exists as Son of God before all ages, indeed as God, of one being with the Father, is seated bodily after He became incarnate and his flesh was glorified' (663).
51. See 1116.
52. Balthasar says, 'From Valentinus to Bultmann the flesh and blood has been spiritualised and demythologised', *The Glory of the Lord, A Theological Aesthetics*, I: 'Seeing the Farm', (Edinburgh, 1982, p.314).
53. 639.
54. 640.
55. 643.
56. 645.
57. 655.
58. 658. In concluding this section, we might fittingly recall the great Ascension Hymn: *culpat caro, purgat caro, regnat Deus Dei caro*, 'flesh hath purged what flesh has stained, and God, the flesh of God, hath reigned'.
59. 478.
60. DS, 3812.
61. Mentioned in a discussion on The Eternal Word Television Network,.
62. 609.
63. See 2599, 2611 and *passim*.
64. Facing p.276. Later the Catechism says, 'sacraments are powers that came forth from the body of Christ (see Luke 5:17; 6:19; 8:46), which is everything and life-giving' (1116).
65. 1115. When speaking of the Anointing of the Sick, the Catechism explains, by means of an example, how the

Sacraments are rooted in the mysteries of Jesus' life. 'He makes use of signs to heal: spittle and the laying on of hands, mud and washing. The sick try to touch him, "for power came forth from Him and healed them all". And so in the Sacraments Christ continues to "touch" us in order to heal us' (1504).

66. See *Summa Theologiae*, 3a, Q.8,2.
67. Idem, Q.62,5.
68. This thesis is argued at lenght by Cardinal Journet in *l'Eglise Du Verbe Incarné*, Vol 2 (Paris, 1962), pp.300-302; 625-630; 1110-1111.
69. See 1374.
70. In *Joannis Evangelium*, Lib.10 (15.1); PG 74.341 AB.
71. DS 1740.
72. 1364.
73. 1366, quotes Trent.
74. 1370.
75. 1085.
76. 1104.
77. 1105.
78. Facing p.364.
79. 1698.
80. 1692.
81. 2074.
82. 1697.
83. 2074.
84. 1966. See *Summa Theologiae*, I, II, Q.106,1.
85. See 1719.
86. 1949.
87. 1717.
88. 2565.
89. 2559.
90. See 27f.
91. See 2566.

92. 2598.
93. 2598.
94. See 2602.
95. 2599.
96. 2600.
97. 2712.
98. See 2825-2827.
99. See 240.
100. 2599.
101. 2798.
102. See 2655.
103. See *Mystici Corporis*, n.89.
104. 2616.
105. 2742.
106. See 2667-2669.
107. See 2715: see also *The Mysteries of Jesus*, 514f.
108. Ibid.
109. 2670.
110. In the *Fullness of Faith* (San Francisco, 1988), p116.
111. See 2683.
112. 2683.
113. 2674.
114. 2679.
115. 2725.
116. 409.
117. 2725.
118. 2567.
119. 2728.
120. 2731.
121. 2740.
122. 2500.
123. From the poem 'The Blessed Virgin Compared to the Air we Breathe', in *Gerard Manley Hopkins: Poems and Prose* (London, 1986).

Chapter 4: Revelation and Faith

1. Christoph Schönborn, 'Major themes and Underlying Principles of the Catechism of the Catholic Church', in Joseph Cardinal Ratzinger and Christoph Schönborn, *Introduction to the Catechism*, (San Francisco, 1994), pp. 37-58, espec. p. 47.

2. 'La Constitution 'Dei Verbum' et ses précedents conciliaires', *Nouvelle Revue Théologique* 110 (1988), 58-73.

3. See Breandán Leahy, 'The Profession of the Christian Faith: the Creeds', Patrick M. Devitt, (ed.), *A Companion to the Catechism: A Reader's Guide* (Dublin, 1995), pp. 39-47.

4. See Cardinal Joseph Ratzinger, 'Christian faith as 'the Way': An introduction to Veritatis Splendor', *Communio* 21 (1994), pp. 199-207.

5. See Alain Boudre (with preface by Vaclav Havel), *Miloslav Vlk: A Praga un lavavetri diventa arcivescovo* (Rome, 1996)

6. This section moves us into the Christological and Trinitarian material found in section two of Part One.

7. See also *Gaudium et spes*, 22 and 24.

8. See also John Paul II, Post-Synodal Apostolic Exhoration on the Consecrated life and its mission in the Church and in the World, *Vita consecrata* (25 March 1996), n. 5.

9. See G.M. Zanghí, 'Vangelo e cultura', *Nuova Umanità* 9 (1987), p.14.

10. See *Theologik II: Wahrheit Gottes* (Einsiedeln, 1985).

11. See Hans Urs von Balthasar, *Theodrama* Vol. 5: *L'Ultimo Atto*, (Milan, 1982), p. 339.

12. Maurus Green, *The Vanishing Root: Eddie McCaffrey's Story* (London, 1994), pp. 87-93.

13. See Enrique Cambóm, 'Nuovo catechismo: un punto di partenza' *Gen's* 1 (1993), pp. 2-6.

14. See Michael Paul Gallagher, 'The New Agenda of Unbelief and Faith', in Dermot Lane (ed.), *Religion and Culture in Dialogue: A Challenge for the Next Millennium* (Dublin,

1993) pp. 133-150.

15. J. Ratzinger, 'Kommentar zu GS 19-22', in *'LThK'*, *Vatican II*, Vol. III, pp. 338 and 343.

16. Address to the participants at the 5th symposium of the Council of European Episcopal Conferences (*L'Osservatore Romano* [Italian edition], 5 October 1982).

17. Homily given during a celebration of the word in honour of St John of the Cross at Segovia (*L'Osservatore Romano* [Italian edition], 4 November 1982).

18. See *Trinity as History: Saga of the Christian God* (New York, 1989), pp. 3-4.

19. Karl Rahner, *The Trinity* (London, 1970), espec. pp. 10-15. See John O'Donnell, 'Revelation and Trinity', in *The Mystery of the Triune God* (London, 1988), pp. 17-39.

20. See *Lumen gentium*, n.4.

21. See Chiara Lubich, *Servants of All*, (London, 1979), pp. 97-99.

22. Christoph Schönborn, op. cit., p. 62.

23. *Verbum Caro* (Einsiedeln, 1960), p. 220. See also Achille Romani, *L'Immagine della Chiesa 'Sposa del Verbo' nelle opere di Hans Urs von Balthasar* (Rome, 1975), pp. 17ff; Jutta Konda, *Das Verhältnis von Theologie und Heiligkeit im Werk Hans Urs von Balthasars* (Würzburg, 1991), pp. 139-145.

24. See *Ut Unum Sint* (25 May 1995).

25. See U. Betti, *La Rivelazione divina nella Chiesa* (Rome, 1970), p. 166.

26. See Antonio Sicari, in 'Theology and holiness', *Communio* 16 (1989), p. 356.

27. *Le Spiritualità nuove* (Rome, 1996).

28. *Glaubenswende: Eine Hoffnungsperspektive* (Herder, 1987), p. 115.

29. Ibid., p. 113.

30. Ibid., p.67.

31. Ibid., p.75.

32. Ibid., p.124.

33. Ibid., p. 136.
34. Ibid., 156.

Chapter 5: The sacramental life in the Catechism
1. *The World as Sacrament*, London, DLT 1966, 14

Chapter 6: The Moral Vision of the Catechism
1. Mary Ann Glendon, *Rights Talk: The Impoverishment of Political Discourse* (New York: The Free Press, 1991), p. 14.
2. *Catechism of the Catholic Church* (Dublin: Veritas, 1994).
3. For a fuller explanation of the compatibility of personalism and natural law see my 'Natural Law and personalism in *Veritatis splendor*', chapter 13 in *Veritatis Splendor: American Responses*, ed. by Michael E. Allsopp and John J. O'Keefe (Kansas City, MO: Sheed and Ward, 1995), pp. 194-207.
4. For a discussion of the emerging interest in autonomy in Church documents, see Walter Kasper, *Theology and Church* (New York: The Crossroad Publishing Company, 1992).
5. The Universal Catechism makes reference to an erroneous view of autonomy:
   (1792) Ignorance of Christ and his Gospel, bad example given by others, enslavement to one's passions, assertion of a mistaken notion of autonomy of conscience, rejection of the Church's authority and her teaching, lack of conversion and of charity: these can be at the source of errors of judgement in moral conduct.(1792)

Chapter 7: The Education of Conscience – a lifelong task
1. Paragraph numbers in parenthesis refer to the paragraphs of the *Catechism of the Catholic Church* (Dublin: Veritas 1994), unless the context indicates otherwise.
2. *Familaris consortio* (FC) (1981), 8.
3. See Vatican II, *Lumen gentium* (LG), 16.
4. FC 8.

5. Ep 4:4-6; see Catechism paragraphs 172-74.

6. These phrases are constantly used by John Paul II. He has chosen explicitly to make 'the good of the person' the central moral category, rather than the 'human goods' themselves, as other Christian authors have done. Thus *Veritatis splendor* (VS) states: '... an act is therefore good if its object is in conformity with the good of the person with respect for the goods morally relevant to him. Christian ethics... is directed to promoting the true good of the person; but it recognises that it is really pursued only when the essential elements of human nature are respected' (78). And, 'It is precisely these which are the contents of the natural law and hence that ordered complex of 'personal goods' which serve 'the good of the person': the good which is the person himself and his perfection' (79).

This is to recognise, and affirm, the human being as an intrinsic good, the primary good, so that all other 'human goods' are aspects of the good of the person. In Letter to Families (1994) 12, he says:

'The person is and must be nothing other than the end of every act. Only then does the action correspond to the true dignity of the person'.

7. This distinction is developed by Patrick K. Bastable in his contribution to the theological discussion of *The Letters of Saint Patrick*, (Maynooth: An Sagart, 1993); chapter three, 'Faith-life and Theology: Saint Patrick as a Pastoral Theologian of His Time', pp. 185-99.

8. By 3.1.1 I mean: Part Three, Chapter One, Article One.

9. For example, in the ethical writings of Aquinas, conscience is treated very summarily while the treatise on prudence is substantial. The role of virtue is more central to Aquinas' ethical theory, making the agent and his acts good. Conscience 'serves' prudence in the Thomistic framework.

10. See particularly section II: 'Conscience and Truth', nn. 54-70 and ff.

11. *Gaudium et spes*, chapter I, can be regarded as the charter on the dignity of the human person. Cf. e.g. 27 which is quoted in VS 80.

12. VS 50.

13. VS 7, and *Redemptor hominis* (1979) 13.

14. See GS 25 and VS 97.

15. See also GS 26.2.

16. See Catechism reference to *Solicitudo rei socialis* (1987) 47.

17. VS 31, my emphasis.

18. For the study of this theme see the excellent treatise on *Conscience in the New Testament* by C. A. Pierce (London: SCM Press, 1958).

19. See VS 54. The following important footnote is added to this paragraph:
    'The development of the Church's *moral doctrine* is similar to that of the doctrine of the faith. (Cf. First Vatican Ecumenical Council, Dogmatic Constitution on the Catholic Faith *Dei Filius*, chapter 4; DS 3020, and Canon 4: DS, 3024.) The words spoken by John XXIII at the opening of the Second Vatican Council can also be applied to moral doctrine: 'This certain and unchanging teaching (i.e. Christian doctrine in its completeness) to which the faithful owe obedience, needs to be more deeply understood and set forth in a way adapted to the needs of our time. Indeed, this deposit of faith, the truths contained in out time-honoured teaching, is one thing; the manner in which these truths are set forth (with their meaning preserved intact) is something else'. ASS 54 (1962), 791; Cf. *L'Osservatore Romano*, 12 October 1962, p. 2.

20. See what VS 53 says in this respect.

21. J. H. Newman, *Apologia pro Vita Sua*, (London: Longmans Green, 1888), p. 195.

22. This idea is developed in VS 39-40.

23. VS continues to affirm that 'the autonomy of reason

cannot mean that reason itself creates values and moral norms', in the sense that it would mean 'a denial of the participation of the practical reason in the wisdom of the divine Creator and Lawgiver' (40).

24. This idea of Newman's is one that pervades the Christian understanding of conscience beginning with Saint Paul. VS quotes Saint Bonaventure in this respect:
'conscience is like God's herald and messenger; it does not command things on its own authority, but commands them as coming from God's authority, like a herald when he proclaims the dictate of the King. This is why conscience has binding force' (58).

25. J. H. Newman, *Parochial and Plain Sermons* (PPS) (Westminster Christian Classics Inc., 1966), Vol I, p. 227.

26. See the work of C. A. Pierce referred to in note 18 above.

27. VS 58.

28. See reference in note 18 above.

29. Socrates speaks of his 'inner voice' that he has to obey, e.g. in the *Apologia*; Plato speaks of the 'divine element is us', e.g. in the *Republic*, 590d.

30. VS 89.

31. Aquinas refers to it as '... a Divine court such as is the court of conscience'; see *Summa Theologiae*, II-II, Q. 96, article 4.

32. An excellent treatment of remorse from a philosophical point of view can be found in Raimond Gaita's book *Good and Evil: An Absolute Conception* (London: Macmillan, 1991).

33. See VS 59.

34. Ibid. 64.

35. Ibd. 55.

36. See C. A. Pierce, op. cit., p. 123-4.

37. This is a thesis well developed in the later philosophy of L. Wittgenstein, in his *Philosophical Investigations* (1953).

38. See VS 32.

39. See GS 16.

40. For a development of this theme see Herbert McCabe, 'Aquinas on Good Sense', *New Blackfriars*, Vol 67, 1986, pp. 419-431.

41. Leon R. Kass, 'Practising Prudently' in *Towards a More Natural Science: Biology and Human Affairs* (New York, The Free Press, 1985), p. 206.

42. T. Gilby, commentary on *Summa Theologiae,* Vol 18, Qq. 47-56, Appendix 3, p. 180.

43. J. H. Newman *Selected Sermons,* Edited by Ian Ker (New York: Paulist Press, 1994), p. 9.

44. VS 64.

45. See 'The Indwelling Spirit' in J. H. Newman *Selected Sermons*, op. cit. p. 129.

46. The reality of 'soul-pain' as it appears in those close to death, and the need at that time to move to healing and inner unity responding to the soul's inner powers, is beautifully treated by Michael Kearney in his book *Mortally Wounded* (Dublin: Marino Books, 1996).

Appendix to Chapter 7

Guide to the Catechism's 'Treatise on Conscience' Part Three, Section One, Chapter One, Article 6, Paragraphs 1776-1802.

MORAL CONSCIENCE

1776 Conscience: most secret core and sanctuary. There... alone with God

i. The Judgement of Conscience

1777 [Conscience a moral sense]
  Commands to do good and avoid evil
  Judges particular choices, approving, denouncing
  Bears witness to the supreme Good
  Welcomes the commandments

1778 Conscience is a judgement of reason
By the judgement of his conscience the person perceives and recognises the prescriptions of the divine law. J. H. Newman on conscience

1779 Requirement of interiority to listen to conscience

1780 Requirements of Uprightness of Conscience
Perception of the principles (truths) of morality(synderesis: law of the mind)
Application of those principles in the concrete:
– practical discernment of reasons and goods
– judgement about the concrete act
– [guided by the virtue of prudence] [resulting in choice]

1781 Conscience and responsibility
Witness to the universal truth of the good and to the evil of a particular choice
[Urging: recognition of evil done, repentance, asking forgiveness, good to be practised, virtue cultivated, acceptance of mercy and grace].

1782 The person's right to act in conscience and freedom

ii. The Formation of Conscience

1783 Conscience must be informed. The well-formed conscience makes judgements according to reason and in conformity with the true good

1784 Education of conscience – a lifelong task

1785 Requirements in the formation of conscience:
The Word of God to be assimilated in faith, prayer and the practice of virtue
Examination of conscience
Assistance of the Holy Spirit
Witness [example] and advice of others
Guidance of Magisterium

iii. To Choose in Accord with Conscience
[Conscience and discernment for choice]
1786 Right and erroneous judgements of conscience
1787 Difficult decisions of conscience: [discernment/conflicts]
1788 Discernment: Interpreting the data of experience [facts]
  Interpreting the signs of the times [facts]
  With the virtue of prudence
  Advice of competent people
  Help of the Holy Spirit
1789 Three rules which apply in every case:
  −never do evil
  −golden rule of sense of self-worth and the worth of others
  −charity always: respecting one's neighbour and his conscience

iv. Erroneous judgement [of conscience]
1790 Obligation to obey the judgement of conscience if certain, even if erroneous
1791 Culpable ignorance in erroneous judgement
1792 Sources of erroneous conscience
  −ignorance of Christ and his Gospel
  −the bad example of others
  −enslavement of one's own passions
  −mistaken notion of autonomy of conscience
  −rejection of Church's authority and Magisterium
  −lack of conversion [no repentance]
  −lack of charity [virtue]
1793 Invincible ignorance in conscience
1794 Purity of Conscience and charity

MORAL CONSCIENCE: IN BRIEF
[1] 1795 Conscience person's most secret core and sanctuary
[2] 1796 Conscience is a judgement of reason
[3] 1797 The verdict of conscience

[4] 1798 [Education of conscience] Everyone must avail himself of the means to form his conscience

[5] 1799 [Possibility of] erroneous and right conscience in moral choice

[6] 1800 A human being must always obey the judgement of his conscience when certain

[7] 1801 Conscience can remain in ignorance or make erroneous judgements culpably or inculpably

[8] 1802 Moral conscience is formed by the Word of God: by assimilating it in faith, prayer and putting it into practice [virtue].

Other Paragraphs in the Catechism Related to Conscience:

33   the human person and the voice of conscience

912   Christian conscience

1014 death and conscience

1385 good conscience and receiving the Eucharist

1435 conversion and examination of conscience

1453 contrition and the stirring of conscience

1454 sacrament of penance and examination of conscience

1458 formation of conscience by confession of venial sins

1480 sacrament of penance and the word of God to illuminate conscience

1700 the dignity of the human person [see 27; 356]

1706 the call to do good: a law of conscience

1749 human person a moral being: freedom and judgements of conscience

1806 prudence guides the judgement of conscience

1848 Holy Spirit and the gift of the truth of conscience

1849 Sin: offence against reason, truth, right conscience; failure of love of God [self] and neighbour

1860 principles of the moral law written in conscience

1903 unjust laws not binding in conscience

1907 sound norm of conscience and common good

Chapter 8: The Decalogue in the Catechism

The *Catéchisme de l'Église Catholique* was the first version to be put into circulation (Paris: MAME/Plon, 1992), at the same time as the Latin text (Rome: Città del Vaticano, 1992). It is not surprising therefore that the earliest reactions to and commentaries on the new work appeared in the French language, and that the English-speaking world has lagged considerably behind. One of the earliest presentations of the Catechism was written by Mgr J. Honoré, Bishop of Tours, who was involved in its preparation: 'Le Catéchisme de l'Église catholique', in *Nouvelle Revue Théologique* 115/1 (1993) 3-18. In the same review (vol. 115/2, pp. 161-168), see Mgr Christoph Schönborn, 'Les critères de rédaction du Catéchisme de l'Église Catholique'. In this same number of the periodical Père Albert Chapelle SJ published the first part of a commentary on the new work in which he was himself a collaborator: '"La vie dans le Christ". Le Catéchisme de l'Église catholique', (ibid., pp. 169-185). The second part of the commentary was written by I. Baumer, 'Le Catéchisme de l'Église catholique. Première partie: la profession de foi' (vol. 115/3, pp. 335-355). P. Gervais SJ then published 'La célébration du mystère chrétien. Le Catéchisme de l'Église catholique' (vol. 115/4, pp. 496-515). The commentary on Part

Three, 'Life in Christ', was again given by A. Chapelle: "'La vie dans le Christ". Le Catéchisme de l'Église catholique' (vol. 115/5, pp.641-657). Mgr Honoré added, 'L'enjeu doctrinal du Catéchisme de l'Église catholique', ibid., 115/6, pp. 870-876. The most recent theological study of the Ten Commandments in a work of consultation is the art. 'Dekalog', in *Lexikon für Theologie und Kirche*, 1995, Bd 3, col. 62-68; several writers address, successively, the Decalogue in the Old Testament, the New Testament and Jewry; the Decalogue in a theological-ethical context, and in practical theology. The author of the last-named section (J. Gründel) was also responsible for the article 'Dekalog' in *Theologische Realenzyclopädie*, 8, 418-428. Also of recent date is the article 'Dekalog' in *Lexikon des Mittelalters*, III, 649-651, by L. Hödl (=from St Augustine to G. Biel). Hödl stresses how much research still has to be done on fourteenth- and fifteenth-century catechetical and homiletic literature, both in Latin and in the vernacular languages). In the encyclopaedia *Catholicisme: hier, aujourd'hui, demain*, R. Brouillard wrote an interesting article (vol. 3, cols 500-505). The oldest general article of all was excellent for its time: E. Dublanchy, in *Dictionnaire de théologie catholique*, vol. 4, cols 164-176. There is a worthwhile contribution by J.-M. Aubert, 'Loi et évangile', in *Dictionnaire de spiritualité*, vol. 9, Paris, 1976, cols 966-984.

The biblical material is examined by Helen Schüngel-Straumann, *Der Dekalog–Gottes Gebote?* (Stuttgarter Bibel-Studien, 67), Stuttgart, 1973, and in brief compass by Seán P. Kealy CSSp, *The Vision of the Ten Commandments. Charter of Freedom*, (The Living Flame Series, 33), Dublin, 1979. The best general work on the theology of the commandments known to me is by the late Philippe Delhaye, *Le Décalogue et sa place dans la morale chrétienne*, Bruxelles–Paris, 1963. A Jewish viewpoint is represented in B.-Z. Segal (ed.), *The Ten Commandments in History and Tradition*, Jerusalem 1990. The classic Reformed perspective was developed by Karl Barth, *Church Dogmatics*, II. *The Doctrine of God*, 2nd volume, Edinburgh, 1957, pp. 583ff., 609 ff. For an evangelical popularisation of Barth's theology, see R.S.Wallace, *The Ten Commandments. A Study of Ethical Freedom*, Edinburgh and London, 1965.

1. It was reported of an American general of the Civil War period that he lived his life according to the strict application of two law codes: the Ten Commandments and the US Army Rules!

2. Origen, *Hom. in Ex.* 8,1; PG 12, 350; cf. Ex 20:2; Dt 5:6.

3. St Irenaeus, *Adv. Haeres.* 4,16,3-4: PG 7/1, 1017-1018.

4. 'Surprisingly enough, there are more explicit references to the Ten Commandments in the New Testament than in the Old, even though the latter is almost four times as long as the former', Raymond F. Collins, *Christianity, Morality and Biblical Foundations*, Notre Dame, 1986, p. 64. Seven New Testament passages explicitly cite the Decalogue. Three are in the Synoptics (the Sermon on the Mount, Mt 5:17-48; the dispute over ritual purification, Mt 15:1-9; Mk 7:1-13; the exchange between Jesus and the rich young man, Mt 19:16-30; Mk 10:17-31; Lk 18:18-30). Four explicit allusions are made in Epistles: St Paul (the relationship between law and love, Rm 13:8-10; Eph 6:1-4, the household code; James, on the fulfilment of the royal law, Jas 2:8-13). NT allusions to the commandments are quite frequent: Mt 15:19, Lk 23:56; sabbath controversies such as Mt 12:1-14; Mk 2:23-28; Lk 6:1-11; John, sabbath controversies (Jn 5:9-18; 9:13-17), and 7:23. St Paul's allusions include Rm 1:30; 3:21-22; Col 3:20; Eph 6:1-2; 2 Tm 3:2.

5. Henning Graf Reventlow, *Epochen der Bibelauslegung*. Bd I. *Vom Alten Testament bis Origenes*, Munich 1990; C.F. Evans *et al.*, 'The New Testament in the Making', in *The Cambridge History of the Bible*, vol. I. *From the Beginnings to Jerome*, ed. P.R. Ackroyd and C.F. Evans, Cambridge 1970, 232-411.

6. James McEvoy, 'The Patristic Hermeneutics of Spiritual Freedom and its Biblical Origins', in *Scriptural Interpretation in the Fathers: Letter and Spirit*, ed. T. Finan and V. Twomey, Blackrock, Co. Dublin, 1995, pp. 1-25.

7. St Augustine, *Contra Faustum Manichaeum* 15.7 (PL 42:310).

8. Justin, *Dialogue with Trypho*, XI,3.

9. Philippe Delhaye, *Le Décalogue et sa place dans la morale chrétienne*, Bruxelles-Paris, 1963, develops the application of these three principles, and likewise their consequences, in some detail (pp.45-66).

10. The Catechism quotes from St Irenaeus (*Adv. Haeres.* 4.15,1: PG 7/1,1012): 'From the beginning, God had implanted in the heart of man the precepts of the natural law. Then he was content to remind him of them. This was the Decalogue.'

11. God was said to have written the commandments 'with his finger'. Augustine's identification of the Holy Spirit with the *digitus Dei* became a stock part of the imagery of the Spirit in medieval times; see, for instance, the hymn, 'Veni creator spiritus...digitus paternae dexterae.'

12. St Augustine, *De Spiritu et Littera*, ch.21 (PL 44:222).

13. From the anonymous English version printed in the *Library of the Fathers*, vol. 5, Oxford/London, 1840, pp. 80-81.

14. The Catechism acknowledges St Augustine's contribution. Ever since St Augustine the Ten Commandments have occupied a predominant place in the catechesis of baptismal candidates and the faithful... (2065). The division and numbering of the Commandments have varied in the course of history. The present catechism follows the division of the Commandments established by St Augustine, which has become traditional in the Catholic Church.' (2066). Attention is drawn to the different division which is found in the Orthodox Churches and the Reformed communities.

15. St Augustine, *De Decem Chordis* (=Sermon 9, PL 38,79; CCL 41, 117-122): 'Habet enim decalogus decem praecepta, quae sunt decachordum psalterium. Quae sic sunt distributa, ut tria quae sunt in prima tabula pertineant ad Deum, scilicet ad cognitionem et dilectionem Trinitatis; septem quae sunt in secunda tabula ad dilectionem proximi.'

16. The scholar who may be said to have rediscovered this pastoral literature is the Very Rev. Leonard E. Boyle OP, Prefect of the Vatican Library. Among his many publications, see 'The Inter-conciliar Period 1179-1215 and the Beginnings of Pastoral Manuals', in F. Liotta, ed., *Miscellanea Rolando Bandinelli, Papa Alessandro III*, Sienna 1986, pp. 43-56. See also the same author's 'Summae Confessorum', in *Les genres littéraires dans les sources théologiques et philosophiques médiévales. Définition, critique et exploitation*, Louvain-La-Neuve, 1982, pp. 227-237.

17. Robert Grosseteste, De *Decem Mandatis*, ed. Richard C. Dales and Edward B. King (Auctores Britannici Medii Aevi X), Oxford 1987, xix-107pp. For a study of the work see James McEvoy, 'Robert Grosseteste on the Ten Commandments', in *Recherches de Théologie ancienne et médiévale* 58 (1991) 167-205; reprinted in James McEvoy, *Robert Grosseteste, Exegete and Philosopher* (Variorum Collected Studies Series, 446), Aldershot, 1994.

18. St Augustine thought of love as an inexhaustible source of action. Its capacity is unfailing, but ambivalent, for love is the cause of crime as well as of heroism. To become ordered, love must be unified, under grace, by a will which has taken the true order of reality, as it is, to be its own internal ordering principle. By doing so, the will then accords to each of the varied objects of our experience only so much of desire and love as is that thing's due, in view of the measure of its participation in being. Ordered love loves material

things for their intrinsic goodness, usefulness, and place within the entire order of goodness and beauty, which creation is; spiritual beings on a plane equal to oneself, in ideal equality and unity; and God, the unmeasured measure of all that is, without measure.

19. St Anselm, *Proslogion*, ch.2.

20. Happily, the Catechism does likewise. Examples of the Church's teaching on matters of urgent, contemporary concern are: world poverty (2269); abortion and euthanasia (2270-2276); suicide (2280); respect for life and scientific research (2292); the safeguarding of peace (2302); the integrity of creation (2415); justice and solidarity among nations (2437). The chapter on the death penalty (2266) has provoked some controversy.

21. Robert Grosseteste, *Expositio in Epistolam Sancti Pauli ad Galatas*, ed. J.McEvoy, (CCCM, 130), Turnhout, 1995.

22. *Summa Theologiae*, IaIIae qu.98-108.

23. See, for instance, the distinguished collective work, *Lex et Libertas. Freedom and Law According to St Thomas Aquinas*, ed. L.J. Elders and Kl. Hedwig, (Studi Tomistici 30), Vatican City, 1987.

24. The treatises on these two subjects are widely separated in the *Summa*. The Ten Commandments are expounded in the IaIIae, the virtues and vices in the IIaIIae. The latter treatise is widely regarded at the present time as Aquinas's masterpiece in theology.

25. The reading of Aquinas' moral theory put forward here *brevissime*, owes much to writings by J.M. Finnis, A. MacIntyre and S. Pinckaers OP; see, in particular, the article by the last-named in the volume referred to in n.23: 'Liberté et préceptes dans la morale de saint Thomas', pp. 15-24.

26. In the apt formulation of S. Pinckaers; see the art. referred to in n. 25.

27. Something similar may be said to hold true of the moral

philosophy which resulted from the secularisation of Lutheranism. Kant's ethical theory can be viewed as his attempt to retain the theological notion of strict moral obligation, while at the same time emancipating the moral conscience from all external tutelage. The pure practical reason of the individual replaces God as the fully autonomous lawgiver. The reason gives the law to itself; heteronomy is overcome and the autonomy of the human subject is assured. However, the form of the obligation remains that of a command, categorically imperative and admitting of no exception. That this (the strictest form of obligation-morality ever to come from a philosophical pen), is a secularised form of the Lutheran theology of law and obligation, and hence the lineal descendant of the Ten Commandments (while being radically removed from the notions of covenant and providence, which gave the Decalogue its original meaning), seems evident. Even the examples of the categorical imperative to which Kant resorts repeatedly, are commandments of the Decalogue.

Chapter 10: The Catechism in the Irish context

1. Rolheiser, R., *The Shattered Lantern*, (London: Hodder and Stoughton, 1994), p.35.
2. Rolheiser, op. cit., p. 27.
3. op. cit. pp. 30-31.
4. op. cit. pp. 168-169.
5. John Paul II, *Centesimus annus*, 24.
6. John Paul II, *Centesimus annus*, 24
7. John Paul II, *Redemptoris missio*, 52.
8. Eliot. T. S., 'Tradition and the Individual Talent' [1919], in *Selected Essays* (London: Faber & Faber, 1951), (3rd ed), p. 14.
9. *Centesimus annus* 49.
10. Belfast, 13 October 1994.

11. Cf. *Centesimus annus* 41.
12. *Centesimus annus* 41, cf. *Gaudium et spes* 24.
13. John Paul II, Address at Limerick, 1 October 1979.
14. *Veritatis splendor* 16, cf. 12.
15. *Veritatis splendor* 24, cf. Catechism 1722.
16. Cf. Vatican II, *Gaudium et spes* 45.
17. Cf. *Veritatis splendor*.
18. Paul VI, *Evangelii nuntiandi* 80 (my italics).
19. *Veritatis splendor* 17, cf. CCC 2057.
20. *Veritatis splendor* 7.
21. Prayer after Communion, Confirmation B.
22. Cottier G., Address to Meeting of Congregation of the Clergy, 26 April 1993.
23. John Paul II, *Catechesi tradendae* 53.
24. John Paul II, *Evangelium vitae*, 83.
25. John Paul II, 13 December 1992.

Chapter 12: Homily

1. Loewith, K., *Nature, History and Existentialism*, edited with a critical introduction by A. Levison, Evenston, 1966, p.70.
2. *Against the Heresies*, Book 1, 10,2.
3. *Against the Heresies*, Book 1 10,1.

BIOGRAPHICAL NOTES ON THE CONTRIBUTORS

Sean Collins OFM, formerly Director of Irish Institute of Pastoral Liturgy, is now a member of the Franciscan Community, Multyfarnham, Co. Westmeath.

Archbishop Desmond Connell, formerly Professor of General Metaphysics at University College, Dublin, is now Archbishop of Dublin and Primate of Ireland.

His Eminence Cardinal Cahal B. Daly, formerly Professor of Scholastic Philosophy at Queen's University, Belfast and Primate of All Ireland.

Teresa Iglesias is Lecturer in Ethics, Department of Psychology, University College, Dublin.

Breandán Leahy, is lecturer in Systematic Theology at Clonliffe College and Mater Dei Institute of Education, Dublin.

James McEvoy, formerly Professor of Scholastic Philosophy at Queen's University, Belfast, is now Professor of Philosophy at St Patrick's College, Maynooth.

Bede McGregor OP is Professor of Missiology at St Patrick's College, Maynooth.

Bishop Donal Murray, formerly lectured in Moral Theology at Clonliffe College and Mater Dei Institute of Education, and in Catechetics in University College, Dublin, is now Bishop of Limerick.

Archbishop Michael Neary, formerly Professor of New Testament at St Patrick's College, Maynooth, is now Archbishop of Tuam.

John Saward is Professor of Systematic Theology at St Charles Borromeo Seminary, Philadephia, USA.

Archbishop Christoph Schönborn, principal redactor of the Catechism, is now Archbishop of Vienna.

Janet Smith is Associate Professor, Department of Philosophy, University of Dallas, USA.

INDEX OF NAMES